FIGHTING CRIME TOGETHER

JENNY FLEMING is a former Fellow with Security 21, in the Regulatory Institutions Network at the Research School of Social Sciences at the Australian National University. She is a former Research Fellow with the Key Centre for Ethics, Law, Justice and Governance at Griffith University, from which she holds a doctorate in politics and public policy. In July 2006 she took up the Professorial Research Chair at the Tasmanian Institute of Law Enforcement Studies at the University of Tasmania.

JENNIFER WOOD is a Research Fellow with Security 21, Regulatory Institutions Network at the Research School of Social Sciences, Australian National University. Prior to joining Security 21 she was an Assistant Professor at the University of Toronto, from which she holds a doctorate in criminology.

the Australia and New Zealand

School of Government

ANZSOG Program on Government, Politics and Public Management

The Australia and New Zealand School of Government (ANZSOG) is a network initiative of five jurisdictions (the Australian and New Zealand governments, plus New South Wales, Victoria and Queensland) and nine universities. Established in 2003, ANZSOG represents a new and exciting prospect for the development of world-class research and teaching in the public and community sectors.

ANZSOG has announced an extensive research program that promotes innovative and cutting-edge research in partnership with academia and the public sector (<http://www.anzsog.edu.au>). In association with UNSW Press, ANZSOG has undertaken to publish a series of books on contemporary issues in Australian government, politics and public management. Titles in this program will promote high-quality research on topics of interest to a broad readership (academic, professional, students and general readers) and will include teaching texts relevant to the ANZSOG consortia in the areas of government, politics and public management.

Series editors are Professor John Wanna and Professor R.A.W. Rhodes, Research School of Social Sciences, Australian National University, Canberra.

Recent titles include:

Terms of Trust: Arguments Over Ethics in Australian Government, by John Uhr;

Yes, Premier: Political Leadership in Australia's States and Territories, edited by John Wanna and Paul Williams;

Westminster Legacies: Democracy and Responsible Government in Asia and the Pacific, edited by Haig Patapan, John Wanna and Patrick Weller; and

The Australian Electoral System: Origins, Variations and Consequences, edited by David M. Farrell and Ian McAllister.

FIGHTING CRIME TOGETHER

The challenges of policing and security networks

Edited by
Jenny Fleming and Jennifer Wood

UNSW
PRESS

A UNSW Press book

Published by
University of New South Wales Press Ltd
University of New South Wales
Sydney NSW 2052
AUSTRALIA
www.unswpress.com.au

National Library of Australia
Cataloguing-in-Publication entry

Fighting crime together: the challenges of policing and security networks.

Includes index.
ISBN 0 86840 923 5.

1. Crime prevention - Australia. I. Fleming, Jenny. II.
Wood, Jennifer Dawn.

364.40994

Design Ruth Pidd
Cover photos Brian Hartigan, Australian Federal Police

CONTENTS

PREFACE AND ACKNOWLEDGMENTS

As an edited book, this project has been a co-operative venture. The editors invited both practitioners and academics to contribute to a volume that would bring a broader understanding to issues relating to policing and security partnerships and networks.

The papers in this collection were aired at a workshop held at the Australian National University (ANU) in Canberra, Australia in June 2005. Apart from the contributors themselves, many people attended the workshop sessions and gave us the benefit of their thoughts, ideas and experience. We thank them for that. The workshop dinner proved to be particularly illuminating!

Workshops don't happen by themselves. The editors were extremely grateful for the talents of Jessica Robertson, who administered the workshop with apparent ease and ensured a smooth and efficient two days. There were three discussants who took pains to read the papers and offer some valuable insights into themes and ideas that emerged from them. Special thanks to Rob McCusker from the Australian Institute of Criminology, Andrew Goldsmith from Flinders University, Rob Floyd from the Department of the Prime Minister and Cabinet, Professor John Wanna from the Australian National University and Benoît Dupont for making the seemingly endless journey from Montreal.

The project was made possible by the generous sponsorship of the National Institute of Social Sciences and Law from the Australian National University and the Academy of Social Sciences in Australia. The Regulatory Institutions Network at the Research School of Social Sciences at the ANU has also been very supportive, both financially and by providing the venue and infrastructure for the workshop. Jenny Fleming and Jennifer Wood would also like to acknowledge the support of the Australian Research Council. Special thanks also to the Security 21 team, particularly Monique Marks and Juani O'Reilly, for their continual support. Thanks to Laura Bevir for the index, to Jessica for the range of contributions she has made to this effort and to John Wanna and Rod Rhodes for their encouragement. Thanks also to John Elliot from UNSW Press, whose enthusiasm and patience has finally been rewarded.

As editors we would like to thank the contributors for their goodwill, co-operation and punctuality, and above all for their participation in this project.

CONTRIBUTORS

JULIE AYLING is a Research Officer in Security 21: International Centre for Security and Justice in the Regulatory Institutions Network, Research School of Social Sciences at the Australian National University. She has a Bachelor of Arts and a Bachelor of Laws with Honours from Macquarie University and a Masters in International Law from the Australian National University. She has undertaken research in a number of areas, including intellectual property and development, and the governance of illicit synthetic drugs. She is currently engaged in a project researching the resourcing of public policing.

JENNINE BOUGHTON is a senior intelligence analyst in the Australian Federal Police and holds a degree in International Relations and Strategic Studies. Jennine has worked in the intelligence field for 20 years in a variety of military and law enforcement intelligence roles. She was the recipient of an Australia Day Award for her work as the Middle East desk officer at the Australian Theatre Joint Intelligence Centre in 1998, and was a co-author of the *Australian Illicit Drug Report* in 2000–01 and 2001–02.

DAVID BRADLEY is the Victoria Police Research Fellow. In a long career associated with policing, David has endeavoured to progress the professionalisation of the police. He has taught at a number of police colleges, including the Scottish Police College. He co-founded the Centre for Police Studies, University of Strathclyde, co-authored the text, *Managing The Police: Law, Organisation and Democracy* (1986), has published extensively on police education and reform, was Foundation Dean of Studies, New South Wales Police, and has facilitated the relocation of foundational and post-foundational police education and research into the university system.

PROFESSOR JOHN BRAITHWAITE is interested in applying regulatory theory to crime prevention and peacemaking in international relations. He has been a consultant to many regulatory agencies, served between 1983 and 1987 as a member of the Economic Planning Advisory Council (which was chaired by the Prime Minister), was a part-time Commissioner with Australia's national antitrust and consumer protection agency between 1985 and 1995 and served as a member of the Council on Business Regulation (1994–96), which reported directly to Cabinet on all laws which impose a regulatory impact on business. He has been active for 30 years in social movement politics in Australia and internationally. In May 2006 Professor Braithwaite was awarded a Federation Fellowship from the Australian Research Council (for the second time) for a project called 'Restorative justice and responsive governance: Fresh challenges, new theory, global networks'.

MARK BURGESS, a police officer in the NSW Police Force who is on leave without pay and former President of the NSW Police Association, is currently the Chief Executive Officer of the Police Federation of Australia. He holds a Bachelor of Social Science (Justice Studies) from Newcastle University and a Master of Public Policy and Administration from Charles Sturt University. He was a member of the Wood Royal Commission Implementation Unit.

PROFESSOR BENOÎT DUPONT is Professor of Criminology at the University of Montreal and Deputy Director of the International Centre for Comparative Criminology. He holds a PhD in Political Science from the University of Toulouse. He is the editor of three books: *Policing the Lucky Country* (with Mike Enders, 2000), *La militarisation des appareils policiers* (with Frédéric Lemieux, 2005), and *Democracy, Society and the Governance of Security* (with Jennifer Wood, 2006).

DR JENNY FLEMING is a former Fellow with Security 21 in the Regulatory Institutions Network at the Research School of Social Sciences at the Australian National University. She is a former Research Fellow with the Key Centre for Ethics, Law, Justice and Governance at Griffith University (Brisbane, Australia), from which she holds a doctorate in politics and public policy. She is the editor of two books (with Ian Holland), *Motivating Ministers to Morality* (2001) and *Government Reformed: Values and New Political Institutions* (2003). She publishes widely in the areas of police–government relations, police labour relations and police management. In July 2006 she took up the Professorial Research Chair at the Tasmanian Institute of Law Enforcement Studies at the University of Tasmania.

PROFESSOR PETER GRABOSKY holds a PhD in Political Science from Northwestern University (Illinois, US) and has written extensively on criminal justice and public policy. His general interests are in computer crime and in harnessing resources outside the public sector to further public policy. He was previously Deputy Director of the Australian Institute of Criminology. From 1998 to 2002 he was President of the Australian and New Zealand Society of Criminology. In 1999 he was elected to the Board of Directors, and as Deputy Secretary General, of the International Society of Criminology.

POLICE COMMISSIONER MICK KEELTY is a career police officer with more than 30 years' experience at local, national and international levels. He is the first Commissioner appointed from within the ranks of the Australian Federal Police (AFP). Since his appointment as AFP Commissioner in April 2001, Commissioner Keelty has led the expansion and transformation of the organisation, with major new responsibilities for Counter Terrorism, Aviation Security and Transnational Crime. He has also overseen the creation of the International Deployment Group, a regional assistance and capacity-building initiative which has already undertaken missions in the Solomon Islands, East Timor, Papua New Guinea and the Middle East.

ASSOCIATE PROFESSOR COLLEEN LEWIS is the head of the School of Humanities, Communications and Social Sciences at Monash University, Melbourne. She researches and publishes in the area of police accountability and anti-corruption institutions. She is the author of *Complaints*

Against Police: the Politics of Reform (1999) and co-editor of: *Civilian Oversight of Policing: Governance, Democracy and Human Rights* (with Andrew Goldsmith, 2000); *Un-Peeling Tradition: Contemporary Policing* (with Keith Bryett, 1994); *It's Time Again: Whitlam and Modern Labor* (with Jenny Hocking, 2003); and *Corporate Management in Australian Government* (with Glyn Davis and Patrick Weller, 1989).

DR MONIQUE MARKS holds a PhD in Sociology from the University of Natal, South Africa. She is a Research Fellow with Security 21 in the Regulatory Institutions Network at the Research School of Social Sciences at the Australian National University. She is the author of two books, *Young Warriors: Youth Identity, Organisation and Violence in South Africa* (2001) and *Transforming the Robocops: Changing Police in South Africa* (2005).

COMMISSIONER CHRISTINE NIXON is the Chief Commissioner of Police, Victoria. In a police career spanning over 30 years, she has occupied a range of policy, operational, research and educational positions in which she has strongly progressed her ideas on police reform. Her higher education quali-fications include a Master of Public Administration from Harvard University. Her extensive organisational involvement has included member-ship of the Harkness Fellowships Selection Committee, the Presidency of the Australasian Council of Women and Policing, membership of the Council of the Victorian Institute of Forensic Medicine, and Advisory Fellow of The Australian University Regulatory Institutions Network.

PROFESSOR ROD RHODES is Professor of Political Science and Head of Program in the Research School of Social Sciences, Australian National University, and Emeritus Professor of Politics at the University of Newcastle (UK). He is the author or editor of 25 books, including: *The Oxford Handbook of Political Institutions* (2006); *Governance Stories* (with Mark Bevir, 2005); *Interpreting British Governance* (2003); *Transforming British Government Volume 1: Changing Institutions, Volume 2: Changing Roles and Relationships* (2000); and *Understanding Governance* (1997). He has been editor of *Public Administration* since 1986. He is a Fellow of the Academy of Social Sciences in both Australia and Britain.

PROFESSOR CLIFFORD SHEARING holds a PhD in Sociology from the University of Toronto, Canada. He has undertaken research into trends and directions in global governance through the window of the 'governance of security' (that is, how societies are policed). He served as a Commissioner on the Independent Commission on Policing for Northern Ireland and has published widely on policing reform. His work seeks to fuse theory, policy and practice.

DR GRANT WARDLAW was appointed to the position of National Manager, Intelligence in the Australian Federal Police (AFP) in July 2003. Grant came to the AFP from the Australian Crime Commission, where he was National Director, Criminal Intelligence. Grant has held senior executive positions in intelligence, research and policy organisations, including being the inaugural Director of the Office of Strategic Crime Assessments and Acting Director of the Australian Institute of Criminology, and has published widely in the fields of terrorism, illicit drug policy and law enforcement intelligence. He is the author of *Political Terrorism: Theory, Tactics and Countermeasures* (1989 [1983]).

DR JENNIFER WOOD has a doctorate in Criminology from the University of Toronto, Canada. Prior to joining Security 21 she was an Assistant Professor at the University of Toronto and taught courses in policing, security and governance. Her publications include: *Democracy, Society and the Governance of Security* (edited with B. Dupont, 2006); Brazil (with N. Cardia), in T. Jones and T. Newburn (eds), *Plural Policing: A Comparative Perspective* (2006); and Understanding global trends in policing: Explanatory and normative dimensions (with M. Kempa), in J. Sheptycki and A. Wardick (eds), *Transnational and Comparative Criminology* (2005).

ACRONYMS

AAP	Australian Assisting Police
ACTU	Australian Council of Trade Unions
AFP	Australian Federal Police
AFPA	Australian Federal Police Association
APMC	Australasian Police Ministers' Council
APPSC	Australasian Police Professional Standards Council
COAG	Council of Australian Governments
CSO	Community Support Officer
DfES	Department of Education and Skills
DWP	Department of Work and Pensions
ECP	Enhanced Co-operation Program
FLO	Fairtrade Labelling Organisations International
FoI	Freedom of Information
FSC	Forest Stewardship Council
GOs	Government Offices for the Regions
IDG	International Deployment Group
ILP	intelligence-led policing
INP	Indonesian National Police

IPA	International Police Association
JCLEC	Jakarta Centre for Law Enforcement Co-operation
LECP	Law Enforcement Co-operation Program
MNC	Multinational company
NPM	new public management
NSMD	non-state market-driven governance system
NZPA	New Zealand Police Association
NTAC	National Threat Assessment Centre
PCC	Police Commissioners' Conference
PCSO	Police Community Support Officer
PFA	Police Federation of Australia
PNG	Papua New Guinea
PM&C	Department of Prime Minister and Cabinet
PMF	private military firm
PPF	participating police force
RAMSI	Regional Assistance Mission to the Solomon Islands
RPNGC	Royal Papua New Guinean Constabulary
SOG	Senior Officers' Group
SPOCTU	South Pacific and Oceanic Council of Trade Unions
TTN	transnational targeting network
TUC	Trade Union Congress
UNMISET	United Nations Mission to Support East Timor
UNOTIL	United Nations Mission in Timor-Leste
UNPAA	United Nations Police Association of Australia
VPLSD	Victoria Police Licensing Services Division

INTRODUCTION: NEW WAYS OF DOING BUSINESS: NETWORKS OF POLICING AND SECURITY

Jenny Fleming and Jennifer Wood

The terrorist attacks of September 11, 2001 reminded citizens the world over that contemporary arrangements for policing and security provision services can no longer be taken for granted. The collapse of the Twin Towers in New York City has forced security experts and policy-makers to come to terms with the inadequacies of a system designed for a past era. It is now the case that local terror can, and will, be waged in the course of political and ideological struggles originating in far-off lands. Contemporary processes of political, cultural and economic globalisation have generated a new world of security risks resulting from the illicit activities of 'nodes' and networks whose methods of organisation defy sovereign boundaries. These require those who are concerned with these issues to develop more effective security networks both within and across these boundaries. At the transnational level, state institutions no longer monopolise the 'governance of security' (Johnston & Shearing 2003; Wood & Dupont 2006).

The growing pervasiveness of 'dark networks' (Raab 2003) has served to fundamentally challenge the capacity of any one state to regulate them effectively. Since September 11, governments are no longer complacent about the need to reinvent institutions and practices of policing and security in order to thwart acts of global violence and local terror. Indeed, much innovation – in the form of developments in networked security delivery – has taken place on the part of both state and non-state actors, including private policing companies and commercial military firms. These developments have occurred at such a rate and speed that it is sometimes difficult to assess their normative implications in an empirically robust and theoretically sophisticated manner. Nevertheless, the recently published *9/11 Commission Report* contends that 'ways of doing business rooted in a different era are just not good enough' and that Americans 'should not settle for incremental, ad hoc adjustments to a system designed generations ago for a world that no longer exists' (2004: 399). In the context of new nodes and networks of security delivery, countries all over the world are also seeking to enhance state power and authority through strengthened legislation and new counter-terrorism policy (Gill 2006: 43).

There is much being done 'in the name of security', and often what is being done is based on the assumption that we all agree on what 'security' actually is or could mean (Valverde & Wood 2001). Security is less a 'thing' than it is what we imagine, construct and dramatise (Manning 2006). As a problem of public sector governance, it is increasingly understood as a 'wicked issue' (Rittel & Webber 1973; Clarke & Stewart 1997; Rhodes 1998; Perri 6 1997; Hennessey 1998), where the problem and/or the solution are either hard to define and/or not available or sub-optimal and often carry consequences that might lead to further problems (Rittel & Webber 1973: 155–59). A wicked issue crosses international and national boundaries and involves multiple agencies and sectors at all levels of government. And of course new forms of 'private authority' (Hall & Biersteker 2002) and non-state governance that operate 'above' and 'below' states (Sheptycki 1998) present complex challenges for scholars and practitioners of policing and public policy.

What do we mean by 'nodes' and 'networks'? It is not always the case that distinct providers of policing and security, or 'nodes', come together in the form of networks. The degree to which nodes co-operate, share resources, develop trusting relationships or more generally align interests is an empirical matter to be verified rather than an untested theoretical assumption (Johnston & Shearing 2003; Johnston 2006). With respect to 'dark' nodes, like those involved in carrying out acts of terror, they may come together in the form of 'loosely coupled alliances' (Dupont, Chapter 2) or they may operate as redundant functional units that, if terminated through anti-terror efforts, would not be of consequence to the resiliency of a broader dark network and its operations (Gross Stein 2001).

Notwithstanding the above conceptual distinction, this book, as its central unit of analysis, focuses largely on networks (and purportedly 'bright' ones). It does so through a variety of disciplinary lenses, from academia and the practitioner community. In general terms, networks are characterised by interdependence between organisations, continuing interactions between network members (caused by the need to exchange resources and negotiate shared purposes) and game-like behaviour, rooted in trust and regulated by rules of the game negotiated and agreed to by network participants (Rhodes 1997; Castells 2000). While such attributes are key features of networks, and are useful for diagnostic purposes, they should not serve to obscure the fact that networks take many forms and mean different things to different people.

Variations in the distribution of resources and in the bargaining skills of participants explain in part both differences in outcomes in a network and variations between networks. Networks often have a significant degree of autonomy from government and are often not directly accountable to the state. Issues of democracy then become pertinent. They are self-organising, although the state can indirectly and imperfectly steer them. Such characteristics are, as Rhodes suggests (Chapter 1), not 'cost free'. Networks can be insular, difficult to penetrate and at times unaccountable for their actions. They can be conflictual on a number of levels and can be difficult to co-ordinate (Fleming, Chapter 4; Fleming & Rhodes 2005). Furthermore, even if networks are, *in theory*, being accomplished through formal practices and policies, there is much that occurs informally, through mundane operational routines and daily troubleshooting, that results in new networking habits, systems and structures (Dupont, Chapter 2). Thus it is practical actors that accomplish networks just as much as it is policy-makers and other authoritative voices 'at the top'.

While policing and security networks have become the focus of much academic debate in the aftermath of 9/11 (for example, Gill 2006; Lippert & O'Connor 2006; Dupont 2004; Wood & Dupont 2006), we shouldn't make the mistake of thinking that they are an entirely new addition to police management and strategy. The use of networks in policing has been the focus of public police organisations in most western democracies for at least two decades. In Europe particularly, local policing is increasingly involved in complex networks of relationships and interests. This trend is also true for centralised police organisations, where the rhetoric of community/partnership policing places an onus on the police to collaborate with government agencies, local communities and non-government organisations to develop and implement crime prevention and security strategies (McLaughlin & Murji 2001, cited in Virta 2002: 191). This signals a widespread acknowledgment that police can no longer 'do it alone'. Policing through local networks, also known as 'partnerships', is established policy in both Australia and Britain (Crawford 2005).

Most crime problems and palliative solutions in present-day society are interlinked with other public policies. These policies include the delivery of urban services such as transport, housing and street lighting; educational matters such as school bullying and truancy; and health and community welfare issues such as inadequate parenting (Cope 2001; Edwards 2005; Brereton 2000). There is increasing recognition that given these linkages and the prevailing climate of fiscal constraint, crime control needs a 'whole-of-government approach' and indeed a cross-sectoral approach involving a variety of communities (Cabinet Office 2000; Garland 2001; Mulgan 2001). Such an approach would emphasise locally shared responsibility for security and be a way of organising multi-agency co-operation in community policing strategies (Community Policing Consortium 1994).

The practitioner community generally recognises that the demand for policing and security services exceeds the capacity of governments to provide it. Not only do networks provide the opportunity for different forms of knowledge and capacity to be integrated in the furtherance of shared outcomes; they also provide the opportunity for resources (material and human) to be leveraged. The chapter by Ayling, Grabosky and Shearing (Chapter 3) provides a rich description of the seemingly innumerable ways in which police harness outside resources to bolster their strategic capability.

The need for regional and international networks is increasingly recognised, as seen in Keelty's chapter on regional and international engagement by the Australian Federal Police (AFP) (Chapter 5) and in Wardlaw and Boughton's chapter on the AFP's intelligence-led policing agenda (Chapter 6). Networks assist in identifying potential problems and allow for flexible responses. They also provide frameworks within which goals and strategies can be negotiated and provide opportunities for joint decision-making that potentially reduce the scope for disagreement during implementation. As CEO of the Police Federation of Australia, Burgess (Chapter 7) argues that for 'police organisations to operate effectively, they must develop intricate networks at the local, jurisdictional, national, and importantly in today's world, international level'.

While the strategic appeal of governance networks is widely accepted, they inevitably pose challenges for those seeking to establish and maintain them. While acknowledging that resource allocation, conflictual governing structures, political inertia and cultural differences can represent significant challenges for successful networking, the contributors explore new strategies for integrating the knowledge, capacities and resources of different security providers and recognise that what is required is a better understanding of the conditions that allow for effective and successful governance networks. This collection of essays thus addresses the challenges of policing and security networks from a police, practice and research perspective. The book is intended as a way of bridging the gap in knowledge that exists regarding what police and other security agencies do, how they address security issues and how they seek to serve their communities.

Bringing together practitioners who are active in the field and those who are involved in academic research is – as Bradley, Nixon and Marks (Chapter 8) remind us – essential for innovative police work. At a workshop conducted in June 2005 at the Australian National University, practitioners and researchers from within the academy and across the fields of policing and security practice and policy came together to consider the wicked issue of security and policing and the nature of networks in the governance of these policy areas. Other points of debate considered were: what are the weaknesses and limitations of existing institutions and practices of policing and security in relation to networks? What are the challenges for public police organisations in the context of networks? What new institutional and strategic models should be designed, implemented and evaluated? How do we design, assess and manage these new networks? How do we ensure that these networks are instrumentally effective as well as democratic?

The robust discussion and rigorous debate at this workshop resulted in this collection of essays. Each chapter contributes to our understanding of the nuances and complexities that surround networks as a concept and as a practical ideal, as well as the various ways they are utilised in policing and security environments. They demonstrate the multifaceted perspectives of the various actors involved in networks. In many cases they point to the unlimited potential of networks and nodal arrangements to clarify and manage the complex issues that constitute the governance of security on a number of levels. The essays in part identify the 'pros and cons' of network formation in policing and security, and provide an opportunity for readers to assess the various roles that agencies, individuals and organisations play in their respective networking agendas.

This book brings together scholars and practitioners involved in designing and informing new models for policing and security that meet the challenges of a changing world of security risks at the local, national and international level. The scholars are not all primarily involved in criminology. Taken together, political scientists, sociologists, lawyers and those well versed in public administration and management provide a multi-disciplinary voice. The title of this book captures its emphasis on the *challenges* of policing and security networks, on the idea that in some way (or in many instances in a variety of ways), the founding of security networks at local, national or international levels and the maintenance of such networks is a difficult and complex business. Of course the nature of such challenges is contextual. Organisational requirements, international diplomatic relations and global crime all provide environments within which networks are established. The management of policing and security arrangements in these various contexts is bedevilled by different collective interests and political agendas. Variance in terms of context, interests and agendas and, perhaps significantly, the lack of rigorous evaluation and analysis of 'successful' networks precludes the offering of tight guidelines or standard solutions for the establishment and continuing development of networks of any shape or size. The best we can hope for is to identify the challenges associated with them and provide basic principles by example. After all, any innovation will need to be 'tailor made' to suit the social, political, cultural and economic environments that surround it (Wood 2006), a point that Keelty makes when he underscores the need for acute cultural awareness on the part of AFP members working in different parts of the Asia-Pacific region (Chapter 5).

This book has an implicit three-part structure. The first section, containing works by Rhodes, Dupont, Fleming, and Ayling, Grabosky and Shearing (Chapters 1 to 4), looks specifically at the key explanatory concepts, themes and debates surrounding networks and networking behaviour generally. It draws from empirical research as it provides theoretical insights into issues such as existing network models and designs, mapping networks, and managing networks. It also flags some issues of relevance to democratic theory and practice.

Rhodes' view of the basic principles of network practice, and guidelines for 'thriving networks', are the focus of the book's opening chapter. Written from a public administration perspective, Rhodes challenges 'the dominant, instrumental or tool view of networks' and argues that 'the lessons of public sector reform over the past twenty years are as applicable in police and security studies as anywhere else'. Rhodes demonstrates that networks are no longer a metaphor or a site for arcane theoretical disputes, but a live reform issue for governments that are increasingly aware of the pertinence of resource allocation and the importance of collaboration and partnerships generally. His chapter identifies the characteristics of networks, the factors that support and develop networks, and the weaknesses that can inhibit them.

The growing body of literature on the features and organisation of security networks, and the normative contribution of these publications, can only benefit from the development and analysis of more detailed datasets. Dupont's chapter introduces some considerations of the methodological tools that can be mobilised to map and model complex organisational sets. Dupont argues that if we are to verify the existence and extent of networks, an empirical toolbox must be created and tested. Such a toolbox must take into account the specifics of the security field or 'securisphere'. He shows how different types of networks can be mapped, what challenges must be faced in the process, and what data such exercises can yield. He is particularly interested in assessing whether or not the mapping of security networks can provide us with new insights into the governance of security (confirming or contradicting existing theories) and improve our understanding of contemporary security provision in western societies.

In their discussion of resource networks, Ayling, Grabosky and Shearing (Chapter 3) look at the integration of state and civil resources and the mechanisms of 'coercion', 'sale' and 'gift' that work to 'pull in', and thus network, the physical, financial, technical, informational and human resources necessary for effective public policing. The authors tackle the somewhat thorny issues of accountability, regulation and democratic practice in managing resource integration and allocation and identify the central challenge as managing such practices 'in a manner that is generally considered to best serve the public interest – consistently, fairly and with the result of overall effective outcomes for society'.

The final chapter in this section addresses the challenges associated with multi-agency networks in police organisations and provides an 'inside' perspective on how police view networks and 'make sense' of a governing structure that they perceive as being in conflict with command and control strategies, the contracting out of police services and performance measure-ment mechanisms. Fleming suggests that the attributes that are purported to promote thriving networks provide significant challenges for police offi-cers seeking to establish and maintain effective networks with other public agencies. Fleming's chapter, dealing as it does with a strong practitioner per-spective, is an appropriate precursor to the second section of the book, which allows three senior police practitioners to reflect on the various chal-lenges that confront them in their everyday practice.

Commissioner Mick Keelty is the Police Commissioner of the Australian Federal Police (AFP). Internationally, the AFP's networks with international agencies and its subsequent liaison work are increasingly inte-gral elements in the investigation of transnational crime. Its role in regional engagement and its international peacekeeping missions are also strategic priorities. In his discussion of the challenges associated with international networking, Commissioner Keelty emphasises the importance of context and identifies the ongoing maintenance of network facilitation as vital to successful network practice. He identifies the challenges of imposing a country's own values and cultures on other jurisdictions when facilitating such networks, and points to the importance of firm political commitment and ongoing support from national governments.

Wardlaw, working for the AFP as the National Manager for Intelligence Services, and Boughton, a senior intelligence analyst in the AFP, pick up Keelty's theme of the importance of international liaison networks in the context of intelligence gathering and sharing. Wardlaw argues for a more proactive networked approach to law enforcement. He identifies the central importance of effective internal networks for intelligence gathering and analysis but concedes that 'no matter how true law enforcement tries to be to the doctrine of being intelligence-led, an ever-present challenge will always be the widening sphere of influence of global events on our daily activities'.

Burgess, formerly a NSW police officer, is now Chief Executive Officer of the Police Federation of Australia (PFA), an umbrella body that represents Australian police unions, which Fleming et al. (2006) identify as 'a growing network of stakeholders in policing'. Like Wardlaw, Burgess also emphasises the importance of internal networks to the success of external networks and strategic alliances. One of the most significant challenges recognised by Burgess is how to meet the local (and often insular) needs of the organisation's constituents while establishing national networks that address more global issues. Burgess suggests that there needs to be a more integrated, networked approach to local law enforcement and crime reduction, and like many of the contributors here, identifies the importance of recognising security issues as being 'national' concerns, deserving 'national responsibility, attention, and resourcing' for successful networks, particularly those that involve communities.

Fittingly, practitioners and an academic come together for the final chapter in this second section. Bradley, Nixon (Chief Commissioner of Victoria Police) and Marks reflect on the research partnership between police and academics and argue for a supportive professional network that would involve police and researchers working together in participative action research to address ways in which research might inform network practice. They argue that both '[p]olice and academics need to climb out of their boxes and enter the labyrinth of research and modelling programs together'. There is much about the history of police–academic relationships, as well as the current ways in which joint research and innovation is governed, that makes this a daunting task. Nevertheless, the authors contend that such collaboration is vital to the advancement of progressive, professional and democratic policing.

The final three chapters of the collection have a normative orientation in their reflections on the future of networking practices and arrangements in the delivery of policing and security services, and in the governance of this provision. These chapters are designed to prompt readers to think more clearly and strategically about the future of the public police in terms of its proper place(s) in the ever-changing 'securisphere' (Dupont, Chapter 2). Braithwaite (Chapter 9) conceptualises the police role within his theoretical framework of 'responsive regulation' (Ayres & Braithwaite 1992), of which 'restorative justice' is an important normative component (Braithwaite 2002). In his chapter on peacemaking networks and restorative justice, Braithwaite argues that police peacekeepers have an important role in building peace in nations that have been riven by armed conflict and that the role of such peacekeepers may be conceived in terms of participating in and sustaining networks for the governance of peace. He maintains that at the core of effective peacekeeping endeavours is a humanitarian ethic concerned with the safety of civilians and non-combatants in times of war and conflict. Beyond this dimension there is a more pressing long-term requirement to nurture restorative justice practices that draw from local knowledge and capacity. Restorative justice allows for the truths of harms to be revealed, acknowledged and discussed so that all of those affected by them can heal and move forward in peace and hope. Police must play a crucial role in the identification, protection and support of 'islands of civility' (Kaldor 1999) deemed to be present in even the most war-torn environments. Braithwaite's vision involves 'circles of reconciliation' that 'bubble up from civil society with support from outside NGOs, from the World Bank and others with the resources that count for peace'.

Lewis and Wood (Chapter 10) examine some key challenges associated with governing nodes and networks of policing and security provision. Traditionally, questions of accountability and governance have centred on the activities of public policing organisations, and in particular on the potential for police to be unduly invasive, coercive and partial in their dealings with members of the public. This traditional framing of the governance problem remains an important one in light of the extraordinary powers and authority being granted to police and other state security institutions in the context of the 'war on terror'. Notwithstanding this, Lewis and Wood begin with the premise that this conceptualisation of the governance problem is much too narrow in light of the changing field of policing and security delivery. Drawing inspiration from scholars who have sought to widen this debate (Loader 2000; Loader & Walker 2001, 2006; Johnston 2000, 2006), Lewis and Wood frame the governance question as one about the protection of democratic values within and across the field of policing and security delivery generally. Following from the insights of Stenning (2000), they stress that it is no longer acceptable to assume that mechanisms developed to govern the conduct of the public police are naturally more desirable or effective than those established to govern the conduct of private individuals and groups. As they refer to the broader literature on accountability and regulation, they remind us that each mechanism is in itself limited and insufficient. The future of governance thus rests on the development of new 'hybrids' that shape, through different strategies, the behaviour of diverse policing and security providers towards democratic ends.

What the current governance problem raises is the potential for seemingly 'bright' networks of policing and security delivery to have a 'dark' side. This is the focus of the final chapter in this collection, by Wood. The public police, along with other public sector agencies and individuals involved in security policy and practice, must participate in the formation of networks that at least meet, or ideally exceed, the competencies of the 'dark networks' (Raab & Milward 2003) that are involved in complex activities such as organised crime and terrorism. Even at local levels, as the chapter by Fleming reminds us, police are required to forge all manner of partnerships to tackle the wicked problems of crime and disorder. Wood argues that the question of how precisely the police should *normatively* position themselves in local, national and transnational networks should be given careful consideration in the future. What could be at stake is the very identity of the public police as a symbolically important institution, with the authority and legitimacy that comes with that symbolism, as well as a professional institution that has carved out, and will continue to carve out, an 'exclusive domain of practice' (Australasian Police Professional Standards Council 2006). The positioning of the police within networks is not simply about engaging in power struggles (Dupont 2006) in ways that contribute to police dominance, although this may be desirable for police leaders and unionists as a normative agenda. The positioning of the police is more fundamentally about the responsibility that police have to advance the democratisation of the policing and security field generally. Wood's chapter pulls together strands from previous chapters in this volume in depicting what is, or ought to be, distinct about the police identity and role as they participate actively in the constitution of bright and democratic networks.

We are grateful to the contributors of this volume for the manner in which they came together to exchange ideas about what we know about policing and security networks, about the conceptual and pragmatic challenges that they pose, and about the normative, and sometimes disturbing, implications they present us with. It may be inevitable that networked arrangements for policing, security and governance generally will be our future. There is much we can do, however, to ensure that networks operate in the most bright and transparent ways and in ways that effectively meet the security challenges of the 21st century.

References

9/11 Commission (2004) *The Final Report of the National Commission on Terrorist Attacks Upon the United States.* New York: W.W. Norton & Co.

Australasian Police Professional Standards Council (2006) *Defining the Australasian Policing Profession.*

Ayres, I. and Braithwaite, J. (1992) *Responsive Regulation: Transcending the deregulation debate.* New York: Oxford University Press.

Beynon, J. and Edwards, A. (1999) Community governance of crime control, in G. Stoker (ed.), *The New Management of British Local Governance.* Houndmills, Basingstoke: Macmillan.

Braithwaite, J. (2002) *Restorative Justice and Responsive Regulation.* Oxford: Oxford University Press.

Brereton, D. (2000) Policing and crime prevention: Improving the product, in D. Chappell and P. Wilson (eds), *Crime and the Criminal Justice System in Australia: 2000 and beyond.* Sydney: Butterworths.

Cabinet Office (2000) *Wiring It Up.* London: Cabinet Office.

Castells, M. (2000) *The Rise of the Network Society* (2nd edition). Oxford: Blackwell Publishing.

Clarke, M. and Stewart, J. (1997) *Handling the Wicked Issues: A challenge for government.* Birmingham, UK: University of Birmingham, Institute of Local Government Studies.

Crawford, A. Lister, S., Blackburn, S. and Burnett, J. (2005) *Plural Policing: The mixed economy of visible patrols in England and Wales.* Bristol: The Policy Press.

Community Policing Consortium (1994) Understanding community policing: A framework for action, Bureau of Justice Assistance Monograph. Washington DC: US Department of Justice.

Cope, S. (2001) Analysing criminal justice policy-making: Towards a policy network approach, in M. Ryan et al. (eds), *Policy Networks in Criminal Justice.* Houndmills, Basingstoke: Palgrave Macmillan.

Dupont, B. (2004) Security in the age of networks, *Policing and Society,* 14(1): 76–91.

—— (2006) Power struggles in the field of security: Implications for democratic transformation, in J. Wood and B. Dupont (eds), *Democracy, Society and the Governance of Security.* Cambridge: Cambridge University Press.

Edwards, C.J. (2005) *Changing Policing Theories* (2nd edition). Sydney: Federation Press.

Edwards, A. and Benyon, J. (2001) Networking and crime control at the local level, in M. Ryan et al. (eds), *Policy Networks in Criminal Justice.* Houndmills, Basingstoke: Palgrave Macmillan.

Fleming, J. and Rhodes, R.A.W. (2005) Bureaucracy, contracts and networks: The unholy trinity and the police, *Australian and New Zealand Journal of Criminology,* 38(2): 192–205.

Fleming, J., Marks, M and Wood, J. (2006) Standing on the inside looking out: The significance of unions in networks of police governance, *The Australian and New Zealand Journal of Criminology,* 39(1): 71–89.

Garland, D. (2001) *The Culture of Control*. Chicago: University of Chicago Press.

Gill, P. (2001) Not just joining the dots but crossing the borders and bridging the voids: Constructing security networks after 11 September, *Policing and Society*, 16(1): 27–49.

Gross Stein, J. (2001) Network wars, in R.J. Daniels, P. Macklem and K. Roa, *The Security of Freedom*. Toronto: University of Toronto Press.

Hall, R.B. and Biersteker, T.J. (eds) (2002) *The Emergence of Private Authority in Global Governance*. Cambridge: Cambridge University Press.

Hennessy, P. (1998) The Blair style of government, *Government and Opposition*, 33(1): 3–20.

Johnston, L. (2000) *Policing Britain: Risk, security and governance*. Harlow: Longman.

—— (2006) Transnational security governance, in J. Wood and B. Dupont (eds), *Democracy, Society and the Governance of Security*. Cambridge: Cambridge University Press.

Johnston, L. and Shearing, C. (2003) *Governing Security: Explorations in policing and justice*. London: Routledge.

Kaldor, M. (1999) *New and Old Wars: Organized violence in a global era*. Stanford, CA: Stanford University Press.

Lippert, R. and O'Connor, D. (2006) Security intelligence networks and the transformations of contract private security, *Policing and Society*, 16(1): 50–66.

Loader, I. (2000) Plural policing and democratic governance, *Social and Legal Studies*, 9(3): 323–45.

Loader, I. and Walker, N. (2001) Policing as a public good: Reconstituting the connections between policing and state. *Theoretical Criminology*, 5(1): 9–35.

—— (2006). Necessary virtues: The legitimate place of the state in the production of security, in J. Wood and B. Dupont (eds), *Democracy, Society and the Governance of Security*. Cambridge: Cambridge University Press.

Macauley, S. (1986) Private government, in L. Lipson and S. Wheeler (eds), *Law and the Social Sciences*. New York: Russell Sage Foundation.

Manning, P.K. (2006) Two case studies of American anti-terrorism, in J. Wood and B. Dupont (eds), *Democracy, Society and the Governance of Security*. Cambridge: Cambridge University Press.

McLaughlin, E. and Murji, K. (2001) Lost connections and new directions: Neo-liberalism, new public managerialism and the 'modernization' of the British police, in K. Stenson and R. Sullivan (eds), *Crime, Risk and Justice: The politics of crime control in liberal democracies*. Devon: Willan Publishing.

Mulgan, G. (2001) Joined-up governance, paper delivered to the British Academy Conference on Joined-Up Government, 30 October.

Perri 6 (1997) *Holistic Governance*. London: Demos.

Raab, J. and Milward, H.B. (2003) Dark networks as problems, *Journal of Public Administration Research and Theory*, 13(4): 413–39.

Rhodes, R.A.W. (1997) *Understanding Governance*. Buckingham: Open University Press.

—— (1998) Different roads to unfamiliar places: UK experience in comparative perspective, *Australian Journal of Public Administration*, 57(4): 19–31.

Rittel, H. and Webber, M. (1973) Dilemmas in a general theory of planning, *Policy*

Sciences, 4(2): 155–65.

Sheptycki, J. (1998) Policing, postmodernism and transnationalization, *British Journal of Criminology,* 38(3): 485–503.

Stenning, P. (2000) Powers and accountability of private police, *European Journal on Criminal Policy and Research,* 8: 325–52.

Valverde, M. and Wood, J. (2001). In the name of security, *University of Toronto Bulletin,* 16.

Virta, S. (2002) Local security management: Policing through networks, *Policing: An International Journal of Police Strategies & Management,* 25(1): 169–89.

Wood, J. (2006) Research and innovation in the field of security: A nodal governance view, in J. Wood and B. Dupont (eds), *Democracy, Society and the Governance of Security.* Cambridge: Cambridge University Press.

Wood, J. and Dupont, B. (eds) (2006) *Democracy, Society and the Governance of Security.* Cambridge: Cambridge University Press.

THE SOUR LAWS OF NETWORK GOVERNANCE | 1

R.A.W. Rhodes

Introduction

In this chapter, I tell the distinctive story of the shift from the Bureaucratic State to the Contract State to the Network State, focusing on the problems of the Network State. I explore the intrinsic limits of networks, and the fit between networks, bureaucracy and markets. I provide four brief illustrations of network governance 'in action': joined-up government in the United Kingdom, the whole-of-government approach in Australia, partnership policing in Australia and the United Kingdom, and visible policing in the United Kingdom. My aim is to show the ubiquity of the problems that exist at the national and local level in both Australia and Britain. I also explore the unintended consequences of the shift to networks, arguing that the several problems boil down to three recurrent issues: the holy grail of co-ordination, the mix of service delivery systems, and disputes about ownership. Finally, I challenge the dominant view that networks are a tool of government to be managed to achieve central objectives. Instead, I argue that their strength lies in their independence from government and their role as a weak check on the power of any would-be central co-ordinator.

There is a secondary theme. I am not an expert in police and security studies; I am a political scientist specialising in public administration. This chapter is written out of the conviction that the lessons of public sector reform over the past 20 years are as applicable in police and security studies as anywhere else. Students of public administration have been studying the effects of the NPM (new public management) and equivalent reforms for over two decades (see, for example, Aucoin 1995; Hood 1991; Pollitt 1993; Pollitt & Bouckaert 2000; Rhodes & Weller 2001). I want to suggest that police reform is but public sector reform writ small. Issues that appear old hat in the public administration literature have not been given enough attention in police studies, so this chapter seeks to redress that balance.

This approach has an immediate and direct relevance to the concerns of this book. As the editors point out, scholars of policing and security recognise that the demand for security in western democracies exceeds the capacity of the government to provide it. So plural policing is the order of the day. A networked approach to policing and security is one way of improving effective service provision, especially given the overlap between crime and other public policies such as health and community welfare. So the task is to work with and through networks. My task is to explore the problems posed by this aspiration.

Towards the network state

Table 1.1 provides a brief summary of the Bureaucratic State, the Contract State and the Network State. It encapsulates the story of the shift from bureaucracy to contracts to networks, which has become a prominent, even dominant, account of recent reforms of the public sector (see Rhodes 1977, 2000; Stoker 2004). The story of bureaucracy and contracts has been told often, so I focus on the Network State.

If contracts are characterised by prices and competition and bureaucracies by authority and rules, then networks are characterised by trust and diplomacy. In the Network State, partnerships between public, private and voluntary sectors, in many guises, organise and deliver services for the government. Marketisation may have introduced the private sector and price competition to delivering public services, but it also fragmented the institutional infrastructure of the public sector. The plot of the story about networks is about putting the public sector together again. For example, care of

TABLE 1.1   From bureaucracy to contracts to networks

	The Bureaucratic State	The Contract State	The Network State
Basis of relationships	Employment relationship	Contract	Resource exchange
Degree of dependence	Dependent	Independent	Interdependent
Medium of exchange	Authority	Prices	Trust
Means of conflict resolution and co-ordination	Rules and commands	Haggling and the courts	Diplomacy and mutual adjustment
Culture	Subordination	Competition	Reciprocity

the elderly needs co-operation between several agencies, and if each is to do its job properly, they need to share any or all of such resources as staff, information, money, buildings and expertise.

Governments throughout Europe deliver services with and through networks. It may be thought that such skills characterise the consensual democracies of Western Europe, where governments are coalitions. But network management is now a well-established feature of British government, locally, regionally and centrally (see, for example, Cabinet Office 2000; Cm 4310 1999). Policy networks and communities are a longstanding feature of policy-making (for a general review, see Rhodes 2006). Reform has multiplied the actors delivering services, and produced great pressure for organisations to co-operate and so spread networks. Now the skills of network management are a longstanding feature of the public sector. Thus Caiden (1990: 30) identifies putting oneself in the other person's shoes as a longstanding value and belief of Commonwealth officials; these skills are ever present in Australian intergovernmental relations (see Keating & Wanna 2000). And of the British higher civil service, Sir Douglas Wass said, 'finesse and diplomacy is [sic] an essential ingredient in public service' (cited in Hennessy 1989: 150). Such skills lie at the heart of steering networks. Public servants have been managing networks for years, but either chose not to talk about it or, like Molière's Monsieur Jourdain, did not know that they had been speaking prose all their life. The idea is not new, although it can seem novel; it was just temporarily misplaced. Words like 'diplomacy', 'trust' and 'reciprocity' are central to managing the Network State.

Diplomacy

The defining role of senior public servants used to be to give advice to their ministers. Although this role continues, with public sector reform, increasingly their role has become that of manager of their department. With the onset of network steering, the shift is from management to diplomacy, and the departmental secretary must now combine the potentially conflicting roles of policy adviser, manager, diplomat and regulator. In managing networks, the diplomat's role becomes pre-eminent.

Diplomacy refers to management by negotiation. The diplomat must persuade 'another government to accept and perhaps actually help to promote the policies which it is the ambassador's function to advocate'. The main technique is 'the maintenance by continual persuasion of order in the midst of change' (Watson 1982: 125 and 223). The literature on diplomatic negotiations contains uncanny parallels with intergovernmental relations in a nation state, with its emphasis on negotiation when common interests and issues of conflict coexist. Without common interests there is no interdependence, and functional conflicts are endemic. One way of resolving conflict in international relations is negotiation. Of course the term is not restricted to international relations. It covers all the external relations of government departments; that is, it encompasses other departments, other public agencies (including local authorities), parliament, the media and, where relevant, international agencies.

Trust

At the heart of networks and management by diplomacy is the notion of trust; it is 'the most important attribute of network operations' and the central co-ordinating mechanism (see Frances et al. 1991: 15; Kramer & Tyler 1996). Shared values and norms are the glue that holds the complex set of relationships together; trust is essential for co-operative behaviour and, therefore, the existence of the network. Moreover, trust is non-calculative. As Powell (1996: 63) points out, trust is 'neither chosen nor embedded but is instead learned and reinforced, hence a product of ongoing interaction and discussion'. Preserving trust is, therefore, a reciprocal and endless task. Fox's (1974: 362) conclusions about trust in industrial relations are equally apt for networks. Thus, in networks with high trust relationships, participants:

share certain ends or values; bear towards each other a diffuse sense of long-term obligations; offer each other spontaneous support without narrowly calculating the cost or expecting any equivalent short-term reciprocation; communicate freely and honestly; are ready to repose their fortunes in each other's hands; and give each other the benefit of any doubt that may arise with respect to goodwill or motivation.

Reciprocity

Networks involve friendship, loyalty, even altruism (Thompson 1993: 54–58), but above all, network culture is characterised by reciprocity. As Powell (1991: 272–73) comments, reciprocity is rooted in 'the normative standards that sustain exchange', especially indebtedness, obligation and a long-term perspective. So a lack of equivalence creates a moral sanction, bonds that keep the parties in touch with one another; the books are balanced only in the long term. However, as Thompson (1993: 58) points out, reciprocity is also a symbolic relationship, and 'in the constant ritual of exchange, deep obligations and duties are established, symbolic statuses confirmed, metaphorical social references invoked'. In this way, network co-ordination becomes stabilised.

For a network manager, trust is essential for co-operative behaviour – and, therefore, for the existence of the network. So he or she will build trust to make sure negotiations continue until agreement is reached, and to maintain relationships even when agreement proves elusive. A diplomat does not set other people's objectives for them, but seeks to persuade them that their objectives are shared objectives; the skill is to find agreed objectives. Networks are the context in which the public service exercises diplomatic skills. Implementation depends on many other agencies – states, local governments, the private and voluntary sectors. Increasingly, the public servant is responsible for linking government both horizontally (between departments) and vertically (between levels of government and all other types of organisation involved in delivering services). The search for policy coherence is not confined to the department and its links to other central agencies; it occurs throughout civil society.

Understanding network governance

In this section, I explore when and why governing structures fail, focusing on networks because they are the focal point of this volume. An all-too-common feature of government policies is that one specific reform, such as marketisation, is seen as 'the solution'. But no governing structure works for all services in all conditions. All governing structures fail (Jessop 2000). Bureaucracy and red tape are an old litany. The costs of contracting out also become obvious. The limits of bureaucracy and markets are well known. So I will concentrate on the limits of networks. I provide four brief illustrations: joined-up government in the United Kingdom, the whole-of-government approach in Australia, partnership policing in the Australian state, and visible policing in the United Kingdom. My aim is to show the ubiquity of the problems. I then look at the sour laws of networks, focusing on the problems of co-ordination, mixing government structures, and ownership.

Networks thrive where markets and hierarchies fail, where trust and reciprocity characterise the relationships between organisations, and where management works by negotiation, not command. This much is obvious from Table 1.1. Also, as with any other form of public sector management, success depends on getting the relevant information, skills and resources. When actors husband information and resources, when in effect they refuse to share, then the co-operation that defines networks is unlikely to be forthcoming.

Equally, networks, like all other resource allocation mechanisms, are not cost free. They are often closed to outsiders and unaccountable for their actions. They can generate conflicts: between individual and organisational commitments; between local and national public expectations; between flexibility and rules; and between work goals and national regulators. They can be difficult to steer and they can mix with other governing structures like oil and water (see Fleming & Rhodes 2005).

There is a growing literature on how to manage networks to avoid these problems. How do you manage in interorganisational contexts where no manager can impose the objectives for the other participating organisations? The normal answer is by hands-off management and through persuasion, where independent actors agree on objectives. Senior management does not set them. As Ferlie and Pettigrew (1996: 88–89) found, the web of inter-agency alliances prompts a shift to matrix management styles, with chief executive officers increasingly concerned to build and uphold links and institutionalise strategic alliances. Respondents identified the following key networking skills:

> strong interpersonal, communication and listening skills; an ability to persuade; a readiness to trade and to engage in recip-rocal rather than manipulative behaviour; an ability to construct long-term relationships (Ferlie & Pettigrew 1996: 96).

I give one brief illustration of this growing literature on how to manage net-works (for a comprehensive review of tools for network governance, see Salamon 2000). So, sample the following pearls.

Box 1.1   Local practical solutions

Explore and agree the objectives of cross-boundary working.
Develop a shared understanding of what the network is for.
Develop an appropriate shared strategy.
Clarify roles, expectations and responsibilities for all players.
Create a culture in which cross-boundary working is likely to succeed.
Create appropriate shared service delivery systems.
Have a clear idea of what success would look like.

SOURCE   *Goss 2001: 97–100.*

As Perri 6 et al. (2002: 130) point out, network management 'is not rocket science'. This list of lessons gives credence to that claim. But the aspiring network manager also has to confront the sour laws of network governance. As a first step in exploring these laws, I give four brief illustrations of network governance 'in action'.

Network governance – four examples

Here I describe briefly the British government's experience with joined-up government and Australia's whole-of-government approach to show the dilemmas that are generic to the public sector. I then compare, briefly, Australian and British experience with community policing to show that the same problems recur in this specific context. In each case, I provide a short description of the initiative and a résumé of the key problems.

Joined-up government in the United Kingdom

In the United Kingdom, joined-up government has two dimensions: horizontal co-ordination of central departments and agencies and vertical co-ordination of subnational bodies, irrespective of whether they are part of the government, the voluntary or the private sectors (see Cm 4310 1999; Cabinet Office 2000). In brief, in the United Kingdom, horizontal co-ordination covers strengthening the role of central agencies. Thus the Treasury gets involved in departmental policy-making by striking Public Service Agreements that link budget allocations to a department's performance. The No. 10 Policy Unit and the Cabinet Office similarly seek to co-ordinate across government, most notably through the many new units, including the Social Exclusion Unit, the Performance Innovation Unit, the Delivery Unit, the Office of Public Services Reform, the Strategic Communications Unit, the Regional Co-ordination Unit, the Women's Unit, and Task Forces. There is also much emphasis on interdepartmental co-operation and new delivery structures – for example, there are concordats between central departments (for example, between DfES [Department for Education and Skills] and the DWP [Department of Work and Pensions]), and 'Tsars' to co-ordinate policy on 'wicked' issues such as drugs, rough sleeping, and heart disease.

Vertical joining-up covers such innovations as strategic partnerships at local level, fostered by, for example, GOs (Government Offices for the Regions). There are a growing number of central–regional–local partnerships, action zones for health, education and employment, which seek to bring together local actors to deal with, for example, inequalities in health provision, and innovative joint policy initiatives such as Surestart, which brings together childcare, primary health care and early education provision to combat child poverty.

Six problems recur. First, the existing tensions between the Treasury, No. 10 and the Cabinet Office undermine joining-up initiatives as the various central agencies fight for ascendancy (on the conflicts between the Treasury and No. 10, see Bevir & Rhodes 2006).

Second, joining-up initiatives assume a consensus between central government, local government and other agencies. However, the many bodies outside central government prize their autonomy and resist the central imposition of objectives, preferring to own the initiative. Thus there is an epidemic of zones, to the point where the solution to fragmentation has become part of the problem, since the zones add significantly to the many bodies to be co-ordinated. John Denham (1999), then a junior minister in the Department of Health, conceded that 'zones can sometimes make government look more, rather than less complicated to the citizen' and that there is the danger of 'initiative overload' because the zones do not join up.

Third, most ministers are in their post for 18–24 months, and err on the side of short term-ism. They need quick results. The initiative for joined-up government comes from No. 10, with its own priorities.

Fourth, ministerial responsibility encourages departmentalism, as do the civil service silos and associated culture. In turn, the department-based select committees of the House of Commons reinforce departmentalism.

Fifth, existing management systems undermine joining up. The proportion of budgets earmarked for cross-cutting programs is too small. Targets skew performance because they are internal to the department. Responsibility is diffused between sections of departments and between agencies.

Finally, devolution to Scotland, Wales and Northern Ireland fosters differentiation, not integration (for more detailed discussion, see Kavanagh & Richards 2001; Ling 2002; Mulgan 2001; Perri 6 et al. 2002).

The whole-of-government approach in Australia

John Howard (2001), Prime Minister of Australia, described a whole-of-government approach as a key challenge to the Australian Public Service (APS). The response of the APS was the Management Advisory Committee (MAC) (2004: 1), which defines the whole-of-government approach as:

> Public service agencies working across portfolio boundaries to achieve a shared goal and an integrated government response to particular issues. Approaches can be formal and informal. They can focus on policy development, program management and service delivery (see also Shergold 2004).

The Cabinet Implementation Unit (CID) in the Department of Prime Minister and Cabinet (PM&C) is the focal point of the initiative. CID's work is supplemented by regular meetings of portfolio secretaries and by the annual high-level retreats and the usual Cabinet, ministerial, interdepartmental and intergovernmental mechanisms. Although much emphasis is laid on improved co-ordination at the top of government, the initiative also extends to external groups and across jurisdictions. The report includes several case studies of such joint working. They include the Australian Government Natural Resource Management Team, which is responsible for government strategy on the sustainable use and conservation of land, water, soil and vegetation resources; the efforts of the Council of Australian Governments (COAG) to improve the social and economic well-being of indigenous peoples; and the government's response to the Bali bombings.

As with the British attempt at grand co-ordination, there are problems. First, how do you get ministers to buy into interdepartmental co-ordination? The short answer is that it's difficult: they are reluctant. They want to make a name for themselves, not for their colleagues. Second, departments are competing silos. The rewards of departmentalism are known and obvious. For interdepartmental co-ordination, it is the costs that are known and obvious. Co-ordination costs time, money and staff. Indeed. As Wanna (2005: 9) argues, whole-of-government is a sideshow for most managers. Third, co-ordination is *for* central departments! It serves their priorities, not necessarily those of the other departments involved. Fourth, there is a tension between managerialism, which seeks to decentralise decision-making, and the call for better co-ordination, which seeks to centralise it. Fifth, federalism is a long-standing constitutional check on the power of the Commonwealth. It is brutally simple. Co-ordination is for the Commonwealth, not state governments and other agencies. The Commonwealth does not control service delivery. It has limited reach, so it has to negotiate. As in the United Kingdom, central co-ordination presupposes agreement with the priorities of central agencies, when it is the lack of such agreement that created many of the problems – a genuine Catch 22.

The mixed economy of visible patrols

Policing has many providers, public and private. We live in an era of plural policing (Crawford 2003). Crawford et al.'s (2005) study of visible patrols in the United Kingdom identifies a mixed economy of policing covering sworn officers, special constables, CSOs (community support officers), neighbourhood and street wardens, municipal rangers, private security guards and citizen volunteers. Their key functions include patrol and visibility, crime prevention, community engagement, information gathering and law enforcement. Where there is effective co-ordination, locally dedicated visible patrols foster security, social cohesion, innovative service delivery and the spread of good practice. However, roles and responsibilities in plural policing can be blurred and balancing the several roles can be a problem. So trust between the several organisations is essential for effective working.

These 'mobile scarecrows' (Crawford et al. 2005: 91) confront several problems. First, the contracts are short term and the turnover of personnel is high, hampering communication between the several organisations and impeding efforts to build trust. Second, Crawford et al. (2005: Chapter 5) found that good co-ordination was atypical. Marketisation fragmented service delivery. It is scarcely a surprise to find that there were co-ordination deficits when effective action required joined-up national government initiatives, regional oversight, strategic co-ordination of partnerships, and local operational co-ordination. The problem was clearly spelt out by one Chief Constable:

> The mixed economy has been a reality in policing for some time, it's just it hasn't been quite joined up and still isn't because of rivalries and turf wars, as much between government ministries as anything else ... You can get more out of all these people than the simple sum of their parts if you co-ordinate properly (cited in Crawford et al. 2005: 70).

Third, information exchange is occasional, fragmentary and constrained by concerns about confidentiality. Fourth, accountability is weak. Joint decisions can be taken in partnerships that span hierarchies, leading to the problem of many hands, in which so many contribute that no one contribution can be held to account. Fifth, regulation is segmented, with emphasis on cost rather than quality. In short, as Wakefield (2005) argues, 'reassurance policing' is 'another vague initiative' that police are not good at, like public consultation. But as with the previous examples, the mixed economy of visible patrols is an example of a network model of horizontal partnerships co-producing local security complicated by a market in which providers compete and by the bureaucratic steering by police of their 'junior partners'.

Community policing – 'It's situational'

Fleming and Rhodes (2005), in their exploration of the limits and prospects of community policing in the United Kingdom, report on the views of senior officers and how they deal with the challenges and tensions of co-ordinating the hierarchical network of bureaucratically organised public police departments with their contractual obligations with external networks and the community networks, comprising business, voluntary community groups non-government agencies. The continuing and dominant importance of authority, hierarchy and rules was evident, and many spoke of the pervasive nature of managerialism, outsourcing and contractual obligations. Most acknowledged the difficulties of reconciling these governing structures with 'community networking'.

Officers spoke of the conflict between meeting organisational performance targets and the proactivity work and co-operation associated with networks and partnerships. They questioned the efficiency of number-crunching and bean-counting activities associated with accounting for the efficient and effective delivery of services to the community. The inevitable 'lack of resources' argument was canvassed. Many argued that the police should explain to the community the limits to their ability to provide services. For example, the public's expectations of police response times are out of touch with 'what police have to work with'. The political nature of police work generally was seen as a significant obstacle to working with the community: police usually cannot deliver good news stories of reduced crime rates and faster response times.

Fleming and Rhodes conclude that bureaucracy, contracts and networks need to be managed effectively simultaneously. From the police perspective, any confusion is solved by context and situation:

> Command and control is situational. In my team, I don't have subordinates. I have team members. Years ago a constable wouldn't speak to a superintendent – this is not the case now. I invite their ideas and input and encourage them to talk to me. If they are happy, I have a productive working team. However, as I said, it's situational. Fighting fires is a good example. As a commander, when I want something done, it isn't up for negotiation. We have to rely on command and control (cited in Fleming & Rhodes 2005: 203).

Clearly, the need to match management style to context is a priority for police officers. It may also be something senior police management and their political masters need to consider.

Fleming (Chapter 4) provides another account of police officers' perspectives on networking and partnerships. This account reaffirms what

police see as the conflictual nature of governing structures in police organisations and highlights the challenges they face when confronted with
making partnerships work.

The sour laws of network governance

Here I want, first, to revisit the several problems that cropped up in the four
examples of network governance, and argue that they boil down to: the holy
grail of co-ordination, the mix of service delivery systems, and disputes
about ownership. Second, I want to challenge the increasingly common
view that networks are a tool of government to be managed to achieve
central objectives.

The holy grail of co-ordination

The search for co-ordination lies at the heart of both New Labour's reforms
in the United Kingdom and Howard's call for a whole-of-government
approach. In both countries, the reforms have a centralising thrust. They
seek to co-ordinate departments and other agencies – whether of the centre,
the states or local government, and whether public or private – by imposing
a new style of management on other agencies. The Blair government is
explicit. Although the government does 'not want to run local services from
the centre', it 'is not afraid to take action where standards slip' – an obvious
instance of a command operating code (Cm 4310 1999: 35, 37, 45, 53, 55).
Such a code, no matter how well disguised, runs the risk, at all times, of
recalcitrance from key actors and a loss of flexibility in dealing with localised
problems. Gentle pressure relentlessly applied is still a command operating
code, just in a velvet glove. When you are sitting at the top of a pyramid and
you cannot see the bottom, control deficits are an ever-present unintended
consequence.

Co-ordination is not just an issue for central governments. It is also an
issue in community policing, which is also centralising – co-ordination pre-
sumes a co-ordinator, in this case the police. Thus Crawford et al. (2005)
report the police taking the lead role in managing networks either as a conscious strategy with their 'junior partners' or in frustration because those
'junior partners' are not more like the police. Indeed, Crawford et al. (2005:
89) advocate a hierarchy of co-ordination from national joining-up to local
operational policing.

What we see here is an age-old problem dressed up in fashionable phrases. That problem is co-ordination. We know that despite strong pressures for more co-ordination, the practice is 'modest'. It is 'largely negative, based on persistent compartmentalisation, mutual avoidance and friction reduction between powerful bureaus or ministries'; it is 'anchored at the lower levels of the state machine and organised by specific established networks'; it is 'rarely strategic, so almost all attempts to create proactive strategic capacity for long-term planning ... have failed'; and it is intermittent and selective in any one sector, improvised late in the policy process, politicised, issue oriented and reactive (Wright & Hayward 2000: 33). Co-ordination is the 'philosopher's stone' of modern government: ever sought, but always just beyond reach, all too often because it assumes both agreement on goals and a central co-ordinator (Seidman 1975: 190).

But co-ordination is not confined to central co-ordination by rules. There are alternatives. The all-too-often ignored but classic book on informal co-ordination is Lindblom's (1965) analysis of partisan mutual adjustment. For Lindblom, central co-ordination refers to 'a set of interdependent decisions' that is 'co-ordinated if each decision is adapted to the others in such a way that for each adjusted decision, the adjustment is thought to be better than no adjustment in the eyes of one decision maker'. A partisan is a decision-maker who makes decisions calculated to serve his or her own goals. Mutual adjustment occurs when a decision-maker either simply adapts to decisions around him or seeks to induce changes in other decision-makers. The methods by which a decision-maker can induce such adjustments include bargaining, reciprocity, manipulation and compensation (see also Chisholm 1989; Davis 1995; Peters 1998; Wildavsky 1979: 131–33). The overlap here with the idea of diplomacy is both obvious and inescapable.

It's the mix that matters

One clear effect of marketisation is that it undermines the effectiveness of the networks it spreads. Contracts undermine trust, reciprocity, informality and co-operation. I am not arguing that joined-up government and networks are unworkable. All governing structures fail. Governments have to find the right mix because the several mechanisms can mix like oil and water. One clear, even dramatic, irony of contracting was that it undermined the effectiveness of the networks that it spread. The government promoted competition and contracting out. The effect was to 'corrode ... common values and commitments' and 'to create an atmosphere of mistrust'. Market relations had 'corrosive effects' on 'professional networks which depend on co-operation, reciprocity and interdependence' (Flynn et al. 1996: 115, 136–37). In short, contracts undermine trust, reciprocity, informality and co-operation. We relearn another old lesson.

Support for this interpretation can be found in all four illustrations. In Britain, subnational agencies protect their autonomy from central command and control. In Australia, the states similarly protect their rights. The police struggle to reconcile contracts with partnerships. As Fleming and Rhodes (2005) argue, contracts focus on performance indicators and are characterised by prices and competition (including internal competition for scarce resources). Neither performance measurement nor competition mixes well with resource exchange, information sharing, negotiation, trust and reciprocity. Crawford et al. (2005: 90) see the integration, steering, networked and market models of visible policing 'coexisting in more or less awkward relations', and dispute claims that the network model is dominant.

Disputes about ownership

It is common for the problems of managing networks to be transformed into problems of leadership. Does top management walk the walk as well as talk the talk? Stewart (2000: 50) comments:

> The absence of integrated working is longstanding, culturally embedded, historically impervious, obvious to all concerned and deeply entrenched in central and local government.

Leadership is the new mantra; for example, Dr Peter Shergold (2004), Secretary of PM&C (Department of Prime Minister and Cabinet), sees leadership as one of the key characteristics of COAG's (Council of Australian Governments) indigenous initiative (see also Halligan 2005: 34). Is leadership the new solution? Not if the term applies to central, directive leadership, or even to transformative leadership, aimed at persuading other actors to accept central objectives.

Local networks cease to be local networks when they are centrally manipulated or directed. In effect, when networks are centrally managed, horizontal relationships are transformed into vertical relationships. The centre has to calculate whether the costs of agreement are greater than the costs of imposition, and all too often it finds for the latter. Such relationships are better described as exercises in official consultation; at least this phrase does not imply any local discretion.

The instrumental view of networks sees them as a tool of greater central control (see, for example, Kickert et al. 1997; Perri 6 1997). Thus Taylor (1997) describes how central actors adopt a decentralised negotiating style that trades a measure of control for agreement. This style of hands-off management involves setting the framework in which networks work but then staying an arm's length from those networks. At times, central government has shown sympathy for this approach to steering. For example, the United Kingdom's Department of National Heritage provides the policy framework and policy guidance, prods the network into action by systematic review and scrutiny of its work, uses patronage to put 'one of its own' into a key position, mobilises resources and skills across sectors, regulates the network and its members, and provides advice and assistance (Cm 2811 1995). The same argument applies to the role of police in local networks. If they define themselves as taking the lead role, they can then choose between command and control strategies or arm's length framing strategies. In short, diplomatic means can reinforce control.

There is an alternative to the instrumental view of networks. Local ownership and a degree of independence from central government can be seen as defining characteristics of network governance. From this standpoint, the republican view of democracy, with its stress on freedom from domination, seems apt. For example, John Braithwaite (1997: 312) argues for:

> the ideal of many semi-autonomous powers recursively checking one another rather than a few autonomous branches of governance. The more richly plural the separation into semi-autonomous powers, the more the dependence of each power on many other guardians of power will secure their independence from domination by one power.

So 'it is better to have many unclear separations of public and private powers than a few clear ones'. Multi-level governance, with its many policy networks, approximates to 'many unclear separations of public and private powers' (Braithwaite 1997: 312). The issue becomes, therefore, one of local ownership and ensuring equity of access to the networks.

I can now return to the topic of leadership, but this time understood as local entrepreneurs; leadership is about opening networks. For Stoker (2004: 139), the task of local politicians is 'to facilitate voice in diverse communities, and reconcile differences, develop shared visions and build partnerships to ensure their achievement'. Leadership is not about control, but about supporting people as they find their own solutions (see also Wilkinson & Applebee 1999). The implication of this line of analysis is that the police are not the best partners for the community. For a UK example, the function of CSOs may be better contracted out: this would both avoid the police using them 'as a generic resource to fill service gaps' (Crawford et al. 2005: 91), and maintain a distinct identity for the CSOs, one embedded in the community rather than in the police.

Conclusion

Governmental traditions shape the beliefs and practices of public servants and police alike. It is scarcely any surprise that public sector reform is rarely neat or uniform when traditions vary greatly, not just between countries but also between institutions. Recent changes to network governance compound complexity, giving public servants more balls to juggle as they strive to manage contracts, to steer networks, and to draw on bureaucracy's institutional memory. The central story is about balancing that unholy trinity, the ever-changing mix of markets, hierarchies and networks.

In looking for that balance, the role of the academic is not to deliver instrumental knowledge; to transform networks into another tool of central control. Rather, we can offer narratives that enable policy-makers to see things differently. We can try to find new features of network governance. My story is the shift to networks, the contradictions between networks and other governing structures, the sour laws of unintended consequences, and the role of local entrepreneurs in opening networks and facilitating their role as a check on government. It challenges the dominant, instrumental or tool view of networks. For example, it argues for local ownership over central control. It suggests that the police are not the best way to involve the community in plural policing; for example, that reassurance policing would be better contracted out.

The advantage of wearing public administration spectacles is, therefore, that a different story emerges. As Fleming and Rhodes have noted in the police context, a reluctance to engage with police reform is not always about recalcitrant police officers flexing their cultural muscles (although of course it can be). My version of such a story would stress the inherent limits of bureaucracy, market and network reforms and their incompatibility when used simultaneously. My story would note that police are intrinsically aware of these limits. My story stresses the shared experience of reform in the public sector and the validity of the local knowledge of both public servant and police officer. In short, my story is a new way of seeing the limits and potentialities of network governance.

References

Aucoin, P. (1995) The New Public Management: Canada in comparative perspective. Quebec: Institute for Research on Public Policy.

Bevir, M. and Rhodes, R.A.W. (2006) Governance Stories. Oxford: Routledge.

Braithwaite, J. (1997) On speaking softly and carrying big sticks: Neglected dimensions of a Republican separation of powers, University of Toronto Law Review, 47: 305–61.

Cabinet Office (2000) Wiring It Up. London: Cabinet Office.

Caiden, G. (1990) Australia's changing administrative ethos, in A. Kouzmin and N. Scott (eds), Dynamics in Australian Public Management: Selected essays. Melbourne: Macmillan.

Chisholm, D. (1989) Co-ordination Without Hierarchy: Informal structures in multiorganizational systems. Berkeley: University of California Press.

Cm 2811 (1995) Department of National Heritage Annual Report 1995. London: HMSO.

Cm 4310 (1999) Modernising Government. London: Stationery Office.

Crawford, A. (2003) The pattern of policing in the UK: Policing beyond the police, in T. Newburn (ed.), Handbook of Policing, Devon: Willan Publishing.

Crawford, A. Lister, S., Blackburn, S. and Burnett, J. (2005) Plural policing: The mixed economy of visible patrols in England and Wales. Bristol: The Policy Press.

Davis, G. (1995) A Government of Routines. Melbourne: Macmillan Education.

Denham, J. (1999) An epidemic of zones: Illness or cure?, speech delivered to the CIPFA/Public Management and Policy Association Conference, International Conference Centre, Birmingham.

Ferlie, E. and Pettigrew, A. (1996) Managing through networks: Some issues and implications for the NHS, British Journal of Management, 7: 81–99.

Fleming, J. and Rhodes, R.A.W. (2005) Bureaucracy, contracts and networks: The unholy trinity and the police, Australian and New Zealand Journal of Criminology, 38(2).

Fox, A. (1974) Beyond Contract: Work, power and trust relations. London: Faber.

Frances, J. et al. (1991) Introduction, in G. Thompson et al. (eds), Markets Hierarchies and Networks: The co-ordination of social life. London: Sage.

Goss, S. (2001) *Making Local Governance Work*. Houndmills, Basingstoke: Palgrave Macmillan.

Halligan, J. (2005) Public sector reform, in C. Aulich and R. Wettenhall (eds), *Howard's Second and Third Governments*. Sydney: UNSW Press.

Hennessy, P. (1989) *Whitehall*. London: Secker & Warburg.

Hood, C. (1991) A public management for all seasons?, *Public Administration*, 69: 3–19.

Howard, J. (2001) The Centenary of the APS oration, speech delivered to the Centenary Conference of the Institute of Public Administration Australia, Canberra, 19 June.

Kavanagh, D. and Richards, D. (2001) Departmentalism and joined-up government, *Parliamentary Affairs*, 54: 1–18.

Jessop, B. (2000) Governance failure, in G. Stoker (ed.), *The New Politics of British Local Governance*. Houndmills, Basingstoke: Macmillan.

Keating, M. and Wanna, J. (2000) Remaking federalism?, in M. Keating and J. Wanna (eds), *Institutions: The future of Australian governance*. Sydney: Allen & Unwin.

Kickert, W.J.M., Klijn, E-H. and Koppenjan, J.F.M. (eds) (1997) *Managing Complex Networks: Strategies for the public sector*. London: Sage.

Lindblom, C.E. (1965) *The Intelligence of Democracy*. New York: The Free Press.

Ling, T. (2002) Delivering joined-up government in the UK, *Public Administration*, 80: 615–42.

MAC (Management Advisory Committee) (2004) *Connecting Government: Whole of government response to Australia's priority challenges*. Canberra: Australian Public Service Commission.

Mulgan, G. (2001) Joined-up governance, paper delivered to the British Academy Conference on Joined-Up Government, 30 October.

Perri 6 (1995) *Holistic Governance*. London: Demos.

Perri 6, Leat, D., Seltzer, K. and Stoker, G. (2002) *Towards Holistic Governance: The new reform agenda*. Houndmills, Basingstoke: Palgrave Macmillan.

Peters, B.G. (1998) Managing horizontal governance: the politics of co-ordination, *Public Administration*, 76: 295–311.

Pollitt, C. (1993) *Managerialism and the Public Services* (2nd edition). Oxford: Blackwell.

Pollitt, C. and Bouckaert, G. (2000) *Public Management Reform: A comparative analysis*. Oxford: Oxford University Press.

Powell, W. (1991) Neither market nor hierarchy: network forms of organization, in G. Thomson et al., *Markets Hierarchies and Networks: The co-ordination of social life*. London: Sage.

—— (1996) Trust-based forms of governance, in R.M. Kramer and T. Tyler (eds), *Trust in Organisations: Frontiers of theory and research*. London: Sage.

Rhodes, R.A.W. (1997) *Understanding Governance*. Buckingham: Open University Press.

—— (ed.) (2000) *Transforming British Governance* (2 volumes). London: Macmillan.

—— (2006) Policy network analysis, in M. Moran, M. Rein and R.E. Goodin (eds), *The Oxford Handbook of Public Policy*. Oxford: Oxford University Press.

Rhodes, R.A.W. and Weller, P. (eds) (2001) *The Changing World of Top Officials: Mandarins or valets?* Buckingham: Open University Press.

Salamon, L.M. (ed.) (2002) *The Tools of Government: A guide to the new governance*. Oxford: Oxford University Press.

Seidman, H. (1975) *Politics, Position and Power* (2nd edition). Oxford: Oxford University Press.

Shergold, P. (2004). Speech to launch *Connecting Government*, Canberra, 20 April.

Stewart, M. (2000) Local action to counter exclusion, in Policy Action Team 17, *Joining It Up Locally: The evidence base*. London: Department of the Environment, Transport and Regions.

Stoker, G. (2004) *Transforming Local Governance*. Houndmills, Basingstoke: Palgrave Macmillan.

Taylor, A. (1997) 'Arm's length but hands on': Mapping the new governance – The Department of National Heritage and Cultural Policies in Britain, *Public Administration*, 75: 441–66.

Thompson, G. (1993) Network co-ordination, in R. Maidment and G. Thompson (eds), *Managing the United Kingdom*. London: Sage.

Wakefield, A. (2005) Ethnography in Private Policing, paper prepared for the Ethnography in Policing Panel, 55th Political Studies Association Annual Conference 4–7 April, University of Leeds (UK).

Wanna, J. (2005). 'Connecting Government' and 'Whole of Government' – meanings, claims and critique, paper delivered to the 17th Annual Government Business Conference, Australian Government Agencies, Queensland Regional Heads Forum, Gold Coast, 19–20 May.

Watson, A. (1982) *Diplomacy*. London: Eyre Methuen.

Wildavsky, A. (1979) *The Art and Craft of Policy Analysis*. London: Macmillan.

Wilkinson, D. and Appelbee, E. (1999) *Implementing Holistic Government*. London: Demos.

Wright, V. and Hayward, J. (2000) Governing from the Centre: Policy co-ordination in six European core executives, in R.A.W. Rhodes (ed.), *Transforming British Government, Volume 2: Changing Roles and Relationships*. London: Macmillan.

MAPPING SECURITY NETWORKS: FROM METAPHORICAL CONCEPT TO EMPIRICAL MODEL

2

Benoit Dupont[1]

The concept of a 'network' is a powerful one. Its appeal lies in its ability to account for the present multiplicity of institutional, organisational and social morphologies. Networks promise to absorb, recombine, and merge the two dominant and competing forms of social organisation (the bureaucratic hierarchy and the market) into a third one to form what Rhodes (Chapter 1) calls the 'unholy trinity'. Networked governance seems to transcend the proclaimed obsolescence of bureaucracies (see, for example, Osborne & Gaebler 1992) and the unsavoury smell of the market.

In the field of security, the myth of the fight against crime and the war-like metaphors on which it relied were seriously undermined by the discovery that organised crime was much less organised than initially thought, and that crime syndicates were loosely coupled alliances of individuals who retained a large degree of autonomy (Naylor 2002). Success in that line of work depends on the position one maintains in broader networks that often overlap and extend far beyond the core group (Morselli 2005). The events of 9/11 and the subsequent revelations about missed opportunities to prevent them were a catalyst for discussions of terrorist networks outperforming police bureaucracies and recommendations that law enforcement organisations adopt flatter and more flexible structures (Williams 1994; Arquilla & Ronfeld 2001).

Police organisations have studied crime maps to identify hotspots and have embraced social network analysis to better understand the structure of criminal and terrorist groups, but they have been surprisingly slow to use these tools to map their own policy and implementation environment. Academics have been more enthusiastic, but the few efforts so far to map existing security networks have either focused on a few nodes (Newburn 2001; Cooley 2005, for three Canadian case studies) or emphasised narrative and statistical data describing the roles of the various actors, their mandates, and their interests (Crawford et al. 2005; Fleming & Rhodes 2005). Quantitative techniques have very rarely been mobilised in this area, despite a long sociological tradition of their use in social, organisational, and political network analysis (Knoke 1990; Freeman 2004). To date, and to the best of my knowledge, only one study (never cited in criminological works) has attempted to measure the role played by social capital in the recruitment strategies of the private security industry (Erickson 2001). No such research has been carried out on the police.

There are two reasons for this. First, institutional fetishism of the dominant paradigm of security forged by Hobbes and Weber makes it difficult to accommodate the current transformations in security provision, where the traditional idea of a state monopoly over the use of legitimate coercion is being challenged by the introduction of dispersed and de-centred security authorisation and delivery (Bayley & Shearing 2001). As Shearing notes (in press), paradigms are theoretically self-sufficient, leaving them open to empirical deficiencies. In that context, the mapping of security networks has never been fully attempted. The discovery of the size (in terms of membership and workforce) of the private and hybrid security sectors refutes the established paradigm, but as long as the rediscovered private sector could be depicted as a homogeneous group, the idea that it constituted a junior partner to the police could be maintained, making the survival of the existing conceptual frameworks possible. This disciplinary blind spot is reinforced by the fact that the mapping exercise advocated here is resource intensive and involves a number of methodological challenges. Hence, in part because of practical difficulties, the concept of network is often used metaphorically, leading to various interpretations of what a network is, what its properties are, and what it does.

The growing body of literature on the features and organisation of security networks, and the normative contribution of these publications, can only benefit from development and analysis of more detailed datasets. This chapter introduces some considerations of the methodological tools that can be mobilised to map and model complex organisational sets, and the way the results such tools yield can be used to improve our understanding of contemporary security provision in western societies. In order to provide a more concrete approach, I focus on data collected in a large North American city that shares many characteristics with Australian cosmopolitan centres such as Melbourne or Sydney. The focus is mainly on the analysis of quantitative data, first by looking at the macro-structure of the network and then by detailing the micro-properties of the partnerships involved. The purpose of this case study is not to advance the case for shared or universal features but to explore the methodology, its challenges, the insights it can offer, and the ambitious research agenda it could frame.

The first part of this chapter clarifies the definition of networks that informs this approach, and describes their most salient properties in the security field. The second section examines the methodology that can be used to sketch security networks and their many dimensions empirically, as well as the challenges that must be overcome in order to do this. Finally, in the last two sections I provide some examples of how the data can be analysed and interpreted at the macro- and micro-sociological levels, suggesting that the notion of a 'securisphere' is more useful than the static idea of a state monopoly in understanding the authorisation and delivery of security.

Framing the conceptual nature of security networks

The concept of network lends itself to a number of ambiguities that have contributed to its attractiveness and wide use in sociology, political science, and criminology circles. When the term is not used metaphorically,[2] researchers have often relied more on intuitions of what a network is or how it behaves than on the stimulating research that is available on the empirical features of social and organisational networks (for a small sample of this research, see, for example, Burt 1992; Castells 1996; Morselli 2005; for a popular history of graph theory and network analysis, see Barabási 2002). Intuitive use of the term rarely differentiates between formal, informal and technological dimensions, and almost never considers the varied structures and substructures that can be found in a network, such as clusters, cliques, hierarchies, or random distributions of ties (Brodeur & Dupont forthcoming).

Imprecise use of the term allows it to be seen as analogous to communications or transport networks, evoking notions of highly co-ordinated assemblages. It is, however, easy to identify networks (in the sociological sense of the term) within groups of people or organisations that are not explicitly aware of the numerous and indirect links that bind them. This is especially true in the case of large-scale networks, where size obscures the structure, and in secret networks, whose survival depends on the compartmentalisation of links (as in informant or terrorist networks).

It is clear that a precise definition of the concept of security network, and an explanation of its implicit boundaries, is needed. In this chapter a security network refers to a set of institutional, organisational, communal or individual agents or nodes that are directly or indirectly connected in order to authorise and/or provide security for the benefit of internal or external stakeholders (Dupont 2004; Shearing & Wood 2000). The variety of nodes found in such networks is the source of structural heterogeneity and inequality (Castells 2000: 11): large government agencies and transnational corporations operate in the same field as local interests and family-owned businesses, with some entities made up of only one person (consultants, for example). Nevertheless, a complex web of recurrent interconnections and linkages brings these nodes together on a voluntary, contractual or regulatory basis.

One problem commonly found in network analysis is its failure to recognise the importance of determining node identities, thereby blurring the boundaries between nodes and their links. When a node reaches a certain size, it can be described as a network in its own right, which can create problems with using the concept. Consider, for example, the case of the US Department of Homeland Security, which amalgamated 22 existing government agencies in one of the largest examples of bureaucratic restructuring in the United States in the past 50 years. In its current form, the level of fragmentation and competition between sub-units makes it possible to consider the new entity an unco-ordinated network (or dysfunctional hierarchy) (Carafano & Heyman 2005).

For methodological reasons, nodes in security networks will be considered to consist of organisations and individuals that operate as discrete entities and are viewed as such by the overall membership of the security field. This restriction is a simplification of reality, where, for example, the same organisation can tap into networks through various different sub-units that promote various agendas. In other cases, an individual can represent more than one entity at the same time, for example as manager of a company and also president of a professional association. It is possible to compensate for these modelling limitations by collecting qualitative data that can more easily capture the nuances and meanings attached to particular nodes.

Security networks are formed around the authorisation and delivery of security, through a range of processes and services that extend from the identification of needs and the resources available to respond to them, to the management of risks and the deployment of human and technological assets. Nodes can be specialised in the authorisation or delivery aspects or can integrate both dimensions: while some businesses choose to outsource to private security companies, others prefer to develop in-house expertise. Security networks differ from the policy networks familiar to political scientists (Marsh 1998; Rhodes Ch 1.), which are designed to shape policies around specific issues (at the sectoral or sub-sectoral levels). Although they may also be involved in policy debates, particularly around the nature and level of regulation, they are established and maintained largely within the context of routine activities associated with the production of security. The need to reduce exposure to uncertainty and contingency is also a strong incentive for belonging to a security network. The terms of exchanges between members of a security network are then guided less by the need to influence government decisions than by the capacity to pool resources in order to increase effectiveness and decrease vulnerability. There is no shared overall objective or value, but instead a myriad of overlapping interests brought together by informal, voluntary, contractual or regulatory ties.

In this respect security networks are very similar to the large social and economic networks discovered by mathematicians and sociologists, which are not designed from the top but emerge progressively from regular interactions between their members.[3] The size of such networks and their multilayered properties often limit members' awareness of the degrees of connection and interdependence within the network. In fact, just as Monsieur Jourdain in Molière's play had been speaking prose for 40 years without knowing it, many nodes are indifferent to their whole security network, focusing their attention instead on the most proximate (geographical or relational) and regular contacts. Security networks are more incidental than teleological, and as such, their normative potential is dependent on a much more detailed understanding of their dynamics than the current metaphorical use of the term allows.

Because networks can potentially include a limitless number of actors through interconnection (the famous six degrees of separation theory), networks whose boundaries are not carefully defined quickly become impractical for empirical study, due to their exponential growth. Such networks are part of the work of mathematicians and physicists, who can use simulations, but are much less practical for social scientists, who are confronted with the colossal task of collecting data in the real world.

Typologies can also be used both to clarify the area to be studied and to introduce some degree of scale to the study of networks. One useful variable to consider is the geographical scope of a network's mode of exchange: from the local to the international, through the national. We can reasonably expect security networks that operate at the local level to differ significantly in their membership and structure from national institutional networks and their international counterparts, which are concerned largely with transnational organised threats (Dupont 2004). Social and organisational networks have also benefited from the development of technological or informational networks (Castells 1996; Arquilla & Ronfeldt 2001). However, even if these two kinds of networks are intricately integrated, they should not be expected to operate in the same way. As a few observers have already noted, the fact that data or information is available to a network is not in itself a sufficient condition to ensure its diffusion and use by all institutional nodes. Social processes similar to those that facilitate the creation and transfer of tacit knowledge (Polanyi 1967; Nonaka & Takeushi 1995; Brown & Duguid 2000) can block the circulation of explicit knowledge within a security network (NCTAUS 2004; Sheptycki 2004).

Obviously the tentative typology presented here does not preclude overlaps and connections between categories. Nor does it necessarily capture all the relevant and significant variables of security networks, whose complexity challenges any analysis that relies exclusively on theoretical tools. The empirical approach seems at the moment to provide the most promising avenue for increasing our knowledge in this domain.

Counting nodes and ties:
Methodological considerations and challenges

In order to capture the essence of security networks, extensive data must be collected about the nodes they are composed of and the properties of these nodes, as well as about the webs of linkages that bind nodes together. There is a growing body of statistics that attempts to measure the size of the private security sector in terms of employee numbers (Prenzler & Sarre 1998; De Waard 1999) and is then used to design crude indicators such as the ratio of private to public security employees. Such indicators are useful to chart the diffusion of responsibilities in the security field – what Bayley and Shearing (2001) call the multilateralisation of security – but although these methods are useful in assessing the size of the submerged part of the security iceberg, they cannot tell us who is doing what, with whom, and how frequently. Any methodology we develop must fill this gap.

The amount of data required and the resources available for this research led me to limit this work to the geographical area of a large metropolitan centre of 1.8 million people. This city covers an area of 500 square kilometres, and had an estimated GDP of US$100 billion in 2003; 28 per cent of its population are immigrants; the unemployment rate is 9.2 per cent; and 50 per cent of the inhabitants have a college or university degree. In 2004 the annual city budget was US$3.15 billion, 18.7 per cent of which was spent on public security. One of its features is a 30km underground network of public and private pathways that connect 10 subway stations, 2 bus terminals, 2 train stations, 4 universities, 10 cinemas and theatres, 200 restaurants, 1600 apartments, 1700 retail stores, and 80 per cent of the city's office spaces. Each day, half a million people use this network. This web of private properties (Shearing & Stenning 1981) provides a powerful incentive for public and private security nodes to co-ordinate their activities in order to prepare for emergencies and prevent some forms of criminal activity.

The nodes of this local security network were defined as public and quasi-public organisations involved in the production of security, in-house (proprietary) security services for industrial or service-oriented businesses, and private security companies. Nodes were thus defined as entities or segments of entities whose primary function is the authorisation and/or delivery of security for communities, individuals, and organisations residing, working, studying, shopping, consuming services, or producing goods in this large metropolitan area. Relevant entities were formally identified through membership lists of the two main professional security associations active at the local level, the latest registration data of the regulatory body in charge of private security, the yellow pages of the telephone book, and snowball sampling during the collection itself.

One difficulty with this way of 'counting' the nodes is that it does not take into account variations in terms of size. A small number of nodes (such as the public police and large private security companies that employ thousands of workers) account for most of the workforce, while a large number of nodes are composed of only a few employees. In this respect, the impact certain organisations have on the field has nothing in common with the light footprints left by others. This inequality is reflected, to a certain extent, in the distribution patterns of ties – and power or influence are not, of course, exclusively derived from size. It is nevertheless important to remember that the visualisation tools used in network analysis have a tendency to discard many node properties in their representations, and that two very different nodes might end up looking the same on a diagram.

Data was gathered through interviews with each node's manager and covered the formal and informal dimensions of existing partnerships. The choice of managers as the primary respondents introduces some limitations, as they are unlikely to be aware of all the ties their employees maintain with colleagues in other nodes. However, their decisions are more likely to result in changes in policy and to affect the structure of the field than those made daily by frontline workers, whose practices are more routine (Erickson 2001). Managers can thus provide a satisfactory overview of the more important ties.

Exceptions were made for larger and more complex organisations such as the police, whose division of labour and long hierarchical chain require access to more than one respondent in order to map the numerous linkages activated daily. In those cases, key informants from various units of the organisation were interviewed. The interviews consisted of a qualitative component, which attempted to establish a profile of the node in terms of tasks accomplished, resources, expertise and governance structure, and a quantitative component, which took the form of a multivariable contact matrix. Each respondent was given a 'node generator', a constantly updated list of all the nodes in the security field under study.[4] Respondents were asked to name the nodes with which formal and informal ties had been maintained over the past 12 months. Because of the exploratory nature of this research, questions about ties were deliberately framed in the most general terms in order to include the many forms of partnerships and exchanges that might occur. (Future research should involve more detailed questionnaires that can discriminate between various layers of linkages by nature or perceived usefulness). For each contact, respondents were asked to specify nine variables:

- the number of individual contacts within the partner organisation;
- the existence of more privileged relationships with one of these contacts;
- extra-professional socialisation with those contacts;
- the context in which meetings with professional contacts occur outside the workplace (friendship, kinship, love affair ...);
- the frequency of contacts with the privileged partner or the group of contacts;
- the general distribution of responsibilities for activation of ties;
- the preferred technological tools used to interact with the contact;
- the contact's perceived level of responsibility (as compared to the respondent's); and
- the formal or informal nature of the partnership.

There were a number of challenges associated with collecting the data. The decision to complement quantitative data with qualitative data and the repetitive process of going through nine variables for each recorded contact made data collection time-consuming in a context where respondents had extremely busy schedules and unexpected circumstances often delayed the arranged interviews. Nevertheless, 50 respondents were interviewed over a period of 16 months, from January 2004 to April 2005. The breakdown of their organisational affiliation is provided in Table 2.1. In order to facilitate analogies with the Australian context, the right-hand column lists the security nodes that would be found if the research were duplicated in a city such as Sydney.

TABLE 2.1   Respondent's organisational affiliation

	N	%	Australian equivalents (Sydney area)
Public police	4	8	Australian Federal Police; NSW Police; ASIO
Hybrid sector	23	46	City of Sydney (Safe City Program); Customs Australia; Australia Post (corporate security); CityRail (Transit officers); University of Sydney (security service); Department of Immigration; Sydney Opera House (security)
Professional associations	1	2	Australian Security Industry Association; ASIS International NSW Chapter
In house (proprietary) private sector	14	28	Westpac Banking Corporation; Telstra; Woolworths; Qantas
Contract generalist	3	6	Chubb Security; Unified Security Group
Contract investigations and expertise	3	6	Bassett Risk Management; Control Risks Group; Harris Security Management
Contract equipment	2	4	ADT; Automa Biometric Solutions
Total	50	100	

Unless the network we are studying is randomly structured, the sampling strategies used in statistical analysis cannot be applied. Ideally, mapping a network should include identification of all its components, because we are trying to measure inconsistencies (the extreme values are the most significant). Considering only a sample of the components might miss a key node of the network, even, perhaps, the 'hub' that allows the network to function properly. Relying exclusively on snowball sampling or other self-selection methods such as membership lists runs the risk of mistaking a sub-component (albeit a large one) for the whole of a network.

Unfortunately, real-life networks are sprawling, and may include large numbers of nodes which can be catalogued only by reducing data thickness. In our case, for example, the 207 nodes listed by our 50 respondents certainly did not include all actors in the city's security system. However, the high density and connectivity uncovered, coupled with the fact that the data originated from diversified nodes, make it unlikely that key parts of the local network were omitted. Compromises and an element of arbitrary judg-ment are unfortunately unavoidable when partitioning a network (deciding where it ends for the purpose of the study).

The fact that networks have quasi-organic properties also represents a challenge for the researcher. During the study a few respondents accepted new responsibilities with other nodes; others were demoted or lost their position through downsizing. This constant evolution of networks (including possible collapse) is invisible in the snapshots provided through the tools used here, but more recent methodological developments add a temporal dimension to the mapping of nodes (Powell at al. 2005).

The collected data was imported into three distinct software packages: Ucinet, a social network analysis package that performs basic operations such as measurement of centrality, subgroup identification, role analysis, and elementary graph theory routines (Borgatti et al. 1999); SPSS, which was used to perform basic statistical analysis of tie variables; and NVivo, a qualitative analysis software that facilitates the coding and linkage of large and complex datasets.

The 'securisphere': Embedding pluralities

The respondents belonged to 47 discrete organisations,[5] which, taken together, employ 17,480 people[6] and provide security as a public service, internally, or on contract. (This last category includes the municipal police service with its 3,900 officers, a few large private security companies, such as Securitas, that offer guard services and employ more than 1000 people, and a large majority of in-house or for-contract security organisations that rarely have more than 100 employees). The average length of respondents' experience in the security field was 19.75 years (median: 20 years; standard deviation 12.16), including experience acquired in the public police by those who had started a second career in private security. This group, whose expertise and contacts were transferred from the public to the hybrid or private sectors, has often been described as the 'old boy network'. It accounted for 26 per cent of the respondents and its members can be found mainly in two categories of organisations: hybrid para-public organisations and in-house security of large companies. Very few of these individuals chose to join the generalist, investigation, or technology-related private security companies.

Despite the fact that respondents used the generic term 'security' to describe what they were doing, a diversity of meanings, rationalities, and outcomes is associated with the processes of authorisation and delivery. While the consensus around the police mandate is that it authorises the use of coercive force when needed to maintain order and enforce the law on behalf of all citizens, hybrid and private security nodes are more inclined to work proactively to manage risks and cannot mobilise exten-sive – and legal – force to achieve that end. In the case of mass private properties (Shearing & Stenning 1981), the risks to be managed are mainly those that threaten the routine activities of customers or users, while manufacturing or high-tech companies are more concerned with the integrity of their assets (such as intellectual property or costly equipment). The financial and governmental sectors emphasise the reliability of their procedures and want to make sure that these are not compromised by fraudulent behaviours.

FIGURE 2.1 Complete network (Gower)

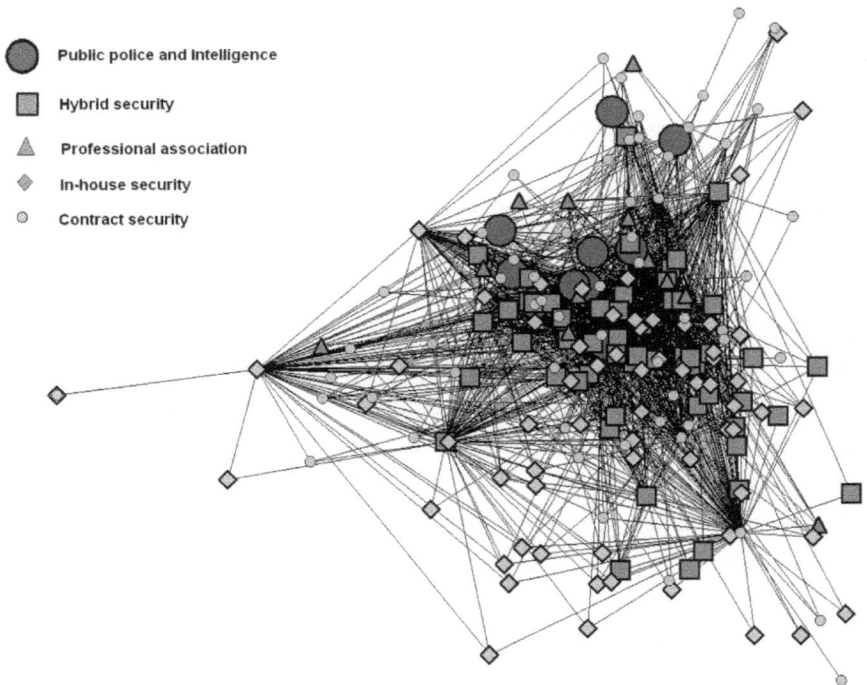

Legend:
- Public police and intelligence
- Hybrid security
- Professional association
- In-house security
- Contract security

Each actor, depending on the sector of activity and the demands of its stakeholders, develops a distinctive form of expertise, suited to its resources and constraints. One privileged strategy for significantly enhancing the quantity and quality of resources and lowering the impact of external constraints is to resort to partnerships. These partnerships, formal or informal, represent the 'bones' of the network. They can consist of the exchange of information about threats, best practices, potential providers, clients or employees; the pooling of resources such as CCTV (closed circuit TV) feeds; the joint management of training programs; or the implementation of new standards of practice. Figure 2.1 represents the patterns of partnership revealed by 47 security nodes, which belong to an overall network of 207 organisations. (Due to the density of the network and the ties, a few nodes might be superimposed.) Each line represents a partnership that was active over the previous 12 months (the frequency of contacts is discussed in a following section).

The intricate network pictured in Figure 2.1, which resembles a bird's nest, represents only a fraction of all potential ties, with bidirectional data covering no more than 23 per cent of the whole network (nodes interviewed/nodes cited). In order to properly measure the characteristics of the network, it was necessary to restrict the analysis to nodes that provided us with their complete list of partners. Due to this restriction, only 990 out of 1600 registered ties are used in this segment of the analysis. Although this meant a loss in comprehensiveness, it increased the validity of our findings.

The sample network, represented in Figure 2.2, has an average density of 46 per cent, meaning that 46 per cent of all possible partnerships between nodes are considered active. This appears high given the number of organisations being considered and their heterogeneity. This high density is confirmed by the high connectivity of the network: when we compute the distance between nodes, we see that the average geodesic distance is 1.5, which implies that actors can reach all the other nodes of the network through only one intermediary (this would be the shortest path, but many more or less efficient connections could be made). In such a tightly knit environment, information travels fast and is easy to retrieve, exchange costs are relatively low, and new trends will be adopted rapidly. Reputations can be undone at an equally fast pace.

Figure 2.2: Core network (spring embedding)

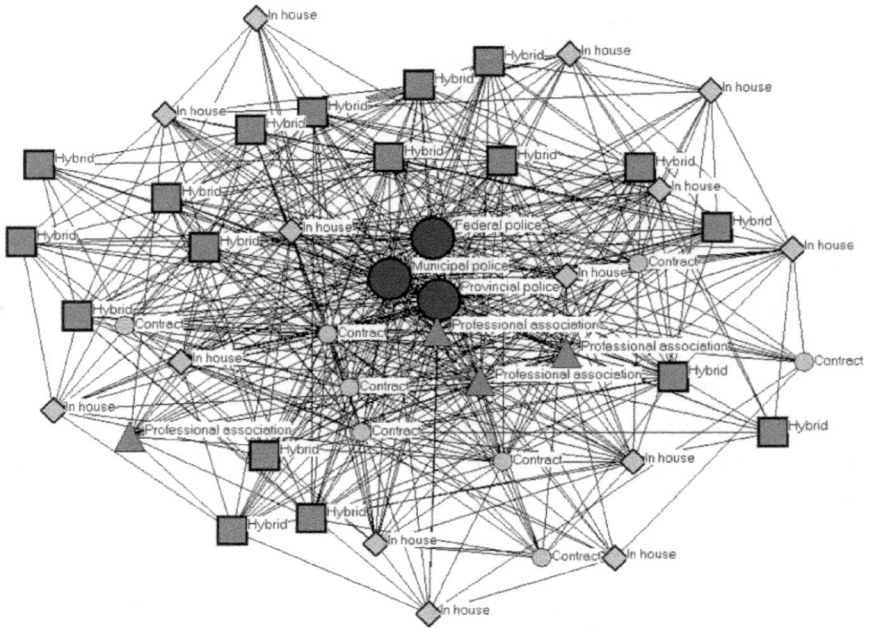

Another essential dimension in network analysis is centrality, which refers to the distribution of power within a network: the more central a node's position, the more opportunities it will have, the fewer constraints it will experience, and the more influence it will derive from its position. The amount of power derived from centrality also depends on the density of the network, but the two are not systematically correlated: dense networks can be highly centralised around a dominant player, but they can also be structured with a cliquish distribution of power. In the field of security, the public police are without any doubt the hub to which all actors converge because of their control over two essential assets: the legitimate use of force and the legal access to identity and crime-related information. But the core of the network is not the exclusive domain of the police: professional associations also play a central role. They provide continuing training to their members and allow them to tap into a vast reservoir of expertise, which flows freely between members. They are also a privileged marketplace where technology and service vendors meet prospective customers and where potential buyers can check the credentials of existing providers with their former or current clients, who attend the same meetings.

One striking aspect of this core is the fact that it is made up of two very loosely linked components: very few police respondents mentioned formal or informal ties with professional associations and the representatives of those associations lamented the lack of interest on the part of the police. Only a few hybrid organisations were members of the provincial association of chiefs of police, included apparently because of their limited legal powers to investigate or their mandate to act in the public interest (such as overseeing the security of an international airport). The police and professional associations seem less likely to be connected to each other than to the rest of the network and to be in competition – albeit with different resources at their disposal and different costs incurred – for the central role in the overall network. While the police officers interviewed had a lower-than-average number of ties outside the public police sector and appeared to be comfortable with this situation, their organisation is the largest 'sink' of partnerships in the network, with 96 per cent of nodes stating that they maintained a link of some sort with the municipal police. The percentage of those with links to the provincial and federal police, whose jurisdictions are more narrowly defined, is marginally lower (87 per cent and 83 per cent respectively).

By way of comparison, the number of incoming ties declared for each member of the network was an average of 29 per cent. The legitimacy of the police, confirmed by the efforts of all other actors to maintain a privileged relationship with them, is in sharp contrast to the more laborious process of expertise exchange and certification offered by professional associations. Professional associations were constantly involved in recruitment drives and initiatives aimed at keeping their members interested.

In both groups, less powerful members sought ways to reduce constraints and exposure to external contingencies. This is the reason nodes maintain numerous transverse ties, which avoid excessive dependence on the centre and permit them to hedge their exposure to risk in case of emergency. When police organisations and professional associations are removed from the matrix before connectivity tests are run, the average distance between two nodes remains constant at 1.6 (it was 1.5 for the complete network). This indicates an absence of decay: the network is still active and can operate effectively without its core, even if efficiency decreases slightly because fewer options are available. The network clearly acknowledges the power and authority of the police, but it does not depend on them to mediate its exchanges on a routine basis.

The existence of many cliques or subgroups where members' ties with each other are stronger than with the rest of the network[7] attests to this lack of dependence on the police. In our dataset, there are 247 cliques of 7 nodes or more and 78 cliques of 10 nodes or more. As would be expected, there is a large degree of overlap between these denser subgroups, corresponding to functional or personal affinities: the heads of security for educational and cultural institutions share common problems and therefore exchange more information more frequently, as do their public transport counterparts or any particular subset of security providers. In our interviews, the banking sector, the high-tech industry (aerospace, pharmaceuticals), large retail malls, hospitals, and public transport entities tended to exchange information and resources more intensely, sometimes creating their own specialised association or seeking linkages with counterparts at national or international levels.

Clusters of exchanges can also form along geographical lines, such as a large subway station located within a university campus, itself surrounded by the red light district, or the interconnected system of underground retail spaces and high-rise office towers, where millions pass seamlessly every year, oblivious to the co-ordinated security grid humming in the background.

Finally, the personal experiences of the members of a node are defined to a certain extent by the radius and nature of their relational neighbourhood. One example should be sufficient to illustrate this point. Among the five university security chiefs interviewed, the size of the immediate network varied from 10 to 28 nodes. The size of the institutions they worked for and their mandates were relatively identical, but their professional trajectories differed greatly. One of them is a retired police officer who has also tried his hand at security consulting, while others are general managers who have no prior experience in security and do not plan to continue in it as a long-term career. They therefore come to the position with little specific social capital and do not invest heavily in new partnerships beyond those that are essential.

Cliques, whether based on functional, geographic or personal dimensions, mobilise varied levels of trust and reciprocity in order to function. While superficial trust is sufficient for the overall network to operate, resilient trust is necessary at the subset level (Smith Ring 1997). This stronger form of trust is reinforced through frequent exchange of favours and displays of accommodating behaviours, which must be bidirectional.

The equilibrium, however, is fragile, and some dominant players may attempt 'hostile takeovers' of weaker nodes. For example, the municipal police force recently led a carefully orchestrated campaign in the media to discredit the special constable subway force by leaking statistics that showed higher-than-average crime rates in subway stations. As a result of these campaigns, the police managed to absorb subway security, effectively extending their reach to the underground city – and probably making other public transport security providers nervous.

If a shared set of occupational values acquired in an earlier career can come in handy at times, membership in the 'old boy network' is not sufficient to secure a management position in the hybrid and private security sectors. More than law enforcement skills *per se*, what is valued and transferable from police organisations to the broader network is a well-filled address book and direct access to specialist units.[8] Furthermore, the development of university courses in the field of security (at the bachelor level or in the context of continuing education) is creating a growing number of candidates whose academic qualifications are gradually being considered relevant and who are likely to form cliques of their own as a defensive (or offensive, depending on the perspective) strategy to ensure that they are not pushed to the periphery of the network.

The security network depicted here is the result of the amalgamation of many smaller overlapping organisational and personal subsets of relationships, whose common denominator is the authorisation and delivery of security in the most general definition of the term. The multiplexed nature of this network is expressed through varied levels of co-operation, competition, trust and reciprocity, but provides the institutional fabric of urban security. In this sense, the term 'network' is used to describe a multidimensional set of interactions and interdependencies.

The neologism of 'securisphere' might actually be a more appropriate name for the institutional space within which security is produced and, by extension, for the actors that fill it, their fluid partnerships, and the security deficits that develop through negligence or lack of co-ordination. The term emphasises the emergent properties produced by the interactions and interdependencies of nodes or, stated more simply, what transcends the sum of all parts. One intangible manifestation of these emergent properties is the trust and reciprocity that are instrumental in achieving much more favourable outcomes than would normally be expected.

Building trust: The power of reciprocating ties

A micro-analysis of the ties that connect the members of the network will help clarify the nature of reciprocal ties. Our 50 respondents declared an average of 34 ties per node (range: 2–120). However, depending on the sector of activity of the node, the average number of contacts ranged from 9 in the case of the police to 104 in the private technology sector (see Table 2.2).

TABLE 2.2   Number of mean ties by respondent's sector of activity

	N	Mean	Std. Dev.
Public police	4	9	7.05
Hybrid sector	23	30	19.77
Professional association	1	64	19.77
In house (proprietary) private sector	14	36	14.89
Contract generalist	3	30	43.04
Contract investigation and expertise	3	31	12.29
Contract equipment	2	104	22.63
Total	50	34.78	24.73

The low number of contacts maintained by police officers can be explained by their central position, in which they are more in demand than in search of contacts, but also by the size and specialisation of their organisation, which allows a broader distribution of incoming and outgoing linkages. The contract technology sector displays an unusually high number of contacts, reflecting their constant need to find new clients and the ferocious competition in this field, where investments are booming and innovations are constant – an interpretation confirmed by the fact that our sample declared an average of 3.5 technology providers, with high rates of turnover between them.

The frequency with which these contacts were activated (the rate of communication between the nodes) did not follow a predictable pattern, with an average of 46 interactions per year but a standard deviation of 478. The median of 6 interactions per year is a more accurate point of reference, but the broad distribution seems to confirm the multifaceted nature of the ties. The flows of communication these numbers reveal add a layer of intensity to the density already uncovered in the previous section. With a median of 1 contact between each dyad every second month, the network is characterised by a regular monitoring of changes, and responds accordingly to needed adjustments.

These partnerships are based on individualised contacts, with 81 per cent of the respondents having privileged access to three persons or fewer in the partner organisations and 52 per cent having a sole point of entry. This dependence on a few individuals to keep partnerships alive is both a source of strength and a potential weakness. The personalised contacts are beneficial to the development and reinforcement of resilient trust, but can also undermine – or at least temporarily disable – existing relationships: when a member leaves his/her organisation, for example. It should therefore not come as a surprise that replacements must often demonstrate their 'trust-ability' through a certifiable amount of social capital (Erickson 2001).

The importance of trust is also shown through an assessment of hierarchical equivalence between partners: 61 per cent of contacts were believed to have responsibilities similar to those of respondents, a clear sign that a majority of lasting partnerships involve equals, whose trust rests on a shared body of experiences and preoccupations. This perceived egalitarian feature of the network is confirmed by answers to questions that measure dependency towards other nodes: 40 per cent of contacts were described as the result of equal initiatives, and 20 per cent were derived from demands of the partner, while 40 per cent followed a request of the respondent. This relatively balanced distribution suggests a level of exchange reciprocity that fosters trust. The 15 per cent of contacts reported as being located higher in the network hierarchy provide more sporadic strategic advice, information, or support, but their impact is, of course, incommensurable with the frequency of contacts.

Contrary to what was expected, little socialisation seemed to take place other than at work-related events such as conferences, golf tournaments and industry banquets. Only 8 per cent of our respondents stated that they maintained ties with their contacts outside the professional realm. The few occurrences of outside socialisation seemed to occur more often when ties were linked with personal friendships (it is possible that these friendships had been forged in the context of highly successful partnerships). These results constitute a powerful reminder of Nadel's paradox: while structural modelling allows us to study and compare networks systematically, each node – or even the employee of a node – will nevertheless act according to a unique understanding of the network's membership, constraints and utility (Nadel 1957; DiMaggio 1992; Berry et al. 2004). This finding confirms the importance of collecting quantitative and qualitative data simultaneously and analysing them together.

Conclusion

Notwithstanding its primary functions of law enforcement and order maintenance, public policing is embedded in a broader security network, which it helps to shape (both intentionally and incidentally) but which also develops its own answers to the problems of crime, insecurity and safety. In this chapter I have refrained from making normative claims about security networks, focusing instead on the conceptual and method-ological approaches and the challenges such approaches represent. The complexity inherent in the structure of the 'securisphere' was highlighted through a case study mapping the nodes and linkages of an urban security network. The methodological tools presented here can easily be adapted by Australian scholars and practitioners to map local, state and national security networks.

In the post-9/11 era, characterised by increased counter-terrorism efforts, interorganisational mapping tools can also be used to chart move-ment and bottlenecks in the exchange of information and expertise through bilateral or multilateral international co-operation programs. The interest generated by network analysis routines should, in the next few years, lead to methodological refinements that will allow us to follow the evolution and transformation of nodal structures over time, or to combine richly textured qualitative data with dynamic models grounded in strong quantitative approaches. These empirical efforts can contribute to the growing body of theoretical literature on the pluralisation of security in two different ways.

First, they can introduce a dose of reality – and messiness – which tends to be easily 'forgotten' in our attempts to put forward elegant and neat explanatory frameworks. The proposed artificial opposition between those who refuse to concede that state monopoly over the authorisation and delivery of security is obsolete, on one hand, and those who preach the gospel of the market, on the other, is an oversimplification of the much more intricate blend of arrangements that often materialise in an *ad hoc* fashion. Second, they provide some tools that allow us to capture the essence and constants of this complexity (within the limits stated above) and can support more appropriate normative frameworks that take advantage of the nodal properties highlighted above.

More concretely, scholars could use this methodology to assess the rele-vance of current internal and external oversight mechanisms, and to explore the potential of meta-regulation (Parker 2002; Braithwaite 2003) to better ensure the just and equitable distribution of security. Are there security holes or deficits in the 'securisphere' that need to be filled?

Another preoccupation is the the ability of security networks to evade accountability requirements. By facilitating the offloading of certain tasks to other nodes of the network which are under lower levels of scrutiny, do security networks undermine democracy by diluting the effectiveness of mono-institutional control mechanisms? The question of co-ordination should also be examined in greater detail: to what degree can security networks be co-ordinated, and what mechanisms are best suited to provide the optimal level of collaboration? Should a single node be given the mandate for this role? Should encouraging co-ordination be a task given to an existing node or do we need to design a new type of governing institution that is more appropriate for the pluralised struc-ture of security delivery? The methodological challenges alluded to earlier in this chapter are likely to translate into normative challenges, as networks prove excessively hard to shape.

Security practitioners, whether they belong to public, private or hybrid organisations, are not necessarily captivated by such conceptual debates, but they will still find the methodology introduced in this chapter useful. Police and intelligence organisations, for example, have adopted network analysis techniques to disrupt criminal organisations and terrorist groups, analysing their structure and using this knowledge to selectively remove key nodes or undermine the trust that sustains those dark networks (Arquilla & Ronfeldt 2001; Klerks 2001; Arkin 2002; Van Meter 2002; Tita et al. 2004). It is ironic that this offensive use (in the strategic sense) has never been applied for managerial purposes; the scepticism shown by police offi-cers when questioned by Fleming (Chapter 4) seems to indicate strong resistance to the idea of governing by networks advocated in some public management circles. While one can easily understand their reservations about the applicability of readymade recipes, particularly in the context of existing governing structures (Rhodes Ch. 1; Fleming & Rhodes 2005; for an example of a 'how to' manual, see Goldsmith & Eggers 2004), acquiring a more detailed understanding of the institutional environment and its rela-tional properties can be of great benefit to an organisation.

Knowing the organisation's position in comparison with its partners, and understanding who the privileged partners are, what forms of assistance and expertise they can offer, and what the patterns of interaction with those actors are can help a node manage its limited resources more effectively and avoid duplication. Similarly, less beneficial partnerships can also be identified and ended or adjusted to better suit needs and expectations. Within an organisa-tion, managers will benefit from being able to identify those linkage brokers who are particularly gifted at establishing and nurturing partnerships.

These hubs are intangible assets that crystallise social capital, but they are not always captured by organisational charts and hence have to be iden-tified with network analysis tools. But whether these tools are used to deepen our understanding of security production or to achieve the more modest aim of improving the efficiency of particular nodes, the modelling techniques described here should not be overestimated: they are only lenses that allow us to see what they have been crafted to show. If we want them to provide images that are as sharp as possible, it is essential that we consider security in light of all it can be instead of just what we think it ought to be.

Notes

1   The author wishes to acknowledge the research assistance provided by Mathilde Turcotte, Julie Charest, Frédéric Diaz, Massimiliano Mulone and Marie-Noelle Royer, and their unrelenting efforts to secure interviews with busy security executives. Carlo Morselli was an inexhaustible source of knowl-edge on social network analysis. The participants and organisers of the 'Policing, Security and Democracy Workshop' held at the Australian National University also provided some invaluable comments and suggestions on an earlier draft of this chapter. This research was made possible by a grant from the Quebec Research Fund for Society and Culture.
2   This metaphorical usage is often unintentional.
3   For an example of a network simulation involving more than a million and a half nodes and concerned with the transportation and health patterns of a large urban area, see Barrett et al. 2004.
4   However, all the respondents in the sample were included in the initial list and the additional nodes are only located in the periphery of the full network.
5   Open source data (memoranda of understanding and joint operations) and con-fidential membership lists (in the case of professional associations) were also used to complete the contact matrix, which explains why a few nodes are repre-sented without a formal interview. In those rare cases, no data other than the existence of a partnership could be collected.
6   Special care was taken to avoid double-counting of employees provided by secu-rity companies to guard the premises of clients who also had their own in-house security detail. However, this was possible only to the extent that information provided by our respondents was accurate.

7   A clique is defined as a group with a complete set of ties, or one where all nodes are connected to all others.
8   Government contractors hiring retired high-ranking public servants to serve on their boards, such as generals in the case of the defence industry, can attest to the widespread nature of this phenomenon (Johnston 2006).

References

9/11 Commission (2004) *The Final Report of the National Commission on Terrorist Attacks Upon the United States.* New York: W.W. Norton & Co.

Arkin, W. (2002) Mapping the minds in Iraq's regime; Social scientists take aim at Saddam Hussein, *The Los Angeles Times,* 1 September: M1.

Arquilla, J. and Ronfeldt, D. (eds) (2001) *Networks and Netwars.* Santa Monica CA: Rand.

Barabási, A.-L. (2002) *Linked: The new science of networks.* Cambridge: Perseus Press.

Barrett, C.L., Eubank, S., Anil Kumar, V.S. and Marathe, M.V. (2004) Understanding large scale social and infrastructure networks: A simulation-based approach, *SIAM News,* 37(4): 1–5.

Bayley, D. and Shearing, C. (2001) *The new structure of policing: Description, conceptualization and research agenda.* Washington DC: National Institute of Justice.

Berry, F., Brower, R., Ok Choi, S., Xinfang Goa, W., Jang, H., Kwon, M. and Word, J. (2004) Three traditions of network research: What the public management research agenda can learn from other research communities, *Public Administration Review,* 64 (5): 539–52.

Borgatti, S.P., Everett, M.G. and Freeman, L.C. (1999) *UCINET 6. Version 6.59.* Natick: Analytic Technologies.

Braithwaite, J. (2003) Meta risk management and responsive regulation for tax system integrity, *Law and Policy,* 25: 1–16.

Brodeur, J.-P. and Dupont, B. (forthcoming) Knowledge workers or 'knowledge workers'? *Policing and Society.*

Brown, J.S. and Duguid, P. (2000) *The Social Life of Information.* Boston: Harvard Business School Press.

Burt, R.S. (1992) *Structural holes.* Cambridge MA: Harvard University Press.

Carafano, J. and Heyman, D. (2005) *DHS 2.0: Rethinking the Department of Homeland Security.* Washington DC: The Heritage Foundation and Centre for Strategic and International Studies.

Castells, M. (1996) *The rise of the network society.* Oxford: Blackwell.

—— (2000) Materials for an exploratory theory of the network society, *British Journal of Sociology,* 51(1): 5–24.

Cooley, D. (ed.) (2005) *Re-imagining policing in Canada.* Toronto: University of Toronto Press.

Crawford, A., Lister, S., Blackburn, S. and Burnett, J. (2005) *Plural policing: The mixed economy of visible patrols in England and Wales.* Bristol: The Policy Press.

De Waard, J. (1999) The private security industry in international perspective, *European Journal on Criminal Policy and Research*, 7: 143–74.

DiMaggio, P. (1992) Nadel's paradox revisited: Relational and cultural aspects of organizational structure, in N. Nohria and R.G. Eccles (eds), *Networks and Organizations: Structure, form, and action*. Boston: Harvard Business School Press.

Dupont, B. (2004) Security in the Age of Networks, *Policing and Society*, 14(1): 76–91.

Erickson, B.H. (2001) Good networks and good jobs: the value of social capital to employers and employees, in N. Lin, K. Cook and R.S. Burt (eds), *Social capital: theory and research*. New York: Aldine de Gruyter.

Fleming, J. and Rhodes, R.A.W. (2005) Bureaucracy, contracts and networks: The unholy trinity and the police, *The Australian and New Zealand Journal of Criminology*, 38(2): 192–205.

Freeman, L.C. (2004) *The development of social network analysis*. Vancouver: Empirical Press.

Goldsmith, S. and Eggers, W. (2004) *Governing by network*. Washington DC: The Brookings Institution.

Johnston, L. (2006) Transnational security governance, in J. Wood and B. Dupont (eds), *Democracy, society and the governance of security*. Cambridge: Cambridge University Press.

Klerks, P. (2001) The network paradigm applied to criminal organisations: Theoretical nitpicking or a relevant doctrine for investigators? Recent developments in the Netherlands, *Connections*, 24(3): 53–65.

Knoke, D. (1990) *Political networks: The structural perspective*. Cambridge: Cambridge University Press.

Marsh, D. (1998) The development of the policy network approach, in D. Marsh (ed.), *Comparing policy networks*. Buckingham: Open University Press.

Morselli, C. (2005) *Contacts, opportunities and criminal enterprise*. Toronto: University of Toronto Press.

Nadel, S. (1957) *The theory of social structure*. London: Cohen & West.

Naylor, T. (2002) *Wages of Crime*. Ithaca: Cornell University Press.

Newburn, T. (2001) The commodification of policing: Security networks in the late modern city, *Urban Studies*, 38 (5–6): 829–48.

Nonaka, I. and Takeushi, H. (1995) *The Knowledge-creating Company: How Japanese companies create the dynamics of innovation*. New York: Oxford University Press.

Osborne, D. and Gaebler, T. (1992) *Reinventing Government*. Reading MA: Addison-Wesley.

Parker, C. (2002) *The Open Corporation: Effective self-regulation and democracy*. Cambridge: Cambridge University Press.

Polanyi, M. (1967) *The Tacit Dimension*. New York: Anchor Books.

Powell, W., White, D., Koput, K. and Owen-Smith, J. (2005) Network dynamics and field evolution: The growth of interorganizational collaboration in the life sciences, *American Journal of Sociology*, 110(4): 1132–1205.

Prenzler, T. and Sarre, R. (1998) Regulating private security in Australia, *Trends and Issues in Crime and Criminal Justice No. 98*, Australian Institute of

Criminology, Canberra.

Shearing, C. (2006) Reflections on the refusal to acknowledge private governments, in J. Wood and B. Dupont (eds), *Democracy, Society and the Governance of Security*. Cambridge: Cambridge University Press.

Shearing, C. and Stenning, P. (1981) Modern private security: Its growth and implications, in M. Tonry and N. Morris (eds), *Crime and Justice: An annual review of research*. Chicago: University of Chicago Press.

Shearing, C. and Wood, J. (2000) Reflections on the governance of security: A normative enquiry. *Police Practice*, 1(4): 457–76.

Sheptycki, J. (2004) Organisational pathologies in police intelligence systems, *European Journal of Criminology*, 1(3): 307–32.

Smith Ring, P. (1997) Processes facilitating reliance on trust in inter-organizational networks, in M. Ebbers (ed.), *The Formation of Inter-organizational Networks*. Oxford: Oxford University Press.

Tita, G., Riley, J.K., Ridgeway, G., Grammich, C., Abrahamse, A.F. and Greenwood, P.W. (2004) *Reducing Gun Violence: Results from an intervention in East Los Angeles*. Santa Monica CA: RAND Press.

Van Meter, K.M. (2002) Terrorists/liberators: researching and dealing with adversary networks, *Connections*, 24(3): 66–78.

Williams, P. (1994) Transnational criminal organisations and international Security, *Survival*, 36(1): 96–113.

3 | HARNESSING RESOURCES FOR NETWORKED POLICING

Julie Ayling, Peter Grabosky and Clifford Shearing

Introduction

More than two decades ago, Shearing and Stenning published a paper entitled 'Snowflakes or good pinches', in which they explored the use of what Buerger and Mazerolle (1998) have termed 'third-party policing'. 'Third-party policing' is defined as 'police efforts to persuade or coerce nonoffending persons to take action which are designed to indirectly minimize disorder caused by other persons or to reduce the possibility that a crime may occur' (Buerger & Mazerolle 1998: 301). Since 1998 their definition has been extended to include actions by non-offending persons to respond to law violations (Mazerolle & Ransley 2005: 156).

Grabosky has pursued this issue of 'citizen co-production' (Grabosky 1990) of social order in a variety of contexts (Grabosky 1994; Gunningham & Grabosky 1998); in particular, the use of 'non-governmental resources to foster regulatory compliance' (Grabosky 1995a) as a way of furthering the regulatory objectives of state governments.

These and similar developments, rather than 'hollowing out' states (Rhodes 1994), have arguably served instead to strengthen them. At the same time they have transformed states to become more regulatory in nature

(Rhodes 1997: 91–93; Braithwaite 2000; Levi-Faur 2005). Where states have emphasised the importance of mobilising and integrating the resources available through state agencies, the term 'whole of government' has been used to recognise these initiatives. Where governments have sought to mobilise resources available both within and outside state agencies, the term 'whole of society' is appropriate.

Perhaps the arena in which building third-party forms of governance has been most dramatically advocated has been in the report of the 9/11 Commission in the United States (9/11 Commission 2004). The report argues that just as terrorists adopt a decentred nodal approach in mobilising resources, so too must governments if they are to effectively respond to terrorist threats. One way in which the report suggests that this can be done is through adopting a whole-of-society approach to governance. Together these networked strategies, it argues, will make for 'smart government'.

The report argues that the United States must adopt third-party tactics that involve civil society organisations – and especially the private sector – in its response to terrorism. Such tactics have indeed been adopted by the United States: in its use of private military companies in the war in Iraq, for example.

In recognising the fact that governance now takes place increasingly through whole-of-society mobilisation, Shearing and colleagues have proposed a 'nodal governance' framework (Johnston & Shearing 2003; Shearing & Wood 2003a; Burris et al. 2005). In focusing on a variety of institutions, or nodes, as sites of governance which may or may not network with each other, they seek to focus attention on the importance of understanding the nature of nodes within networks as well as on the nature of networks of which they might be a part.

Mapping mobilisation

In the following pages we set out a framework for mapping the variety of arrangements that have evolved for integrating state and civil society resources to enhance public policing. Grabosky (2004) suggests that a useful framework within which to organise this mapping is one provided by anthropologist and historian Natalie Zemon Davis (2000), who proposes a typology of three forms of exchange: coercion, sale and gift. These exchange mechanisms are expressed in practice through a variety of over-lapping and hybrid forms. This typology allows us to map the way in which civil society resources are being mobilised to contribute to public policing objectives through state law and other state-directed and state-supported mechanisms.

In the context of public police organisations, Davis's typology of exchange translates to circumstances in which the police as an organisation:

- command co-operation from the private sector in order to further law enforcement objectives (coercion);
- buy and sell services (sale); and
- benefit from private generosity in the form of donations or sponsorship (gift).

The following matrix illustrates many of the mechanisms of coercion, sale and gift that work to 'pull in', and thus network, the resources (physical, financial, technical, informational and human) necessary for effective public policing.

TABLE 3.1   Mechanisms of exchange

Forms of Exchange / Resources	Coercion	Sale	Gift
Services	• duties to act	• outsourcing	• donated services • volunteers
Monies/Goods	• civil forfeiture	• user-pays policing • merchandising • procurement	• donations • private sponsor-ship
Information	• mandatory reporting • compulsory processes	• informants • human sources (rewarded)	• human sources (volunteering)

There are three principal interests that might be served by some combination of police–private interface: the interest of the private actor, that of the public police service, and that of the general public. The answer to the question 'Who pays and who benefits?' will not always be obvious. Sometimes serving a private or otherwise parochial interest will also benefit the public interest, as when police ensure that a minority is free to go about its business, be it religious worship or a street march (Shearing & Wood 2003b). The public interest in freedom of worship or expression is upheld, together with the private interest in safety and free speech. But private and public interests will not always converge. Occasionally, policing on behalf of a private interest will draw already limited resources away from general policing services.

Asking the question about whose interests are being served raises the question of whose interests *should* be served. Consumption of police resources is often rivalrous: that is, their consumption will prevent them being available to others. Some measure of rationing is therefore needed. The challenge facing policing today is how to manage that rationing in a manner that is generally considered to best serve the public interest – consistently, fairly and with the result of overall effective outcomes for society (Loader & Walker 2005). Although policing is not wholly a public good, it is still expected to be *for* the public good (Eng 2001).

Coercion

'Command and control' strategies continue to be relevant and important (Fleming & Rhodes 2005). In the governance of security, the state, together with its coercive capacities, remains central. There are many ways in which states command co-production of public order. Mandatory reporting, for example, allows law enforcement to gain valuable information on particular routine or anomalous activities (see Table 3.2). Aside from reporting requirements, other types of actions may also be mandated, with third parties being conscripted to help enforce the law – for example, the requirement that employers withhold a proportion of their employees' wages and pay them directly to tax authorities.

The following matrix draws on examples from around the world to illustrate various forms of coercive networking. It is clear that coercion may be directed at both third parties and 'first parties' – the direct targets of policing.

TABLE 3.2   Forms of coercive networking

	First Party	Third Party
Action	• Mandatory self-regulation • Required record keeping, for example, environmental records • Required private interface, for example, requirement to be audited or to have liability insurance • Bail or probation conditions, for example, requiring compliance with a curfew or regular reporting to a police station • Driver not to leave scene of an accident (1st or 3rd party) • Anti-loitering or 'move-on' powers • Civil and criminal forfeiture • Criminal restitution • Drug testing of prisoners and parolees	• Duty to rescue • Withholding of taxes by employers • Garnishing of wages by employers in satisfaction of a court order • Requirements that ISPs archive traffic data • Requirements that telecommunications carriers assist with interception • Record keeping by second-hand goods dealers • Checking of travel documents by airlines • Requirements that carriers use due diligence to prevent importation of illicit drugs • Emergency powers: commandeering of infrastructure (transport, media etc) • Special taxation to fund law enforcement (for example, fees on vehicle registration)

Information	• Corporate disclosure:
	  - Financial
	  - Environmental
	  - OHS
	  - EEO
	• Compulsory processes, for example:
	  - Requirements to attend and answer self-incriminating questions if asked by a Royal Commission
	  - Requirement to provide encryption key
		• Mandatory reporting of, for example:
		  - Child/spouse/elder abuse
		  - Statutory rape
		  - Medical error
		  - Patients whose health prevents them safely driving a motor vehicle or, as a health professional, practising their profession
		  - Child pornography discovered on computer
		  - Illegal immigrants applying for certain US welfare programs
		  - Suspicious financial transactions
		  - Violent medically ill patients
		  - Precursor chemicals and chemicals used to manufacture explosives
		• Informants (when coerced)

Mandatory reporting

Mandatory reporting requirements may create information networks. They are generally imposed legislatively and are found in a wide range of areas. The benefits of mandatory reporting for both law enforcement and the general public are numerous. Very often mandatory reporting replaces an existing system of voluntary reporting that has proved inadequate to address a significant social problem, such as exploitation of the vulnerable (children, the elderly, consumers, investors, etc), money-laundering, illegal immigration and so forth. Mandatory reporting of child abuse, for instance, may provide both law enforcement and welfare authorities with a more comprehensive understanding of the breadth and distribution of the problem.

Reporting requirements remove the opportunity for capricious decision-making by professionals (provided there are clear guidelines about the circumstances in which reporting should occur). This may reinforce a client's or patient's trust in them and in the institution or profession in question.

The very fact of the existence of a reporting requirement can also act as a deterrent to the commission of an offence. A corporation may think twice about exceeding prescribed pollution emission levels if it has to report on its practices. A company required to disclose financial information may have difficulty disguising illegal accounting practices (Seligman 1983: 45). Wider social objectives, such as investor protection from fraud, are therefore served.

For the police, corporate disclosure requirements may well facilitate law enforcement because of the public availability of information about a company's practices. The cost of and time spent in prosecutions may be reduced. And for the companies themselves, disclosure, albeit mandated, serves as evidence of 'good corporate citizenship', which may encourage investment and improve a company's ability to weather bad times.

However, mandatory reporting is also often associated with increases in costs. Additional costs to law enforcement, welfare and medical systems may be significant and the capacity of existing systems may be overwhelmed due to a sharp increase in reported cases. In New South Wales, for example, the number of child protection authorisations increased by 82 per cent between 1999 and 2002 (Australian Bureau of Statistics 2003). Fear of punishment for non-reporting may result in some degree of over-reporting. Where resources *can* be found to follow up on reports, this may be at the expense of resources for prevention and support. Moreover, sheer numbers may make it more difficult to differentiate between serious cases and the unfounded or relatively trivial. In turn, this may result in potentially tragic inaction or in unwarranted interventions.

There may also be unintended non-financial effects associated with mandatory reporting. For instance, mandating corporate disclosure may create a false sense of security amongst investors who then see no need for independent enquiries into the company's financial stability. One has only to look at the Enron scandal in the United States and the collapse of HIH in Australia to see the possible consequences.

Mandatory reporting allows little discretion for a professional to take a client's or a patient's particular circumstances into account. It is a blunt instrument. Professionals may be perceived by their clients as agents of the state and professional–client relations may be significantly impacted (Schultz 1990). Clients may be less inclined to access the services in question.

In some jurisdictions, mandatory reporting may also make the task of other agencies of government more difficult – networking is not always viewed as beneficial. For instance, requiring state police agencies in the United States to assist in the enforcement of federal immigration laws may jeopardise police relations with some ethnic communities.

Mandatory action

As with mandatory reporting, there are many varieties of action mandated by law or regulation. Consider the following examples.

Good Samaritan laws: Laws requiring bystanders to render reasonable assistance to persons in an emergency exist in most of continental Europe and some states of the United States and Australia. Failure to render this assistance may result in criminal liability punishable by fines and/or imprisonment. This duty may be general (owed to anyone in need of assistance), or it may arise out of special connections between the bystander and the person in need (such as parent and child, or airline and passenger). The duty may arise at common law or be the subject of specific legislation. Usually there must exist, as a trigger for the obligation, an imminent or direct danger to a person of a degree that would probably lead to that person's death. Danger to the bystander and sometimes danger to third persons will excuse a failure to take action in most jurisdictions (Feldbrugge 1966: 636).

Both moral and pragmatic arguments exist for having laws mandating bystander intervention, and these have been extensively debated. But what of the costs? A duty to rescue carries with it costs to both the state and individuals – the costs of increased criminal prosecutions and possibly of increased private civil litigation encouraged by the legislative recognition of a duty of care. Similarly, there are powerful commercial disincentives to effecting rescues at sea (Davies 2003).

There can also be pitfalls for the unwary if such laws are improperly framed. Not all Good Samaritans are competent. They may do more harm than good. A bystander who fails to rescue a drowning man and also drowns him or herself is hardly promoting the general welfare or assisting in law enforcement. Moreover, hindsight is a great thing. What may at the time be an indeterminate situation for bystanders may seem very clear in retrospect. Good Samaritan laws may actually have an unintended antico-operative effect in that witnesses to a crime who have not intervened may be deterred from coming forward or truthfully answering police questions for fear of prosecution (Volokh 1999). Mandating assistance for the benefit of law enforcement can therefore have unintended negative consequences for law enforcement.

Third-party liability systems: Private institutions may be required to supplement public policing efforts through direct action against wrongdoers (Gilboy 1998). Businesses and other entities that are in the position of intermediaries between legal and illegal environments are especially well placed to undertake such an enforcement role. Sanctions for non-compliance with such duties can include not only traditional criminal penalties (such as fines), but also penalties more tailored to the particular activity pursued by the private entity, such as loss of licence. Examples of third-party responsibility for law enforcement include:

- telecommunications carriers being required to assist the state in telecommunications interception;
- airlines having an obligation to enforce immigration laws by checking the validity of travellers' documentation;
- occupiers of certain public premises in some jurisdictions in Australia having a duty to enforce non-smoking laws;
- licensed venues such as hotels and restaurants being obliged to implement Responsible Service of Alcohol practices, such as not serving intoxicated patrons; and
- parents being subject to fines for the truancy of their children, as can occur in the Australian state of Queensland.

Third-party liability systems abound because they provide additional law enforcement resources in areas where they are needed and may also expand, with relatively little expense, the range of specialist expertise and equipment available to ensure compliance with the law.

But coercion of third parties may be costly and have unintended results, especially where the third party is a commercial entity. Mandating action may also influence the relationships between businesses and their clients or customers. There may be a loss of customer or client support, or costs to the intended target of the action itself. There can also be social costs to mandating action by vulnerable sections of the population. Laws mandating parental control could well exacerbate rather than help alleviate social and economic disadvantage for the families caught out by them.

Civil forfeiture: Civil forfeiture is an example of first-party mandatory action. In many jurisdictions police and/or prosecutors have the power to require the forfeiture of a person's assets on the basis of a suspicion that the asset has a connection with a crime, whether or not the owner of the asset has been convicted of the crime or ever will be. Civil standards of proof apply, and it also falls to the person challenging a forfeiture order to establish the lawful origins of the property (a reversal of the usual onus of proof in judicial proceedings) (Lusty 2002: 348–50).

In Australia and the United Kingdom, proceeds from the sale of confiscated property end up in the government coffers. A percentage may eventually be returned to the confiscating agency for use in their law enforcement activities. In many US jurisdictions, however, police forces are able to keep or sell confiscated property to fund their own law enforcement activities, such as by buying office supplies, computers and vehicles (Saltonstall & Rising 1999). Many municipal and county law enforcement agencies are dependent on civil forfeiture as a budget supplement (Worrall 2001). This dependence carries with it the danger that police law enforcement priorities could become skewed in these agencies.

As well as addressing the moral issue that there should be no financial benefit from engaging in crime, forfeiture laws are a practical device to reduce the capacity of criminals to engage in further illegal activities, and may have a deterrent effect by decreasing the expected financial returns of such activities (Lusty 2002: 345). However, such laws may also impose significant costs, not only on the offenders targeted but also on third parties. In some cases the owners of property subject to confiscation have been totally unaware of its misuse by others. In one US case, the court upheld the confiscation of a family car used by the husband when engaging the services of a prostitute. The wife, who held a half interest in the vehicle, was unable to overturn the confiscation or get compensation (*Bennis v. Michigan* 517 US 1163 (1996)). In fact, families are often the innocent victims of forfeiture laws, especially when illicit drugs are involved.

Guidelines for coercive networking

The use of coercion in democratic societies to compel nodes, as loci of resources, to participate in governance networks, is widespread. In the case of security governance, this coercion is applied not to offenders, but to those who are in a position to contribute to the provision of security. We have suggested that while there are costs that need to be balanced against the public benefits, those benefits can be significant. The challenge for those seeking to use networks for coercion is to realise these benefits while at the same time taking the costs into consideration. One avenue for managing this process is through the development of policy guidelines that seek to ensure a proper balance between all relevant interests.

In developing such guidelines for coercive networking, we can, and should, turn to general principles for direction. A principle that we endorse as appropriate is that enunciated by Braithwaite and Pettit (1990): namely, that coercion should be used only when it enhances overall freedom. In applying this principle to specific cases where coercive measures might be appropriate, states in general and law enforcement agencies in particular will need to consider the details of the instances before them in terms of the more general issues that arise from identification of costs and benefits. Are the policy objectives in question of sufficient importance to justify the coercive measures employed? Is there a justifiable relationship between the coercive methods to be employed and the target problem? Are coercive measures the least restrictive means of achieving public interest objectives, having regard to their likely effectiveness and the availability of equally effective but less intrusive alternatives? Are the costs imposed by the coercive methods (be they financial, administrative, or otherwise) outweighed by the benefits secured? Are any costs that result from coercive measures distributed in ways that are not inequitable? And is the exercise of coercive powers grounded in appropriate procedural safeguards, which include clear accountability mechanisms?

The same kind of cost/benefit framework is an appropriate way to look at the issues that arise from public law enforcement's role in obtaining resources through involvement in commercial activities (sale).

Sale

Like other governmental bodies, the public police have been increasingly forced to create, and participate in, market networks. This arises from state policies of privatisation and the adoption of new public service management models based on private sector philosophies and strategies. Terms such as 'performance assessment', 'value for money', 'cost efficiency' and 'fiscal accountability' have entered the lexicon of police management. Standards normally associated with business are now routinely used to evaluate public police performance (McLaughlin & Murji 1997; Fleming & Lafferty 2000; Murphy 2002; Frieberg 2005).

This focus on the 'bottom line' of service delivery has stimulated creative responses from police management to resource acquisition and allocation, including the charging of user fees, new and better use of technology, outsourcing of services to private contractors, a reduction in and/or the elimination of services and the sharing of policing responsibilities with the community. Public policing, like other public services, must now survive in an environment where 'doing more with less' is the driving philosophy.

Examples of sale as a form of networking include police buying goods, services and information, and selling their own services and merchandise to obtain resources. These developments have been traced in a somewhat piecemeal way in the literature (Johnston 1992: 56–70; Davids & Hancock 1998; Loader 1999; Gans 2000; Murphy 2002), with frequent characterisation of them as reflecting the 'commodification' of policing services (Loader 1999; Newburn 2001; Murphy 2002), with associated risks for police priorities and legitimacy and for distribution of policing services. Some of these risks will become evident from the following discussion of several examples of market-based networking.

Procurement and outsourcing

Market networks within public policing are not new. Laundering, catering, cleaning, publishing, and equipment, vehicle and building maintenance have been the subject of 'outsourcing' for decades. What is new is the growing tendency for police organisations to purchase services that might otherwise have been provided from their own ranks. For example, it is not uncommon for recruit training, traffic patrol duties, audiotape transcriptions (of tele- phone interceptions, for example), prisoner custody and transportation and forensic investigations to be outsourced. London's Metropolitan Police have outsourced both the day-to-day operation and future development of their IT and radiocommunications networks. The Australian Federal Police have entrusted the security of their headquarters to a private security firm. Outsourcing of cybercrime investigations has also been contemplated by Australian police forces (Police Commissioners' Conference Electronic Crime Steering Committee 2001; Etter 2001: 12). Even the process of out- sourcing itself is sometimes outsourced (Davids & Hancock 1998: 56).

The benefits of outsourcing for police have been identified as reduc- tions in costs and increases in efficiency, allowing the police to concentrate their activities on 'core activities', with valuable flow-on effects for the public. For the private sector contractors involved, there are the benefits of new profit-making opportunities and, in some cases, even the potential for industry development under the pressure of competition for police busi- ness. Arguably, outsourcing may also result in higher quality services, with contractors bringing expertise and skills not available, or readily available, within police ranks (Verspaandonk 2001).

Reliance on outsourcing and procurement networks can of course also have multiple downsides. The costs of the outsourcing process may be pro- hibitive, especially where the service outsourced is a particularly complex one (Mulgan 2001). If the process of tendering and contract management is not expertly handled, overdependency on a particular supplier, even capture, can result. This is especially so in areas where there are few sup- pliers. Furthermore, quality is not guaranteed even with the most careful selection of a reputable supplier, and large legal bills and rectification costs for police organisations and governments can result. IBM was taken to court by the New Zealand government in 1999 after choosing not to com- plete a project to develop an Integrated National Computerised Information System for New Zealand Police. Not only was completion of the project three years overdue and NZ$30 million over budget; it was also criticised by users as not operating as promised (Dore 1999).

The outsourcing process can potentially be an avenue for corruption. Allegations of bribery and favouritism emerged following the tender process for New Zealand's police dispatch system in 1995. There may also be problems of staff morale if outsourcing of what were previously in-house jobs takes place.

Decisions over which services are 'non-core' and therefore liable to be outsourced have often been made with little or no public consultation (Davids & Hancock 1998: 51). As a result, there is a risk that policing measures that do not fit a classical crime-fighting or law enforcement profile – that is, those that are more community-oriented and preventive – will be outsourced, even though public demand for a more visible community-based police presence is increasing.

There are also issues of service accountability. To bring the complete array of public service accountability standards to bear on private contractors may well diminish the gains in efficiency and costs made through outsourcing.

Finally, depending on the services outsourced, there may be undesirable flow-on consequences for the public. If a service is no longer provided by the police, it may be that the public will have to pay for it; as Murphy notes, this 'favours the advantaged and weakens collective social relationships and obligations' (2002: 32). On the other hand, there is no doubt that expecting police to do everything also has consequences for the equitable application of policing services (Schönteich et al. 2004: 23–24). Moreover, a private sector customer service approach may just not be appropriate to the provision of certain policing services (Davids & Hancock 1998: 60).

Clearly, police outsourcing decisions have very important ramifications for the public. Much thought has been given to the challenge of developing general principles to guide outsourcing decisions in the public sector, with transparency, accountability and the balancing of interests seen as integral to the process (Commercial Activities Panel 2002). Consideration should be given to the special, sensitive and often confidential nature of police work and the institution of public policing in the application of these principles by police organisations.

Informants and other human sources

The offering of rewards to members of the public for information about criminal activities occurred in London as far back as the late 17th century. High levels of crime led the government to offer rewards for information leading to prosecution and conviction of persons involved in serious crimes such as highway robbery. Sometimes victims of crime would also offer rewards. People known as 'thief takers' used their criminal connections to investigate crime and inform on, apprehend and prosecute those responsible in order to obtain the rewards, or they negotiated the return of a victim's property from the thief for a fee (Howson 1970: 36–41). Some thief takers apparently would incite crime in order to reap the financial bounty (Howson 1970: 41; Hitchcock & Shoemaker 2003. By the mid-18th century, thief takers were institutionalised in the form of the 'Bow Street Runners' and their counterparts around the country.

Today the offering of rewards to the general public (for example, through Crime Stoppers) and the paying of criminal informants are common practices in policing. Police organisations are increasingly promulgating formal guidelines on the appropriate circumstances in which to use informants and the ways in which proper relationships with them are to be maintained.

Grabosky (1995b) has pointed out that extrinsic reward can undermine intrinsic motivation (see also Braithwaite 2002: 25). Does the offering of rewards encourage 'a nation of spies and bounty hunters' motivated by greed and not averse to taking the law into their own hands, even to the extent of orchestrating a crime in order to claim a reward? Or does it merely encourage responsible citizenship, with members of the public happily providing information about witnessed crimes in the face of their own fear, time constraints and apathy? The proper structuring of any reward system so as to draw in relevant information while reducing opportunities for subversion is clearly important.

As far as informant networks are concerned, there are issues relating to the risks and costs for police of using them. Pitfalls can arise from cultivating too close a relationship with criminals, or from using contingency fee arrangements which may encourage an overzealous approach by an informant. From the point of view of the public interest, police need to consider the balance between getting results and the means of doing so – for instance, in relation to ignoring, encouraging or soliciting the commission of a crime by the informant in order to further an investigation.

User-pays policing

It is rare today to find a police force that does not sometimes charge users for its service. The practice of charging has been around since the mid-19th century (see the majority judgment of the House of Lords in *Glasbrook*

Brothers Ltd. v. Glamorgan Country Council [1924] 1 All ER 579 at 587).
Gans points out that regulation of paid policing in common law jurisdictions
allows this pre-existing police practice, either not addressing the issue in legislation at all (as in Canada), or providing that 'special police services' may be
charged for as determined by the police (UK Police Act 1964, s. 15(1)), or
setting out in a non-exhaustive list the charging arrangements for various types
of paid policing (Gans 2000: 188) (various state jurisdictions within Australia:
see NSW Police Act 1990 s. 208 and Police Regulation 2000 s. 106).

The policing of sporting and entertainment events run by individuals or
companies for profit are a common target for this 'user-pays policing'.
Similarly, police may charge for traffic control in certain circumstances that
benefit a private interest (film shoot, wide load escorts, etc), for probity
checks of potential employees requested by government and non-government agencies, for certain technical and forensic services (e.g. photography),
for the provision of reports (such as for insurance investigations), for atten-
dance at false alarms, for the provision of training, and so on. The main aim
is to recoup costs (WA Police Service 2002: 8). A number of Australian
police forces have guidelines for these types of market-based networks. Such
guidelines detail when charges may be levied, the conditions of police deployment and the fees for each service (for example, NSW Police Service 2004).

Sometimes there is a more permanent user-pays arrangement in place.
In WA the Gold Stealing Detection Unit (GDSU) has existed since 1907.
Based in Kalgoorlie and charged with investigating gold stealing offences
and deterring organised crime's infiltration into the gold industry, this unit
of 6 or 7 detectives is funded entirely by the WA Chamber of Mines and
Energy (see <http://www.cmewa.com/docs/Annual%20Report%202005.pdf>
and <http://www.police.wa.gov.au/aboutus/supportservices/crimeinvesti-
gation.asp?commercialcrime> [all websites listed were correct at the time of
writing]). This funding covers salaries, as well as accommodation, equipment, infrastructure, travelling allowances and overtime. These costs are
not accounted for in the WA Police budget.

Another example, also emanating from the mining industry in WA, is
the permanent stationing of two police officers at the Argyle Diamond
Mine. The mining company meets the cost of providing and maintaining
buildings, equipment and accommodation for the police in this instance, but
not their ongoing operating costs, which come from the WA Police budget.
The Argyle police officers provide services to the nearby Balgo Aboriginal

community as well as to the mining operation (see <http: //www.police.wa.gov.au/LocalPolice/KimberleyDistrict.asp?Argyle>). In the Northern Territory, remote Aboriginal communities partly fund (by providing vehicles, accommodation, infrastructure and office space) the posting of Aboriginal Community Police Officers in the community, some of whom have fully autonomous police powers.

The lack of resources to perform a service in the light of other demands on the police's service has been suggested as the *raison d'être* of user-pays policing. But as Gans points out, this does not help in determining which services should be, and are, charged for (Gans 2000: 193). He suggests that charging will most typically be imposed for 'activities that create foreseeable dangers beyond levels typical in a locality' (Gans 2000: 196). While this explains special events policing and some other forms, the explanation seems to fall somewhat short for police charges for services such as probity checks and forensic services.

Here one would suspect that some kind of judgments are again being made about the 'core-ness' of certain services to the police role. Berwick speaks about the placing of 'unique demands upon police resources' (1988: 11). Nevertheless, clearly the main benefit of user-pays work to the police is the additional resources obtained that can then be used to provide 'free' policing services, perhaps even simultaneously, for the public's benefit. The deployment of police to a special event might be made up for by paying off-duty police overtime to be on-duty in areas being neglected because of the event. For the private company, individual or community paying for these police, such arrangements are almost always more costly than hiring private security (Gans 2000: 201), but the police bring with them a greater array of legal tools (such as the use of force) as well as the ability to co-ordinate their paid and free policing efforts (Gans 2000: 202).

The main benefit of more permanent arrangements (such as the GSDU) is generally suggested to be the enhancement of the working relationship between the police organisation and those who pay (Department for Transport 2004: 12). Police are in a position to acquire specialist knowledge associated with the particular working environment, including the commercial context, and this enhances their policing skills. Moreover, they bring with them the tools of policing and the legitimacy, or 'symbolic power' (Loader 1997), of the public police role. For the police, such arrangements mean they cannot be accused of ignoring an important site of potential crime, but at the same time there is little or no drain on limited resources.

Is user-pays policing fair and in the public interest, given that the public policing service is paid for equally by taxpayers? Why should those responsible for an activity that creates the necessary conditions for criminal activity to occur (for instance, by drawing together large numbers of people in a limited area), and from which they are going to profit, not pay for the extra policing this entails (Gans 2000: 197), especially if they have requested that assistance from the police? Is it reasonable that promoters of events, in particular, should be assisted in their profit-making through private exploitation of public resources?

Equity issues might arise, however, in relation to some fee-for-service arrangements. Police dependence on a private source of funding may carry with it risks that public safety and security might be sacrificed to a private agenda. For instance, does the fact that one company can pay for an investigation involving overseas travel for police or other large expenditure result in better service for that company over another smaller operation which cannot afford such an extensive investigation? In such cases the accountability and transparency of police operations are of great importance in ensuring continued public trust.

Any charging regime should make clear the boundaries of the police role in providing the particular service. The private interest being served needs to have an understanding of these boundaries so that inappropriate expectations (about the degree of force able to be used, for instance) do not create difficulties on the ground. This need for clear role delimitations applies not only for one-off charged activities, such as events policing, but also for more permanent arrangements. First and foremost, police officers, even if financed by private industry, are public servants, and potential conflicts of interest between industry expectations and the public interest will only be pre-empted by clear police guidelines.

Unambiguous policies on when police should charge for services, how much they should charge and how they should conduct themselves when doing 'user-pays' policing are therefore essential. If these policies are in the public domain, there can be little cause for speculation that police are in the business of chasing dollars rather than crooks.

Market-based networking guidelines

Resourcing networks through sale reflects broader ongoing changes in the provision of public services whereby market imperatives drive, at least in part, their configuration, and citizens are regarded as 'customers' with choices about service provision, rather than as 'clients' or 'public benefici-aries' (Davids & Hancock 1998: 58–61; Loader 1999: 375–76). There are a number of potential consequences of the close relationships that police and private interests, be they vendors or purchasers, establish through these resourcing networks. Exploitation of such relationships by either side can have detrimental flow-on effects for the public, including possible inequities in the distribution of policing services and distortions in the policing agenda, and implications for police legitimacy (Loader 1999: 377–78). Because of this there is a need for ongoing assessment of the costs and ben-efits of these arrangements, for the setting down in the public domain of clear limits for them and for effective controls over their management.

Gift

In his anthropological overview of gift-giving in pre-industrial societies, the French sociologist Mauss suggested that gift-giving represents a mixture of motives on the part of the giver, including the desire to feel that one is doing one's duty, the desire for prestige that may result from giving, and the expec-tation of return gifts (Mauss 1969; see also Dillon 2003: 40–41).

Along these lines, one can envisage the gifts that drive gift-based net-works as located on a continuum of increasing return on investment for the donor. At one end of the continuum is pure donation, where the donor does not expect anything in return, except perhaps a private word of thanks. Examples would include the donation of time and labour by the many volunteers who assist Australian police organisations under Volunteers In Policing programs, or the donation by community groups of needed equipment, such as the topographic maps donated to Western Queensland Police by local Lions Clubs to assist with search and rescue (Murray 2004), or the money raised and donated by a child in Pittsburgh, USA to buy a police dog a bullet-resistant vest under the Vest-a-Dog program (see <http: //www.vestadog.com/howitbegan.htm>).

Moving along the continuum, donation becomes sponsorship when the relationship becomes more of a commercial arrangement and public recog-nition of the donor by the recipient is an important, and sometimes the primary, motivation for the gift. The corporate donation of vehicles to police falls into this category: the display of the company's name on the vehicle being driven by police suffices as acknowledgment of the company's generosity. Similarly, the private sector may make donations in return for police presence on or near their premises. For instance, Westfield Carousel Shopping Centre in Perth donates computer, fax, video interviewing facilities and office space in the Centre to the WA Police Service (WA Police Service 2000: 14). On occasion, a sponsor will receive a concession from police in addition to or instead of acknowledgment. In return for a donation of aerial surveillance camera equipment for the Victoria Police Air Wing helicopter fleet, Melbourne's commercial television stations received permission to broadcast pictures of events involving police via a digital microwave television downlink (Miller 1999).

Sometimes a more overt acknowledgment of sponsorship is given. Government Acquisitions (GA) (see <http://www.gavpd.com/home.asp>), a private company located in the US state of North Carolina, arranges corporate sponsorship of police vehicles. A company pays for a vehicle, which it donates to a public police organisation under an arrangement negotiated by GA. In return for the donation the company may feature advertisements on the vehicle's hood, boot and quarter panels for three years. Police officials have final say over sponsors' identities and the design and placement of the graphics. GA's service has proven very popular with cash-strapped municipal and county police departments, but has also attracted considerable criticism, on the basis that putting police cars 'up for sale' suggests that police and justice are similarly for sale (Mollenkamp 2003: 81).

At the far end of the gift continuum is a grant of resources which is made subject to conditions by the donor concerning its use. In the US state of Virginia, under the HEAT (Help Eliminate Auto Theft) program, insurance companies return a percentage of liability insurance premiums to the criminal justice system, earmarked for auto theft reduction (Pilant 1998: 44). In Florida and several other US states, Purdue Pharmaceuticals has provided funds to investigate diversion of its prescription painkiller Oxycontin and for police training on prescription drug abuse (Pollarito 2002). The Alberta Energy Corporation in 1998 provided the Royal Canadian Mounted Police with computer equipment, software and technical support to enable it to investigate a particular instance of 'oilpatch vandalism' (Blatchford 2000). And in Cornwall in the United Kingdom, the Polzeath Council, plus the town's businesses and residents, have given funds specifically to provide overtime for officers to patrol their popular beach in summer (Gibbons 1996:22-23).

There are also more permanent institutions and arrangements set up for the purpose of supporting police work. In South Africa an organisation called Business Against Crime (BAC) provides training and materiel support to police agencies as well as influencing criminal justice strategy, policy and priorities (Bhanu & Stone 2004; Singh 2005). BAC is funded by business organisations. Many police organisations obtain resources from foundations set up specifically to assist them. The New York City Police Foundation, for example, has raised money for police health screening, scholarships and training, amongst other things (see <http://www.nycpolicefoundation.org/programs.asp>).

Sponsorship of policing in its various guises is becoming increasingly common around the world. In the United States, with its tradition of philanthropy towards public institutions, it is particularly well developed. It is becoming more widespread in the United Kingdom. In Australia, however, it has been relatively uncommon until recently. The growth of sponsorship in the area of policing is part of a broader trend in which governments worldwide are withdrawing from many areas of activity which were previously regarded as core public functions and making explicit and implicit pleas to commercial and non-profit organisations to fill the vacuum.

The benefits for companies of sponsoring police or their activities are obvious. Reputational association with the 'good guys' can bring great cachet to a company, and by so doing increase their profits. For police, sponsorship carries the lure of much-needed resources. However, there are potential disadvantages to these arrangements both for police and for the public. It has been suggested that corporate sponsorship of police vehicles, with its associated advertising, will create the risk of conflicts of interest for police, distortion of police agendas and even of corporate capture, and will undermine the symbolic authority of police (Fleury-Steiner & Wiles 2003: 447–49), turning police into laughing stocks (Mollenkamp 2003:81). These types of concerns are generalisable to most forms of police sponsorship (see Grabosky 2006). As we have seen, the same kinds of concerns have been raised in relation to relationships of sale, such as user-pays policing.

Clearly there is a balance to be aimed for in these gift arrangements, between protecting the law enforcement agency's reputation and integrity, ensuring that the arrangement satisfies both the sponsor (in terms of its return) and the agency's need for resource enhancement, and serving the public interest. Endorsing a product, for instance, may not necessarily damage a police organisation's credibility or reputation, but there are certain industries with which police would be prudent not to be publicly associated – the alcohol, tobacco, gambling, firearms and sex industries would be among them. Similarly, police involved in sponsorship arrangements need to be concerned not only about the effect on police reputation of commercial exploitation, where a provider invokes the police connection for business advantage, but also about the possible risk of liability if the product is defective. It is not only the police who will be concerned with the consequences of such arrangements for their legitimacy. It will also be in the sponsor's marketing interest to be cautious that that legitimacy is not undermined.

Police may need to contemplate carefully any gift arrangement which results in a diminution of their discretion over the uses to which the gift is put. Acceptance and use of a donation of work space, for instance, would suggest a police presence is expected at that location, not down the road. Any provision of funds that comes with conditions attached would need to be carefully considered to ensure that acceptance of the 'gift' does not distort the police organisation's own agenda or result in an unfair distribution of policing services. To their credit, many Australian criminal justice agencies have devoted a great deal of thought to processes by which sponsorship may be managed with integrity (for example, NSW Independent Commission Against Corruption 1993; NSW Police Service 2001; WA Police Sponsorship and Donations Policy AD 54).

Guidelines for gift-based networking

In many cases wise decision-making (for instance, in relation to choice of sponsors), clear policy guidelines and thorough contract negotiation and management by police organisations will ameliorate any possible undesirable effects. Police have as much bargaining power over the parameters of these sponsorship relationships as the corporate sponsors, with this strength lying in the reputational advantages for the sponsor of association with law enforcement and the criminal justice system. Police should not be afraid to use this power to secure the kinds of arrangements they want or, if that is not possible, to walk away from a sponsorship that threatens their legitimacy or their ability to equitably and independently provide policing services.

Some thought should also be given by both police and governments to the long-term effects on law enforcement of an expansion in corporate sponsorship. Is it likely to result in a reduction in core government funding, and if so, is that something police organisations can face with equanimity? It may be that reducing a police organisation's budget appropriation will eliminate any incentive to raise additional revenue for fear of the consequences for the next year's appropriation. Alternatively, it may serve as an invitation to chase paying police work at the expense of other police work that does not bring those rewards, with adverse consequences for the public interest.

Ambiguities and overlaps

We have already noted that similar concerns arise about relationships between police and the private sector in relation to both sale and gift. Grabosky (2004) points out that differentiating between sponsorship and user-pays policing is sometimes difficult. He gives the example of the situation where the managers of a shopping mall offer to underwrite the cost of police presence on site during opening hours and to provide complimentary office space for the police. The sponsorship of police patrols in Cornwall, mentioned above, is another example of an arrangement which might just as easily be characterised as user-pays policing. Perhaps, as Grabosky suggests, the difference lies in who controls the activity – under a sponsorship arrangement, the police; with user-pays policing, the client. However, sometimes, as the above examples illustrate, this is not entirely clear. Both sides may have a say over the nature and limits of police involvement in the activity.

The relationship between police and informants provides an example of the ambiguities that can surround the three dimensions of exchange. We have discussed informants in the context of sale, because the exchange of money for information is often a feature of the relationship. However, it is not unknown for police to use threats, such as the threat of prosecution, to secure informants' co-operation. These relationships would properly be characterised as being of a coercive nature. Similarly, information may be provided as a gift, motivated by a desire to help, or by something more sinister, such as a desire to inflict revenge. Motives may be mixed. Police can use this fact, combining greed with other motives, by offering both carrots and sticks. For example, police may invite information in return for a nominal payment and protection of an informant's illegal activities, with the clear implication that if the information is not forthcoming, not only will the protection be withheld, but there may be police intervention to prevent those activities continuing. How then to characterise this relationship? There is both an element of coercion and an element of sale.

It matters how police–private arrangements are characterised and that these ambiguities are recognised, because this will affect the kinds of considerations the police bring to bear in assessing the benefits and dangers of entering those resourcing networks and the types of controls needed over the relationships within them. More thought is required on the conditions under which 'gifts' should be encouraged. For instance, if sponsorship is seen purely as a gift, police may not recognise that they have something the sponsor wants and with which they can bargain. And if the relationship between informants and police is seen purely as a commercial exchange, there is a danger that appropriate safeguards against the improper use of coercion will not be considered.

Conclusion

Public policing is being reconfigured under the twin influences of practical exigencies and shifts in the way in which governance is being understood. There is a move towards a more holistic approach that mobilises and directs a wider range of knowledge and capacities available in the community. One aspect of this is that police are exploring new and different ways of managing networks that seek to integrate state and civil society resources. We have considered the resourcing networks that coalesce around particular modes of exchange (coercion, sale and gift), examined examples of arrangements within each mode and addressed the challenges presented by these modes.

This paper highlights the variety of interests represented by the nodes in these resourcing networks: the interests of the police themselves, of the private sector and of the public. Those interests do not always coincide and may sometimes conflict. Network relationships are not always harmonious, and are often contested. The police will frequently be in a position to weigh up those interests before entering into an arrangement that pulls in resources to public policing. If this weighing is not done, there can be unintended and undesirable consequences for policing, including distortion of policing agendas and distributive inequities. The key values of democratic policing may be threatened.

It is important, therefore, that police have at their disposal tools to evaluate the potential short-term and long-term effects of resourcing arrangements and to identify how they might best be managed. Police need to be equipped to develop safeguards against unwanted outcomes, and appropriate controls to ensure that these arrangements neither inhibit nor skew the realisation of public policing objectives. Police in Australia have already begun identifying these tools. The challenge will be to continue this process in a direction that both confirms and enhances the values of democratic policing.

Acknowledgments

The authors would like to acknowledge the support of the Australian Research Council (DP0450247) and the research assistance of Lucy Strang.

References

9/11 Commission (2004) *The 9/11 Commission Report: Final Report of the National Commission on Terrorist Attacks Upon the United States.* New York: W.W. Norton & Co.

Australian Bureau of Statistics (2003) *Australian Social Trends – Family and Community Services: Child protection,* at <http://www.abs.gov.au/Ausstats/abs@.nsf/0/7d95127fb3bfd9caca256d39001bc33f?OpenDocument#Links>.

Berwick, D. (1988) *The Application of the User Pays Principle to the Policing of Sporting and Entertainment Events: Principle Considerations.* National Police Research Unit, Australia.

Bhanu, C. and Stone, C. (2004) Public-private partnerships for police reform, Vera Institute of Justice, at <http: //www.vera.org/publications/publications_5.asp?publication_id=230>.

Blatchford, C. (2000) AEC gave RCMP computers and software': Deployed to track 'people of interest', *National Post,* 23 February, A1.

Braithwaite, J. (2000) The new regulatory state and the transformation of criminology, *British Journal of Criminology,* 40: 222–38.

—— (2002) Rewards and regulation, *Journal of Law and Society,* 29(1): 12–26.

Braithwaite, J. and Pettit, P. (1990) *Not Just Deserts: A Republican Theory of Criminal Justice.* New York: Oxford University Press.

Buerger, M.E. and Mazerolle, L.G. (1998) Third-party policing: A theoretical analysis of an emerging trend, *Justice Quarterly,* 15(2): 301–27.

Burris, S., Drahos, P. and Shearing, C. (2005) Nodal governance as an approach to regulation, *Australian Journal of Legal Philosophy,* 30:30-58.

Commercial Activities Panel (2002) *Improving the Sourcing Decisions of the Government,* Final Report, Government Accountability Office, at <http://www.gao.gov/a76panel>.

Davids, C. and Hancock, L. (1998) Policing, accountability, and citizenship in the market state, *The Australian and New Zealand Journal of Criminology,* 31(1): 38–68.

Davies, M. (2003) Obligations and implications for ships encountering persons in need of assistance at sea, *Pacific Rim Law and Policy Journal,* 12(1): 109–41.

Davis, N. Zemon (2000) *The Gift in Sixteenth Century France.* Madison: University of Wisconsin.

Department for Transport (2004) *Review of the British Transport Police*, at <http: //www.dft.gov.uk/stellent/groups/dft_railways/documents/page/dft_railways_032061.pdf>.

Dillon, Wilton S. (2003) *Gifts and Nations*. London: Transaction Publishers.

Dore, C. (1999) NZ sues IBM over police, *The Australian*, 24 August.

Eng, S. (2001) Policing for the public good: A commentary prepared for the Law Commission of Canada Study Panel on Order and Security, at <http: //www.cppa-acpp.ca>.

Etter, B. (2001) Computer crime, paper delivered at the 4th National Outlook Symposium on Crime in Australia, *New Crimes or New Responses*, Australian Institute of Criminology, Canberra, 21–22 June.

Feldbrugge, F.J.M. (1966) Good and bad samaritans: A comparative survey of criminal law provisions concerning failure to rescue, *The American Journal of Comparative Law*, 14: 630–57.

Fleming, J. and Lafferty, G (2000) New management techniques and restructuring in police organisations, *Policing: An International Journal of Police Strategy and Management*, 23(2): 154–68.

Fleming, J. and Rhodes, R.A.W. (2005) Bureaucracy, contracts and networks: The unholy trinity and the police, *Australian and New Zealand Journal of Criminology*, 38(2): 192–205.

Fleury-Steiner, B. and Wiles, K. (2003) The use of commercial advertisements on public police cars in the United States, post-9/11, *Policing and Society*, 13(4): 441–50.

Frieberg, A. (2005) Managerialism in Australian criminal justice: RIP for KPIs?, *Monash University Law Review*, 31: 12–36.

Gans, J. (2000) Privately paid public policing: Law and practice, *Policing and Society*, 10: 183–206.

Gibbons, S. (1996) Sponsored beats, *Police Review*, 104 (26 July): 22–24.

Gilboy, J. (1998) Compelled third-party participation in the regulatory process: Legal duties, culture and noncompliance, *Law and Policy*, 20(2): 135–55.

Grabosky, P. (1990) Citizen co-production and corruption control, *Corruption and Reform*, 5: 125–51.

—— (1994) Green markets: Environmental regulation by the private sector, *Law and Policy*, 16(4): 419–48.

—— (1995a) Using non-governmental resources to foster regulatory compliance, *Governance*, 8(4): 527–50.

—— (1995b) Regulation by reward: On the use of incentives as regulatory instruments, *Law & Policy*, 17(3): 257–82.

—— (2004) Towards a theory of public/private interaction in policing, in J. McCord (ed.), *Beyond Empiricism: Institutions and Intentions in the Study of Crime: Advances in Criminological Theory*. Somerset NJ: Transaction Books.

—— (2006) Private sponsorship of public policing, *Police Practice and Research: An international journal* (in press).

Gunningham, N. and Grabosky, P. (1998) *Smart Regulation*. Oxford: Clarendon Press.

Hitchcock, T. and Shoemaker, R. (2003) Policing in London before the bobbies, The

Old Bailey Proceedings Online Project, at <http://www.oldbaileyonline.org/history/crime/policing.html>.

Howson, G. (1970) Thief-Taker General: The Rise and Fall of Jonathan Wild. London: Hutchinson.

Johnston, L. (1992) The Rebirth of Private Policing. London: Routledge.

Johnston, L. and Shearing, C. (2003) Governing Security. London: Routledge.

Levi-Faur, D. (2005) The global diffusion of regulatory capitalism, The Annals of the American Academy of Political and Social Sciences, 598 (March): 12–32.

Loader, I. (1997) Policing and the social: Questions of symbolic power, British Journal of Sociology, 48(1): 1–18.

—— (1999) Consumer culture and the commodification of policing and security, Sociology, 33(2): 373–92.

Loader, I. and Walker, N. (2005) Necessary virtues: The legitimate place of the state in the production of security, in J. Wood and B. Dupont (eds), Democracy, Society and the Governance of Security. Cambridge: Cambridge University Press.

Lusty, D. (2002) Civil forfeiture of proceeds of crime in Australia, Journal of Money Laundering Control, 5(4): 345–59.

McLaughlin, E. and Murji, K. (1997) The future lasts a long time: Public policework and the managerialist paradox, in P. Francis, P. Davies and V. Jupp (eds), Policing Futures: The Police, Law Enforcement and the Twenty-First Century. London: Macmillan.

Mauss, M. (1969) The Gift: Forms and Functions of Exchange in Archaic Societies (translated by Ian Cunnison). London: Cohen and West.

Mazerolle, L.G. and Ransley, J. (2005) Third Party Policing. Cambridge: Cambridge University Press.

Miller, M. (1999) Police and media: Spirit of co-operation, Police Life, September: 24–25.

Mollenkamp, B. (2003) Corporate sponsorship for law enforcement, Law & Order, 51(1): 80–82.

Mulgan, R. (2001) Accountability the key to successful outsourcing, The Canberra Times, 20 January.

Murphy, C. (2002) The Rationalization of Public Policing In Canada: A study of the impact and implications of resource limits and market strategies in public policing, The Police Future Group, CACP, Electronic series No. 1.

Murray, D. (2004) Why police have to rely on charity, The Sunday Mail, 6 June:2.

Newburn, T. (2001) The commodification of policing: Security networks in the late modern city, Urban Studies, 38(5–6): 829–48.

NSW Independent Commission Against Corruption (1993) Sponsorship Principles: A Discussion Paper. Sydney: Independent Commission Against Corruption.

NSW Police Service (2001) Sponsorship and Endorsement Policy. Sydney: NSW Police Service.

—— (2004) Cost Recovery and User Charges Policy. Sydney: NSW Police Service.

Pilant, L. (1998) Creative funding, Police Chief, LXV(3): 42–46.

Pollarito, K. (2002) Drug co., Fla. make pact to thwart Oxycontin abuse, Reuters Health Information, at <http://cancerpage.com/news/article.asp?id=5107>.

Police Commissioners' Conference Electronic Crime Steering Committee (2001) *Electronic Crime Strategy 2001–2003*, at <http://www.police.govt.nz/resources/2001/e-crime-strategy/e-crime-strategy.pdf>.

Rhodes, R.A.W. (1994) The hollowing out of the state: the changing nature of the public services in Britain, *Political Quarterly*, 65(2): 138–51.

—— (1997) *Understanding Governance*. Buckingham: Open University Press.

Saltonstall, P. and Rising, D. (1999) Drug loot fuels drug war, *Southcoast Today*, 8 August, at <http://www.s-t.com/daily/08-99/08-08-99/a01lo010.htm>.

Schönteich, M. Minnaar, A. Mistry, D. and Goyer, K.C. (2004) *Private muscle: Outsourcing the provision of criminal justice services* (Monograph No. 93). Cape Town: Institute for Security Studies.

Schultz, LeRoy G. (1990) Confidentiality, privilege, and child abuse reporting: Issues in child abuse accusations, *Journal of the Institute for Psychological Therapies*, 2: 4, at <http://www.ipt-forensics.com/journal/volume2/j2_4_5.htm>.

Seligman, J. (1983) The historical need for a mandatory corporate disclosure system, *Journal of Corporation Law*, 9: 1–61.

Shearing, C. and Stenning, P. (1983) Snowflakes or good pinches?: Private security's contribution to modern policing, in R. Donelan (ed.), *The Maintenance of Order in Society*. Ottawa: Canadian Police College.

Shearing, C. and Wood, J. (2003a) Nodal governance, democracy, and the new 'denizens', *Journal of Law and Society*, 30(3): 400–419.

—— (2003b) Governing security for common goods, *International Journal of the Sociology of Law*, 31(3): 205–25.

Singh, A-M. (2005) Some critical reflections on the governance of crime in post-apartheid South Africa, in J. Sheptycki and A. Wardak (eds), *Transnational and Comparative Criminology*. London: GlassHouse Press.

Verspaandonk, R. (2001) Outsourcing – For and against. *Current Issues Brief*, 18, 2000–2001, Parliament of Australia Parliamentary Library.

Volokh, E. (1999) Duties to rescue and the anticooperative effects of law, *Georgetown Law Journal*, 88: 105–14.

Western Australia Police Service (2000) Cannington Police Office, *Newsbeat*, Issue 8 (Summer): 14.

—— (2002) *Fee for Service, Cost Recovery and Third Party Funding*. Research and Projects Co-ordination Unit, Western Australia Police Service.

Worrall, John L. (2001) Addicted to the drug war: The role of civil asset forfeiture as a budgetary necessity in contemporary law enforcement, *Journal of Criminal Justice*, 29: 171–87.

WORKING THROUGH NETWORKS: THE CHALLENGE OF PARTNERSHIP POLICING | 4

Jenny Fleming[1]

Introduction

The language of partnerships pervades present-day conceptions of crime prevention, community and policing. In contrast to a reliance on rigid, hierarchical bureaucracies, 'networks of diverse group interests have become the dominant ethic' (Crawford 1997: 25). The emphasis on community policing has placed obligations on police agencies to focus on crime prevention and working with the community. As a result, police are expected to work through networks and to develop common approaches to such objectives with other agencies as well as with the local community.

In the United Kingdom, working through partnerships is a principal component of the police reform agenda (see Newburn 2003: 88; Edwards & Benyon 2001; Hughes & McLaughlin 2002; Liddle & Gelsthorpe 1994). Policing through networks and managing multi-agencies in crime prevention work are formally encouraged through policy initiatives and legislation. In 1998 the Crime and Disorder Act made working through partnership a statutory requirement for police and local authorities. Police in the United Kingdom are required to collaborate with public agencies and bodies to establish and promote community safety strategies. Importantly, the legislation allows police and local authorities to share information with other agencies (this was previously restricted under the Data Protection Act) in the interests of such partnerships. Crawford's work on networks (1997) has provided significant data on the way in which these partnerships are perceived and implemented by police (see also Crawford & Lister: 2005).

In Australia, most police organisations promote their commitment to working through networks via formal, and publicly available, annual reports and strategic plans (see APMC 2002; Vernon & McKillop 1990; Bayley 1986). There is no official mandate in Australia for police to work through partnerships. While many police organisations have explored the bound-aries of collaboration and multi-agency work, there are no formal policy parameters within which they work. There is no extra funding for such activity, and where organisations have sought to work through networks and partnerships they have done so within existing funding arrangements. In recent years and in some jurisdictions, senior police managers have been formally encouraged, through employment agreements, to pursue a partner-ship approach to crime prevention. However, for the most part, networking and working through partnerships is not a strong performance measure-ment in Australian police organisations.

Accounts of policing networks and partnerships in Australia are rare, but formal evaluation reports[2] and case study-based papers have provided some information about how these networks function (see Young 2000, 2001; Walters 1996; CJC 1999). These accounts, however, are at a level of abstraction that does not provide the data that is available in, for example, Crawford's research (1997), which highlights the potentially conflicting nature of police partnerships and the divergent experiences and attitudes that participants bring to the multi-agency forum (see also Liddle & Gelsthorpe 1994; Ryan et al. 2001).

This chapter explores the idea of partnership policing in Australia using qualitative data collected through a series of recorded interviews and focus groups with police officers of all ranks in one Australian jurisdic-tion. The views expressed here were recorded as part of a general discus-sion about policing practices, organisational issues, community expectations and problem policy areas for operational officers. The views should be considered as a single perspective on networks and partnership policing generally in this jurisdiction; they do not necessarily reflect the views of the author.

The responses identified were taken from conversations relating to several difficult public policy areas for police and the extent to which a more networked approach might alleviate such difficulties. The chapter reports officers' views on networks and agency partnerships and identifies the factors that constrain networking in this police organisation.

An analysis of over 100 hours of conversation with police officers sug-gests that while there is some instrumental support for a concept that clearly has the potential to facilitate an officer's core tasks, a number of issues provided significant challenges for police officers generally. This chapter is structured around these challenges. The implications of the officers' responses for policing networks generally are discussed. I do not give a cultural explanation for their responses. I 'acknowledge that the complexity of police cultures' can 'impede the development of more responsive and advanced approaches to crime management and reduc-tion' (Foster 2003: 222, 199). However, it is important that we do not ignore officers' accounts of their direct work experiences, nor underesti-mate the organisational factors that shape those experiences. Police *make sense* of their work better than most researchers (see Weitz et al. 2005; Chan 2006). Their perceptions of how things work greatly assist our knowledge about police culture and practice. However, their perceptions are not generally taken into account.

Background and data

The research reported in this chapter is part of a larger project looking at ways of enhancing officers' ability to develop partnerships with the commu-nity, network more efficiently and contribute to multi-agency approaches to crime prevention. The interviews and focus groups that were part of the early consultation phase allowed researchers to gain a clearer understanding of the working environment of the police and what could be achieved in that environment.

Thirty semi-structured interviews were conducted with senior officers (from Sergeant to Commander) and senior civilian managers. The inter-views explored the limits and prospects of networking and co-operative policing in the context of 'problem policy areas'. Interviewees were selected arbitrarily, with senior rank being the only requirement. As one would expect given the numbers of women at senior rank in Australian police organisations, only 4 of the 30 interviewees were women. The interviews were conducted in 2003 and 2004.

In the same period, and with the same police organisation, 11 two-hour focus groups were conducted with police officers. The groups represented all ranks – that is, Commanders to Probationary Constables. All contributors (interviewees and focus group participants) spoke voluntarily and candidly about their individual and organisational experiences with the police service under review. All participants were guaranteed anonymity. The transcripts of the focus groups were coded using the QSR NVivo® software qualitative analysis program.

The state police organisation under review is a relatively small police service, with limited resources. A paucity of experienced officers in the middle ranks has resulted in continuous movement within the service to compensate for seniority gaps and other resource difficulties. Like other police organisations in Australia, this organisation is publicly committed to community policing and embraces the importance of networks and building trust relations with the community. Committed to corporate governance, this organisation is output focused and its operational practice relies on hierarchies of objectives, targets and a highly specific system of performance measurement. As with all police organisations, the service is particularly vulnerable to political scrutiny and influence (Fleming 2004).

Yet while the rhetoric of networks and partnerships pervades this organiniation's strategic plan and annual reports, like most other police organisations, in practice, it has not yet formally moved beyond rhetoric (see Magers 2004). Inter-organisational activity is not a major focus or commitment for management and operational personnel generally.

This organisation is required through its formal agreement with the state government to work in partnership with the community, to create a safe and secure environment and demonstrate a high level of community satisfaction with its services. These objectives are achieved, according to its annual report, through the delivery of specific services. The organisation's performance is tested against these services. Performance indicators cover issues such as public order, emergency management, crime prevention and control, road safety and justice services. These indicators are consistent with the demand by governments for outcome-oriented performance information. There is no formal requirement or measurement for successful collaboration or partnership activity.

Network development and management

A variety of terms are used interchangeably at the theoretical and practical level to describe network policing, partnership policing or multi-agency policing. Whatever the term used, the concept embraces co-ordinated action by relevant local agencies to address a specific policy issue – in this instance, crime prevention. The network or partnership may also include business representatives, community groups and other interested parties. Much has been written about such networks and the management of them. Drawing on the literature, we can identify a number of characteristics and attributes associated with networks that provide a context for the data that follows.

Networks are sets of resource-dependent organisations. For an organisation to achieve its goals, it must exchange resources with other organisations. The key resources are money and legal authority, although personnel, information, infrastructure and expertise are also important (see Rhodes 1999a [1981]). At the heart of these networks and their management are the notions of trust and reciprocity (see Rhodes 1997, 1999b). Trust is the essential co-ordinating mechanism of networks in the same way that commands and price competition are the key mechanisms for bureaucracies and markets respectively (Frances et al. 1991: 15). Shared values and norms and an appreciation of divergent organisational cultures are the glue that holds the complex set of relationships together. Earning and sustaining trust is a two-way process and a continuing task (Flynn et al. 1996: 136). Co-operation and consultation (born out of trust and reciprocity) are crucial. A formal network structure, where membership is stable, consolidates trust and reciprocity and allows initially complex relationships to develop positively.

In positive, collaborative networks, network culture is characterised by reciprocity: a 'give and take' culture that acknowledges obligation and encourages the interchange of resources, information and trust. As Thompson (1993: 58) points out, reciprocity has important symbolic elements, and 'in the constant ritual of exchange, deep obligations and duties are established'. For networks to be maintained there needs to be a sense of ownership on the part of the networks' individual members. Participation benefits are important (Liddle & Gelsthorpe 1994b) and reciprocity reinforces those benefits.

The literature on networks identifies two broad sets of challenges associated with networks: intrinsic limits and mixing with hierarchies and markets. First, networks that do not possess or develop the attributes discussed above are unlikely to thrive. So, for example, where there is competition for resources and conflict is generated between individual and organisational commitments, networks may be difficult to develop. Similarly, where there are legislative or policy constraints, about, for example, information-sharing and privacy issues, successful networking is difficult. Other problems arise when the closed nature of the network makes accountability of decision-making obscure, where process and procedures reduce or remove flexibility and where the network is not a budgetary or administrative priority.

The second challenge is the problem of combining bureaucracy and markets (contracts) with network activity. Fleming and Rhodes (2005) show that many of the challenges that police officers confront in their everyday work practices arise from the difficulties of combining a command and control structure with contractual obligations on the one hand and a client-focused approach of community policing on the other hand.

Community policing is a dramatic departure from traditional policing because it adopts a 'long term strategic approach rather than offering a quick fix to an immediate problem' (Edwards 2005: 119). Community policing is about leadership, partnerships, consultation and building trust within the organisation and with the community. It is understood as a 'range of specific techniques that the police and the public use to work in partnership at a local level' (Wright 2002: 143). If one considers the parameters for such a paradigm for policing, community policing 'has many radically different and sometimes incompatible aspects from the rational-legal bureaucratic model' (Magers 2004: 72). As Fleming and Rhodes (2005) demonstrate, police officers are aware of the contradictions between a bureaucratic mentality dominated by rules and process, hierarchical subordination and non-participative decision-making, contracts, with their emphasis on competition and performance assessment, and networks, which stress the importance of trust, the sharing of resources and collegial decision-making across ranks.

There is a third challenge. At a time when security, counter-terrorism and domestic law and order are issues of high political salience, police activity and delivery of services are heavily scrutinised by governments. Police leaders (that is, Commissioners) are under constant pressure to deliver results – results that can be quantified and used as a way of demon-strating good government service delivery (Fleming 2004). As Freiberg notes (2005), such demands require the 'auditing potential of quantifiable activities rather than intangible tasks and the unquantifiable aspects of police services'. As I have argued elsewhere, measured work drives out the unmeasured; that is, contracts, with their performance indicators, under-mine networks, with their intangible outcomes, and may be of limited use in the network context (Fleming & Rhodes 2005).

The following section explores the views and experiences of police offi-cers on networks, partnerships and working with other agencies generally. The focus groups and interviews identified a number of challenges. These challenges fall into five categories: resources, privacy, trust, inter-organisa-tional relations and government and policy issues.

The data

There is a pervasive view that police are unlikely to participate in networks and local partnerships because partnership work diverts officers and other resources away from the real task of 'saving the world' (Novak, Alarid & Lucas 2003; although see also Sampson et al. 1988: 491). In this research, there were many senior officers who believed wholeheartedly in a net-worked approach. They adopted what Crawford (1994: 332–33) refers to as the 'supportive missionary' approach, emphasising the benefits of net-works as a way of facilitating core tasks:

> I think we should work with other government departments more. Roads for example. We could help with road design, intel-ligence about accident rates and black spots. We do assist in some ways but it happens in a piecemeal way – there is no planning, no set goals. Both agencies could contribute a percentage of our funding to road development, for example. We could work with private sector organisations on building and road redesign. (Commander)

> I can see us becoming one arm in a community consultative board – all interlocking – family services, youth services ... all meshing ... with the departments no longer working in isolation. We need to work towards an inter-agency approach – it will be difficult, but if you are determined to make it work there is no physical reason why it shouldn't work. (Senior Sergeant)

These particular officers were speaking in the future tense; they have little experience of formal networks but know that they have to, in principle, support the concept of network-based community policing. As Magers points out (2004: 71), 'to do otherwise invites criticism for not being progressive and [being] out of step with clear political goals of embracing the principles of police involvement with the community'. Management are in the business of 'getting things done' and feel instinctively that initiatives that have the potential to extend resources and facilitate their core business must have value.

Operational officers are a bit more circumspect about their ability to meet some of the challenges. However, enthusiastic or otherwise, officers of all ranks were mindful of the obstacles that constrain working with other agencies specifically and other community groups more generally. Here officers speak candidly as they engage in what Chan (2006) refers to (in the context of police reform) as 'the process of sense-making'. The officers are effectively making sense of networking and partnerships as they understand them and identifying the challenges associated with such practices.

Resources

Scarce resources were a constant problem for officers of all ranks. The more senior officers demonstrated that they were aware of the importance of building trust and the sharing of resources in networking. They were just as aware of the organisational resource problems and 'the way things work' in the organisation when addressing the issue of scarce resources:

> It's always been the case in [our organisation] that when we go for a full collaboration with somebody ... it has resulted in a reduction in our funding ... so most managers are very keen to hang onto what they have, simply because if they don't it's going to cost us ... they'll outsource to this or they will do that ... There is a difference between collaboration and outsourcing insofar as handing off jobs. And time and time again our budget is reduced as a result of doing that. (Sergeant)

The lack of resources internally was a source of frustration for officers. The paucity of potential partnership organisations' resources was particularly an issue for senior officers, whose concerns are largely related to juggling resources and meeting budgetary bottom lines:

> We get calls from the public asking about social services a fair bit. I say, 'You need to ring Family Services' or whatever, and they invariably say, 'They told us to ring you.' Presumably because they have got no one to deal with it. (Sergeant)

> Yeah, we have quite a few of the local government agencies that are having to ring us more and more often, or we ring them for assistance and they are unavailable to help, so we end up having to do the function because they don't have the staffing levels available. (Commander)

The constables, while aware of other organisations' resource issues, were much more concerned with how such issues impacted on their own work practice:

> Mental Health ... have got one doctor, and no doubt they are the same as the police force with budgetary considerations and financial and staffing issues. They never have enough people ... the flow-on effect is that you are tied up, you have to sit there and you have to wait. And the end result is that those police officers were one of three or two patrols on the road and they are gone for X amount of hours, you know, up to a whole shift. (Constable)

The sharing and exchange of resources (this includes, for example, information exchange, the swapping of stories and mutual advising, and should not be measured just in terms of financial exchange) is a core part of networking – particularly at the multi-agency level. Even if officers support such a concept and do not actively seek to contest such arrangements, it may not be financially and administratively viable for them to do so.

Privacy issues – sharing information

Unlike in the United Kingdom, where the government has legislated to allow police to share information with other agencies, in Australia, privacy is seen as a significant challenge for police working with the community generally and agencies specifically. Crawford (2003: 160), speaking in the UK context, has observed that information issues 'constitute a central battleground in interagency conflicts'. In the absence of data protection legislation, the potential for such a battleground in Australia is obvious. Some officers understood this dilemma:

> That's a big issue with everything we do: privacy. A lot of the other agencies ... are very scared about where they stand with regard to divulging information to another agency. In a lot of the cases if it is to investigate a criminal offence there is no problem, they can provide it, but rather than go ahead they'll just go, 'No, because we don't want to be sued, we don't want to be this, that or the other' ... when really they might be quite entitled to exchange that information and it's just they are not aware of it. (Sergeant)

> [T]hey love working with us and we love working with them. And [other agencies] were involved ... it was great ... then we ran into this sort of ... privacy issue. It was like, 'Well how can we get around the privacy issue?' ... They wanted to tell us and we wanted to tell them but it was like, 'Oh we can't tell you that.' (Sergeant)

Others saw agencies' reluctance to share information as a deliberate strategy to lessen their workload:

> We can go [into any organisation] and say, 'Look we are investigating something' ... and they can quite lawfully provide that information but they choose not to ... a lot of agencies too seem to push their requirements onto the police. I think the big catch-cry for a while was core business. Our core business is keep the community safe, lock up the criminals, deal with the crimes that are committed in the community. But a lot of agencies are pushing these extra responsibilities [onto us]. So, for example, family violence pushes X amount of work onto police ... and we are paying for it. We don't have the resources but we are expected to do something. (Constable)

This constable's obvious frustration is grounded in two observations – first, the issue of resources is ever present. The officer is obliquely referring to recent legislation that makes it mandatory for government workers to report suspected abuse to police. This does impact on police resources in many ways. The officer is also suggesting that the core business of police officers is eroded by such activity. This concern is reminiscent of Crawford's (1994: 335–36) 'critical missionary' type, where officers are concerned about neglecting their core tasks and where 'issues of role confusion and organisational boundary blurring represent important anxieties'.

Where officers have worked in multi-agency partnerships, and with the benefit of hindsight, the issue of privacy was also a concern:

> The sharing of agency information would have been useful – as well as from treatment agencies. They had drug users popping in for chats etc ... and their information could have been useful. In the same way, I couldn't give them formal police data. I could give them my view of the data, as I saw it, but that's not the same thing. I think it limited the effectiveness of the network. (Senior Sergeant)

> It was a joint operation between us. We were just trying to clean up the flats [public housing]. And we were working with some people from Public Housing to do it. There were other issues with removing abandoned vehicles and stuff, but there's this privacy thing that they couldn't give us. We said, 'Can we have the master list for the property?' Oh no. But if we had had the master list we could have gone, 'Well none of the people on that list are in Flat 72, so we can just leave them alone, but the guy or the girl in Flat 74 has got a first instance warrant so we will go to that one. We won't go to 76 or 77 but we will go to 81 because they have got an unpaid traffic fine or whatever it is.' So you could have targeted things, but no, we had to do it the hard way. (Sergeant)

Clearly, as Sampson et al. have suggested (1988: 483), 'problems of confidentiality abound in multi-agency working'. The issue of reciprocity is pertinent here too. If there are issues about sharing and providing participants with information, it will be difficult to foster a trusting relationship. As well, such restrictions may lead to agencies working with their own notions of confidentiality, which can further dent notions of trust within the network.

Trust

The issue of trust is important in a number of ways. Just as compliance with the law, police and police directives is directly related to trust and a perception of fairness (Tyler 1990: 200), police officers themselves react to perceptions of distrust. Novak et al. (2003: 63) have suggested that where officers perceive community disrespect and distrust for police generally, they are unlikely to support partnerships and have less favourable attitudes to community policing. Certainly there is a general feeling at the operational level that police opinions are not valued:

I'd like to see [Mental Health] do some work. A little bit more co-operation. [I'd] like them to trust our opinion a little bit more. Like if we think there's a need to green slip[3] them, obviously we feel there is something wrong. (Constable)

Each organisation [has] got certain ways they deal with things. We expect, when we ring Family Services, that they will come straight out. And in reality it's not the case. We spend five hours talking to them trying to get them out here. And eventually we can't. I don't know why they can't trust our opinion ... when we say, 'This kid's here, he needs care, he's going to re-offend, we need help, we need placement for him.' (Constable)

That's what it feels like: that they just don't trust our opinion. Like we're only police, we [don't know anything]. I used to work for one of the other agencies and the amount of support that I used to get even from the police and from Family Services was so much more than what I get in this job. (Constable)

Senior staff are aware of the importance of being part of networks and gaining the trust of potential partners:

We really must go out and be proactive and engender trust, because make no bones about it, our particular vocation is one of the most powerful vocations in the world. We can deprive a person of their life as well as their liberty. When you have that much power and coming from the democratic society we do, for example, you mentioned throwing out the rights of a juvenile. In any forum there would be absolute pandemonium. So there has got to be a certain amount of trust, there's got to be a certain amount of professionalism. (Senior Sergeant)

You have to build up a trust and rapport with the network participants. It took a while. The treatment agencies, for example, were very anti-police at first. You had to work hard to let them know you understood the drug issues and had the same goals. (Senior Sergeant)

I try and get out and about and get myself on boards as a representative. I am on the Liquor Licensing Board. It deals with contraventions, penalties, applications, that sort of thing. The impact of such decisions is important out there. I need to have a feel for things, a feel for who is doing what. This is one way of doing it. You don't often get invited – 'Oh, no cops, you know what they are going to say.' You have to go looking for it, make yourself part of it – police representation is necessary. (Commander)

It is interesting to note how terms such as 'trust' are so obviously part of these officers' everyday language. The issue of trust is closely tied to the varied experiences of offices interacting with other agencies at a workplace level.

Inter-organisational working

Working with other agencies was well canvassed, especially in the focus groups. Some had positive comments to make about working with other agencies despite the obvious operational difficulties:

> One of the things [working with other organisations] I could do was co-opt other agencies quickly to get involved in a particular issue. When that was over they moved out. We had a bit of a core and a periphery, if you like ... The value of the network is that you are speaking with one voice on an issue. This allows you to push a view up to government much more efficiently. (Senior Sergeant)

Others were more circumspect, aware of the different backgrounds and agendas among potential network participants:

> It became obvious over time that stakeholders had different backgrounds and agendas. Often they didn't have a full understanding of issues so they didn't know what was involved. For example, law, legislation processes and procedures – they wanted us [police] to do something and we would have to explain [that] we can't do that – there was a certain amount of frustration around that. (Senior Sergeant)

> [T]here's a large number of government agencies ... that have different agendas, they want to achieve different outcomes, and they are all impacting on us and they all come to us for advice, for information, for support, or for policing duties, and ... in terms of government there is no integration and no one area that we can go to, to say, 'Hang on, we've got these good ideas, let's bring it together.' Some agencies certainly don't seem to want to be part of that unless it's something that they've instigated. (Commander)

> And you have got to wonder whether in fact they are very interested at all. Because they don't see it as their problem. It's not their core business. Our core business, I suppose we can say, is crime, stopping crime. But Housing is about satisfactory housing for people. It could also be a cultural issue too. We tend as police

to be right of centre, where people in more of those welfare type agencies tend to be left of centre, and therefore there are certain difficulties. (Commander)

Officers who interact with other agencies and the private sector as part of their day-to-day tasks are critical of the way 'they do business':

> They can be difficult to work with. Give you an example. Last few months we had a string of government offices getting broken into and laptops stolen. And that was of significant concern to the government agencies, particularly because of the security information that may or may not have been held on these laptops. So we went out to a particular government department asking them to alert all the security officers to just ask their employees to be more vigilant. It was as simple as that. Make sure your computers are locked away. Bang bang bang. And they refused to do that. No that's too ... 'We would have ministers asking questions why, we would have staff asking questions why, why are police on the doorstep day in and day out' and all the rest. So it was as simple as that ... we went out to government agencies and just asked for their staff to be more vigilant, and ended up in a nice old barney about it. Well at the end of the day it was ... just a reminder that if the government departments aren't prepared to work with us on something as simple as that, well then, really, how difficult do they want to make life? (Senior Sergeant)

Such experiences are going to impact on a police officer's views of whether or not more permanent partnerships are going to be rewarding. Liddle and Gelsthorpe (1994: 6–7) have made the connection between 'ownership and durability'. Where ownership is not generated, uncertainty and a lack of direction are inevitably the results:

> I was working with the relevant departments ... there were eight of them, or six of them. ... I think we have all experienced something of a similar nature, where it might be mental health issues [or kids' issues], where you take them out for a weekend camp, they come back, they have got confidence and everything, and what happens to them after that? They just get dumped back in their family home again. And then the schools don't follow up on it. It's not their problem because they didn't fund it. Juvenile Justice don't follow up on it because they are not on an order. You get these kids that within, sometimes within two months/six

weeks they are back on the cycle again because the good work that was done by getting them self-confidence and all the things that you want to give a kid is destroyed because of policy issues with other people: 'I am not going to fund it', 'We haven't got anybody to do that.' (Sergeant)

Many senior officers felt that there were a range of legislative and policy issues that they were not consulted about; issues that had a direct impact on their resources and their budget. For senior management, inextricably involved with such concerns, this lack of consultation was a serious challenge to the way they conducted their business:

I think that there's a real lack of consultation for us and lack of partnership, I guess, between us and the government, particularly in terms of a range of issues including legislation and policy. [One agency] is very good, and a lot of other agencies too are very good at going out and coming up with these ideas or legislation, policy, things they want to implement, but they don't come and consult with us in terms of the real resource implications long term. (Commander)

These comments about interaction with other agencies are informative. Experiences with agencies on a day-to-day basis have fostered both positive and negative views about working towards more permanent networking arrangements. There is a lot of discussion among scholars about police resistance and their ability to obstruct change. In the conversations quoted here, however, what is clear is that many of the challenges identified cannot be wholly rectified by police organisations. Many of the 'solutions', at least in terms of resources and data availability, as the officers well know, lie with government policy and legislation.

Attitudes to government policy and legislation

The role of government is a pivotal one in the minds of police in relation to funding and the administration of network strategies generally:

[M]y point was really [that in] those kinds of areas there seems to be a lack of consultation with legislative reform, so we will often get consulted at the Cabinet submission stage and not beforehand, and by that stage we will be asked to provide comments, but often it is within a few days, and that doesn't really give us the opportunity to have a fully consultative involvement in the whole thing. And often they are things that affect us ... but we've had no involvement in the process of deciding that yes, we will do that, and how will we do that, and have we got the resources to do that, and is it the most effective way to do whatever it is? (Sergeant)

A lot of these agencies are competing for funding. So the way we structure our government and our non-government services is that they are all in a bidding war, and you know you almost have to be the one that has got the new initiative that ... like the Department of Education's ... Project would have been much more effective if it had been integrated at the ground floor with the Minister's blueprint. But because they have got to compete for the funding they do it separately and then try and integrate it later. So I think if government funding was organised in such a way that it encouraged joint projects, you know, 'We want to fund a joint agency initiative, come to us with a joint agency initiative and we will fund that', rather than sitting around waiting for the Department or whoever to come up with their budget bid for their program. (Commander)

It's a policy decision. How serious is the government about addressing this problem in isolation? Okay we will come up with our model, but without our partner agencies you might as well forget it, we will be in the same position as what we are now. (Sergeant)

Officers are aware that government policy is inconsistent with the rhetoric of partnerships and working more closely with the community. Bound by bureaucratic rules and procedures, conscious of contractual obligations and aware of the organisational resource constraints, police often feel powerless to rectify many of the obvious inconsistencies, and look to government to 'put its money where its mouth is'.

The intrinsic limits of networks

This section of the chapter briefly addresses the intrinsic limits of networks identified by the officers in this research. The section uses phrases as pegs on which to hang some observations about these limits and the implications of these limits for the successful pursuit of networks and partnerships.

Satisfying demand – meeting expectations

Police organisations are not alone in being asked to do more to meet community expectations. The corporate culture of managerialism, so prevalent at the public sector level both in Australia and elsewhere, is associated with contracts, competition, performance measurement, output-fixated targets, partnerships and the reclassification of the public as 'customers'. The 'doing more with less' and 'value for money' language of managerialism has seen all public sector agencies 'tighten their belts'. In all public agencies there is a strong focus on productivity and financial accountability.

Community policing exacts 'high internal costs' on police organisations in terms of resources (Edwards 2005: 113). The police are under great pressure to show that resources are being used efficiently and effectively, with each objective maximised simultaneously (Moore 1990: 73). Resources are considered to be scarce and budgets tight. In this police organisation, resources are allocated to separate regions, and managers allocate those resources accordingly. Such resource allocation potentially promotes internal and external competition.

Dupont (2005) has highlighted some of the more competitive elements of police partnerships, particularly with other agencies. For example, on being asked about working with agencies with 'overlapping responsibilities in the security field', Australian Police Commissioners were 'generally scathing and disparaging' in their remarks. This, from one state jurisdiction:

> [W]hat's been the missing element in my view ... is the tendency for the almost absence or, just lip service, co-operation from many other key government agencies. Now, we are running the score-card for that, the local chairpersons are going to be canvassed about who attends and who doesn't, who participates and who doesn't, who you can get to come and co-operate and who can you not, ... and [we'll] say [to these CEOs]: 'Hey Fred! The feed-back from our 42 committees around the state is, you've only got a 30 per cent appearance and participation rate, and we'll tell you where your people are not playing and you'd better fix it or the next stop will be the deputy Premier's office to say Agency X is not playing the ... game.' We had some good committees, but all we had was the police, the good community people and local government, and most of the others were staying away in their droves (cited in Dupont 2006).

Such practices and attitudes are in conflict with the partnership approach that emphasises resource exchange, trust and reciprocity. Networks and partnerships are resource intensive and essentially incompatible with the 'do more with less' corporate culture.

On a need-to-know basis

In the United Kingdom, the Data Protection Act (1998) introduced a set of general data protection principles that apply to the exchange of personal data between police and other agencies, such as housing, health, probation and social services. The legislation was intended to complement the Crime and Disorder Act passed in the same year, which places a statutory duty on senior police officers to partner with police authorities and other bodies in order to formulate and implement strategies to reduce crime. In this context it has been argued that:

> [I]n reality, multi-agency protocols are essentially 'facilitative' rather than restrictive, containing many broad data protection exemptions and 'few meaningful barriers' to the sharing of a wide range and volume of information, with little regard to privacy issues (Maguire 2000, cited in Lee & South 2003: 428).

In the context of this research, as we have seen, where officers had some experience with a drug network – the privacy issue 'limited the effectiveness of the network'. The story of officers working with Housing recited above is almost comical, not to mention time-consuming. In this instance at least, there would appear to be few data protection exemptions for police working in partnership with other agencies.

The challenges associated with information sharing do not bode well for a partnership based on trust and reciprocity. The sharing of information is more than just the exchange of data. It is symbolic – it suggests, 'we're in this together'. There is a sharing of more than information, and such sharing generates reciprocity. More importantly, it adds significantly to the building of trust, which, as noted, is the fundamental mechanism of successful networks.

You can't shake hands with a clenched fist

The responses identified here suggest that trust between agencies is in short supply. While senior officers were more appreciative of the dilemmas faced by other agencies in terms of resources and information-sharing, the officers on the front line were not so tolerant. The lack of information exchange, a sense on the part of junior officers that their opinions were not valued, and a suspicion that police were used as a catch-all facility when the other agencies' lack of resources prevented them from dealing with a problem, did not bode well for building relationships based on trust. As the officers' responses suggest, collaboration, consultation and co-operation are the building blocks for trust in any potential partnership. Such building blocks are not developed overnight, so one of the things they require is some workplace stability.

In this organisation, police officers are moved around the organisation as a matter of course. It is deemed important for professional development and promotion and other merit awards. As well, national security issues have meant that external organisational commitments have at times taken priority over the business of domestic policing. Officers are moved around a lot, often at short notice. As one senior officer pointed out:

> I think one of the great problems from [our] perspective is [that] nothing stays the same. And I mean it in the sense of people holding positions. We move around too much, we can't develop relationships. It's all right for me to go and talk to Tracy, who works for Housing, and develop a great rapport with Tracy, [but] then Tracy gets transferred, or ... it's me that gets transferred, then someone else has got to build that relationship again with Tracy. And Tracy mightn't like the next person that comes along, or they may have different ways of doing business. One might be more stand-offish. And the personalities and the relationships are the keys, I suppose, to success in regard to solving problems and working together to reach decent outcomes. (Commander)

And another:

> Another issue that really impacts on us at [this level] is the lack of corporate history and the lack of corporate knowledge in this place. I mean if you go back five years ago ... who in the executive, who in the commanders' ranks, were here five years ago? Name one! (Senior Sergeant)

Such staff turnover undermines the development and consolidation of trust relations in potential partnerships.

Why can't they be more like us?

Officers interact with other agencies as part of their work on a day-to-day basis. There were those who enjoyed collaborating with other agencies and appreciated the potential of more formal arrangements. Others emphasised their frustration with those agencies that were perceived as 'not pulling their weight' or as 'passing the buck'. In the focus groups, the participants suggested that a network of stakeholder relationships could create additional barriers to effective operational police work. Always aware of the importance of resources, targets and directives, police officers are resentful that other agencies' lack of resources inevitably impact on them:

> They had no court orders, they were calling police because they just wanted her moved and thought she would throw up a fight. Now we have no powers whatsoever to move someone from one place of residence to another just because Family Services want us to. And their expectations of the police are that [when] they have a problem that they can't deal with they pass it on to the police. And it's not just Family Services, its every other government agency in town. And I don't think you'll find too many police that disagree with that. And I don't think that – you know, yes, the police do have a resourcing problem, but I think the people we work with have a resourcing problem that is being passed on to us. That's one of my big issues at the moment. (Constable)

A number of constables spoke of their concerns about doing other agencies' work for them:

> M: Housing could have just moved them and it would have been over.
>
> J: It's their job. And it doesn't take much for someone from Family Services or Housing to go around to this house and see that it was ...
>
> M: Squalor.
>
> B: But they are intimidated by the people.
>
> Facilitator: By the kids, you mean?
>
> B: Yeah. I mean if you were asked to go round to a house full of these kids and the first thing they said was, 'What the f— do you want?', you know, straight up in your face, and you are just a normal average everyday person, you'd be intimidated. And I

mean these people that are in Housing they are just public servants, they are not ...

J: [A] lot of these agencies, when they do actually go out to any
of these situations, whether it's Mental Health or Housing or
Family Services, they often, yeah, they'll feel threatened, so they'll
want us there.

Such stories are told and retold. It is part of the everyday understanding
and 'sense-making' of police officers' activities. These stories represent
informative and representative anecdotes (Shearing & Ericson 1991: 489)
and resonate with officers of all ranks. Officers are all too aware of the problems encountered at the 'pointy end' of business. Much of the evident frustration stems from the perceived contradictory expectations of the
organisations they interact with. Negative experiences are not useful for
preparing the way for more permanent partnership arrangements with these
agencies. As Crawford (1998: 216) observes, 'partnerships by their very
nature *blur the boundaries* between the roles and functions of incorporated
organisations' (italics added). If there is already a sense that agencies are
willing to offload some of their responsibilities onto police, for whatever
reason, this will have implications for how police think about the concept of
wider and more permanent networking practices.

Government: putting its money where its mouth is

In their specific discussions about government policy and legislation, and
indeed in relation to a range of issues and scenarios, police officers frequently identified government apathy to multi-agency partnerships as an
obstacle to more workable arrangements with external organisations. They
are aware that legislation and policy are essentially contradictory when it
comes to agency interaction with police officers:

What I have found, in trying to deal with other agencies, [is that]
they have an attitude of either they don't really care or they'll use
government legislation or policy that restricts them from being
involved with the police ... Privacy legislation has a key side to
that. So you can't build these ... [I] don't use the word 'can't', but
it's difficult to build key relationships to have an impact on specific problems in your particular area. (Commander)

Officers are also aware of the inconsistencies between the rules of bureaucracy, contracts and networks.

The core contradictions

Running through all this commentary are two contradictions. First, working through networks and partnerships is a stated objective of this police organisation, but all governing structures – bureaucracies, markets and networks – fail some of the time. Second, networking and partnerships do not sit easily with hierarchical governance, strict rules, and a command and control structure or markets that favour competition over co-operation.

Jessop (2000: 20–23) argues that all governing structures fail at some point. He points to the three governing structures discussed here and identifies a number of strategic partnership dilemmas. These dilemmas oppose co-operation with competition, openness with closure, governability with flexibility, and accountability with efficiency. These dilemmas, as noted elsewhere, are especially pertinent to the future development of networking in police organisations (Fleming & Rhodes 2005). Co-operation versus competition is particularly relevant in the context of trust relations and reciprocity. The privacy issues discussed here resonate particularly with the accountability versus efficiency dilemma. The principles of managerialism have exacerbated many of these difficulties.

This police organisation is publicly committed to the partnership approach, both with the community and with other agencies. It is also, like most public sector organisations, committed to managerialism. Managerialism is, as Freiberg (2005) has noted, one of 'the most powerful and influential influence[s] on public administration generally, and criminal justice in particular'. Its practice relies on hierarchies of objectives, targets and performance measurement. Managerialism emphasises planning, organising and leading, and favours the auditing potential of quantifiable activities rather than intangible tasks and the unquantifiable aspects of specific services. Such preoccupations are of limited use in networks. Clearly, there is a tension between co-operative behaviour in the form of inter-agency partnerships and the internal, self-interested competition for resource allocations linked to performance measurement. Managerialism provokes a reactive and number-crunching mentality with an emphasis on resources and outputs. That which threatens either is seen as problematic and does not promote co-operation.

Such structures promote an intra-organisational focus that inevitably serves to undermine the complex task of inter-organisational relations. In pursuit of efficiency and productivity, managerialist reforms promote intra-organisational competition for limited resources. Such a focus does not foster the reciprocity and interdependence that is required of successful networks (Fleming & Rhodes 2005).

Scott (1998: 285–87) shows that an organisation that measures itself through targets and surveys – that is, one that has a high performance culture – and at the same time seeks to introduce community partnerships, faces several problems. Tensions over the priorities among objectives may well cause competition within the organisation itself, particularly when it is likely that resources will be allocated mainly to those activities that are deemed quantifiable or are a part of a target initiative. As others have pointed out, activities that are deemed peripheral to the 'main game' are often discarded in favour of activities that organisations will be held publicly accountable for (Rhodes 1996). Such an arrangement undermines the ability of officers and organisations to focus on developing those attributes that characterise successful networks.

If networking, partnerships and multi-agency work generally is to be effective, then police organisations and those they seek to partner require a more sympathetic set of measures than exists at present. It makes no sense to articulate one set of standards and develop policy for another.

If the future of policing lies with networks, then governments at all levels must be prepared to foster structural conditions that are conducive to such activities. Managerialism does not foster them.

There are also contradictions arising from the attempt to combine a command and control structure with contractual responsibilities and a commitment to network practices. Police organisations are essentially crisis driven. We expect them to be ready for any crisis, any situation that arises.

The co-operative behaviour of a network can collapse under the impact of constantly changing priorities. Such changes are a continuing problem in crisis-driven areas such as family services, police and mental health. Personnel are required elsewhere, scarce resources may need to be redistributed at a moment's notice and strict rules and procedures may become appropriate. Some officers appreciate the dilemmas they confront and recognise the need to adjust their managerial strategies to the context. When hierarchical strategies are called for, senior officers will revert very quickly to command and control structures (Fleming & Rhodes 2005:203). As one officer involved in a network arrangement a few years ago said:

> I think the network way allows you to move on issues quickly as they arise; whether or not this is more efficient in the long run, I haven't decided yet. From the police point of view, command and control is still alive and well and some issues need that response – when we get all organised again we go back to the network. (Senior Sergeant)

Like many public sector organisations, police are subject to intense political pressure. The political salience of law and order ensures that governments take a keen interest in the delivery of police services. Whereas Australian police leaders have traditionally enjoyed a significant degree of administrative and operational autonomy, in recent years, state and federal police ministers have sought to play an unprecedented role in police activity (Fleming 2004). As one officer put it:

> Everything needs to go through government first. We don't really do anything that hasn't been okayed by them. If we want to make changes we have to run them past government ... and they are wary nowadays, very wary. (Commander)

When asked about the possibility of moving to a more networked approach, one officer remarked:

> Somebody would need to drive that sort of change – someone with tenacity. But you must have government on board – any change must be backed up legislatively by government. The agencies would fall in line ... if it was directed by government. (Senior Sergeant)

The politicisation of debates about policing in Australia need not concern us here. Suffice it to say that police work in a highly politicised environment and officers' responses come out of this knowledge.

Conclusion

Responses to questions about networks and partnerships are grounded in understandings about 'why things are done the way they are'. Police officers' experience and knowledge of their environment provide the context for their responses. Such responses remind us of the multifaceted perspectives of the various actors involved in networks. These officers' views suggest that networks are always police initiated and owned. This is not, of course, the case. Indeed, in many partnerships police play a 'bit part' or are part of a much broader network that is co-ordinated and led by others. Hesitation and uncertainty, however, need not be interpreted as resistance to change and reluctance to embark on new initiatives (Skogan & Hartnett 1997: 74–76); they may merely signify an awareness of everyday practices, of the limitations of the various ways of working and of the political context in which they work. They are aware of the politics, the performance measurements and the requirements for promotion and merit awards. They are aware that networking and partnerships do not remove the need to work with bureaucracies and to meet contractual requirements. They are aware of the contradictions of such arrangements. They are mindful of how network practices and working with other agencies may impact on police practices. They know that their everyday routines constrain effective network practice. They are aware that their practices have to be negotiated within parameters they neither set nor control. Their 'shared uncertainties' (Holdaway 1986) and concerns are embedded in such knowledge, and are part of how they make sense of that knowledge. If we appreciate that other agencies have very different goals, cultures and traditions, then we begin to appreciate the various challenges that confront partnership policing.

It should be noted that there are very obviously some successful networking stories. Operation Burglary Countdown in Western Australia, the Commercial Burglary Prevention Package in Victoria, the Youth Community Alliance project in the ACT, and various family violence initiatives in the ACT (Young 2001, 2002), Victoria and New South Wales are all examples of partnerships that have produced positive outcomes.[4]

However, challenges exist, and perhaps we need to look further afield for guidance. The United Kingdom's legislation and general policy trajectory would assist in changing the parameters of police activity in Australia. In the United Kingdom, police are statutorily obliged to network, partner and collaborate with the community and other agencies to reach their goals and objectives. Potential problems associated with privacy, confidentiality and data protection issues are legislated for. Performance measurements are developed in line with these statutory requirements at all rank levels. This is not to suggest that the United Kingdom is without difficulties in these areas. As Hale et al. note (2005: 1), 'there is a marked absence of information as to their probable effectiveness and efficiency in achieving the desired results'. As well, there are critical tensions in the United Kingdom around how to generate better service delivery. For example, the principles of, or need for, partnership are not necessarily well understood by street-level officers delivering services, and many officers are uneasy about how partnership sits alongside other government initiatives. While the government insists that police must consult with communities and gather their views on priorities, it then also imposes national targets that can override those negotiated at a local level.[5]

In discussing the problems associated with the UK experience of partnership and collaboration, Homel (2004: 48–49) suggests that if governments wish to successfully promote networking, 'there is a need for [an] investment in time and resources to be sustained to completion' and for ongoing support to be provided for 'significant planning [and] investment in managerial infrastructure', an infrastructure that needs to include an emphasis on resources, training and development. He might have added a commitment to training and development.

There is of course another challenge associated with governments assuming control of network structures that are intended to be autonomous and based on trust and reciprocity. If governments attempt to take the lead in network formation, they run the risk of directing, not persuading. If networks are formalised, the scope for negotiation is reduced. If money and authority are mandated from the centre, then the centre will own the network, not the individual participants. The challenges are there to be met.

Notes

1 I am grateful to Rod Rhodes and Adam Crawford for their comments on an earlier draft.
2 Formal evaluation of networked partnership arrangements is weak and at times difficult. As Liddle and Gelsthorpe point out, 'a fairly narrow conception of evaluation ... may have inhibited wider dissemination of information about successful projects or approaches' (1994: 16).
3 Green is the colour of the document officers use to refer an individual involuntarily to a psychiatric unit for assessment.
4 For further information, see: <http://www.aic.gov.au/avpa/2005.html#1> (all

websites listed were correct at the time of writing); <http://www.aic.gov.au/avpa/2005.html#2>; <http://www.familyviolence.ca/splash.htm>; <http://www.nzfvc.org.nz/accan/papers>.

5   Informal conversation with Janet Foster, London School of Economics.

References

Australian Police Minister's Council (APMC) (2002) *Directions in Australasian Policing: 2002–2005*. Canberra: APMC.

Bayley, D. (1986) Community policing in Australia – An appraisal: Working paper. Payneham (SA): Australasian Centre for Policing Research (ACPR).

Chan, J. (2006) Making sense of police reforms: The making of culture in a changing field, paper delivered to the Australian and New Zealand Society of Criminology Annual Conference, 7–9 February, Hobart.

Crawford, A. (1994) Social values and managerial goals: Police and probation officers' experiences and views of inter-agency co-operation, *Policing and Society*, 4(4): 323–39.

—— (1997) *The Local Governance of Crime Appeals to Community and Partnerships*. Oxford: Clarendon Press.

—— (1998) *Crime Prevention and Community Safety, Politics, Policies and Practices*. London & New York: Longman.

—— (2003) The pattern of policing in the UK: Policing beyond the police, in T. Newburn (ed.), *Handbook of Policing*. Devon: Willan Publishing.

Crawford, A., Lister, S. et al. (2005) *Plural Policing: The Mixed Economy of Visible Patrols in England and Wales* (Researching Criminal Justice Series). Bristol: The Policy Press.

Criminal Justice Commission (CJC) (1999) *Crime Prevention Partnerships in Queensland*. Brisbane: CJC (Research and Prevention Division).

Dupont, B. (2006) Power struggles in the field of security: Implications for democratic transformation, in J. Wood and B. Dupont (eds), *Democracy, Society and the Governance of Security*. Cambridge: Cambridge University Press.

Edwards, A. and Benyon, J. (2001) Networking and crime control at the local level, in M. Ryan et al. (eds), *Policy Networks in Criminal Justice*. Houndmills, Basingstoke: Palgrave Macmillan.

Edwards, C.J. (2005) *Changing Policing Theories for 21st Century Societies* (2nd edition). Sydney: Federation Press.

Fleming, J. (2004) *Les Liaisons Dangereuses*: Relations between Police Commissioners and their political masters, *Australian Journal of Public Administration*, 63(3): 60–74.

Fleming, J. and Rhodes, R.A.W. (2005) Bureaucracy, contracts and networks: The unholy trinity and the police, *Australian and New Zealand Journal of Criminology*, 38(2): 192–205.

Flynn, R., Williams. G. and Pickard, S. (1996) *Markets and Networks: Contracting in Community Health Service*. Buckingham: Open University Press.

Foster, J. (2003) Police cultures, in T. Newburn (ed.) *Handbook of Policing*. Devon: Willan Publishing.

Frances, J. et al. (1991) Introduction, in G. Thompson et al. (eds), *Markets,*

Hierarchies and Networks: The Co-ordination of Social Life. London: Sage.

Freiberg, A. (2005) Managerialism in Australian criminal justice: RIP for KPIs?, *Monash University Law Review*, 31: 12–36.

Hale, C.M., Uglow, S.P. and Heaton, R. (2005) Uniform styles ll: Police families and policing styles, *Policing and Society*, 15(1): 1–18.

Holdaway, S. (1986) Police and social work relations – problems and possibilities, *British Journal of Social Work*, 16: 137–60.

Homel, P. (2004) The whole of government approach to crime prevention, *Trends and Issues Paper*, 287, Australian Institute of Criminology, Canberra, at <http://www.aic.gov.au/publications/tandi2/tandi287.html>.

Hughes, G. and McLaughlin, E. (2002) 'Together we'll crack it': Partnership and governance of crime prevention, in C. Glendinning, M. Powell and K. Rummery (eds), *Partnerships, New Labour and the Governance of Welfare*. Bristol: The Policy Press.

Jessop, B. (2000) Governance failure, in G. Stoker (ed.), *The New Politics of British Local Governance*. Houndmills, Basingstoke: Macmillan.

Lee, M. and South, N. (2003) Drugs policing, in T. Newburn (ed.,) *Handbook of Policing*. Devon: Willan Publishing.

Liddle, M. and Gelsthorpe, L. (1994) *Inter-agency crime prevention: Organizing local delivery*. London: Home Office, Police Research Group – Crime Prevention Unit.

Magers, J.S. (2004) Compstat: A new paradigm for policing or a repudiation of community policing?, *Journal of Contemporary Criminal Justice*, 20(1): 70–79.

Moore, Mark H. (1990) Police leadership: The impossible dream, in Erwin C. Hargrove and John C. Glidewell (eds), *Impossible Jobs in Public Management*. Kansas: University Press of Kansas.

Newburn, T. (2003) Policing since 1945, in T. Newburn (ed.), *Handbook of Policing*. Devon: Willan Publishing.

Novak, K.J., Alarid, L.F. and Lucas, W.L. (2003) Exploring officers' acceptance of community policing: implications for policy implementation, *Journal of Criminal Justice*, 31(1): 57–71.

Rhodes R.A.W. (1996) The new governance: Governing without government, *Political Studies*, 44: 652–67.

—— (1997) *Understanding Governance*. Buckingham: Open University Press.

—— (1999a) *Control and Power in Central-Local Government Relations* (2nd edition, revised). Aldershot: Ashgate Publishing.

—— (1999b) Governance and networks, in G. Stoker (ed.), *The New Management of British Local Governance*. London: Macmillan.

Ryan, M., Savage, S.P. and Wall, D.S. (eds) (2001) *Policy Networks in Criminal Justice*. Houndmills, Basingstoke: Macmillan.

Sampson, A., Stubbs, P. et al. (1988) Crime, localities and the multi-agency approach, *British Journal of Criminology*, 28(4): 478–93.

Scott, Jan (1998) Performance culture: The return of reactive policing, *Policing and Society*, 8(3): 269–88.

Shearing, C. and Ericson, R. (1991) Culture as figurative action, *British Journal of Sociology*, 42(4): 481–506.

Skogan, Wesley G. and Hartnett, Susan M. (1997) *Community Policing, Chicago Style*. New York: Oxford University Press.

Thompson, G. (1993) Network co-ordination, in R. Maidment and G. Thompson (eds), *Managing the United Kingdom*. London: Sage.

Tyler, T.R. and Yeun, H.J. (2002) *Trust in the Law*. New York: Russell Sage Foundation.

Walters, R. (1996) The 'dream' of multi-agency crime prevention: Pitfalls in policy and practice, in R. Homel (ed.), *The Politics and Practice of Situational Crime Prevention*, Crime Prevention Studies, 5. New York: Criminal Justice Press.

Wright, A. (2002) *Policing: An Introduction to Concepts and Practice*. Devon: Willan Publishing.

Vernon, J. and McKillop, S. (1990) *The Police and the Community*. Canberra: Australian Institute of Criminology.

Young, K. (2001) *Evaluation of ACT Family Violence Intervention Program Phase II*. Canberra: ACT Department of Justice and Community Safety.

Young, K. (2000) *Evaluation of ACT Interagency Family Violence Intervention Program*. Canberra: ACT Department of Justice and Community Safety.

5 | INTERNATIONAL NETWORKING AND REGIONAL ENGAGEMENT: AN AFP PERSPECTIVE

Mick Keelty

Networking and relationships are vital to police officers' ability to do their job every day. For police services this includes building strong relationships with many communities. These include: individuals and groups in the community; the government that defines the scope of the police service's functions and provides the powers and resources to carry those out; other agencies of government whose responsibilities and activities bear upon the policing function; private sector organisations; and other policing and law enforcement agencies. But while the building of effective relationships is a key characteristic of the policing profession in general terms, the Australian Federal Police (AFP) finds itself in the fairly unique position in Australia in that AFP personnel need to have the competence and ability to engage successfully at local, state, national and international levels on a regular basis.

The substantial challenges faced by law enforcement agencies today often fall into the category of 'wicked issues', owing to the complexity of policing organised criminal or terrorist activity. The level of complexity increases dramatically in the international environment, as this increases the number of players involved, introduces new challenges such as transnational crime, and brings into play concepts such as sovereignty and different historical and cultural contexts.

Such complex, or 'wicked', problems require a wide-ranging engagement in whole-of-government approaches in order to address all aspects of their causes, to identify potential remedies, and to implement the potential or prescribed solutions.

To meet the challenges that such complex problems present, the AFP is managing a growing and increasingly complex network of relationships with a wide range of stakeholders and partners. Building this international network has been an integral part of the AFP since its inception, and builds on work done previously by the Commonwealth Police, such as the United Nations (UN) peacekeeping commitment in Cyprus, which has been in operation since 1964.

The AFP is well placed to respond to such challenges because it has long placed a strong emphasis on understanding and engaging with other cultures. This focus on engagement has enabled the AFP to respond appropriately to the recent surge in security events and to increase its role in national security and foreign policy development. These changes require, and benefit from, enhanced engagement with regional countries in the promotion of law and order and in addressing the major transnational crime threats of terrorism, illicit drug-trafficking and people-smuggling.

The three specific tools the AFP has available to achieve its objectives in these areas include the AFP counter-terrorism capability,[1] the AFP International Network,[2] and the AFP International Deployment Group (IDG). The latter was established in February 2004 to improve and better institutionalise the preparation and co-ordination of regional policing assistance missions and law enforcement capacity-building projects.

The AFP context

The origin of Australia's international policing network precedes the establishment of the AFP in 1979. The initial establishment of a permanent offshore presence was a police liaison position in Kuala Lumpur in 1973; this was followed by the establishment of a similar position in Bangkok in 1976. Even though the AFP was established in the aftermath of the Hilton bombing in 1978, specifically as a result of the review of that event by the United Kingdom's Sir Robert Mark, it is noteworthy that there were already moves underway to establish a network of international policing relationships as a means of co-operating with regional countries on a more extensive and mature level than had previously been the case.

The 1980s and 1990s saw a gradual evolution of the international role for the AFP; it was not until the late 1990s that the dramatic increase in scope and scale of AFP international activity to today's level began.

The injection of new funding through NIDS (National Illicit Drugs Strategy) in the 1997/98 financial year increased activity in relation to drug-trafficking, and meant a further expansion of the AFP International Network. This in turn led to the establishment of the LECP (Law Enforcement Co-operation Program) the following year. The LECP commenced as an in-house AFP mechanism for funding and managing projects of training and modest equipment provision to regional law enforcement agencies in order to bolster their policing capacity to investigate transnational criminal activity, particularly drug-trafficking. The LECP, now part of the IDG (International Deployment Group), has since matured into a key asset in terms of capacity-building, equipment provision and training for police forces and their personnel throughout the Asia-Pacific region. At the strategic level, the LECP has been instrumental in promoting uniformity and interoperability of the systems and processes that deal with transnational crime.

The AFP further expanded its involvement in the Pacific through its Melanesia Program, which saw $20 million over five years (with an extension of funding approved in 2004) provided to further develop the AFP's level of engagement with the smaller Pacific island states to our north and east.

2001 – A changed international environment

The 11 September 2001 terrorist attacks in the United States led to a wholesale change in the US approach to its security, and to similar changes within the international community. The US-led War on Terrorism remains a dominant influence on the international security landscape, and is expected to be so for the foreseeable future. The federal government took a number of initiatives to enhance the capacity of Australia's intelligence and security organisations, while at the same time stressing the need for a strengthened whole-of-government approach to tackling the new threat of possible terrorist attacks on Australia or on Australian interests offshore.

The 2003 DFAT (Department of Foreign Affairs and Trade) White Paper, *Advancing the National Interest*, clearly states that national security threats are a composite of traditional and non-traditional threats: the latter include terrorism, the proliferation of weapons of mass destruction, regional disorder and transnational crimes, including the illegal movement of people, drugs and arms. In addition, transnational issues other than transnational crime, such as environmental threats, communicable diseases (such as HIV/AIDS), access to clean water and the depletion of maritime resources are noted as threats to countries in Australia's region. Weak and failed states are identified as facilitators of some of these security threats. Notably, co-operation between governments to develop multilateral rules, standards and institutions is identified as crucial, given that they protect the interests of 'outward-oriented' countries such as Australia.

One of the great concerns (and perhaps one of our greatest challenges) about organised criminal groups and terrorist networks is the fact that they both tend to target corrupt, weak or vulnerable countries with poor governance structures and social, political and/or economic unrest. These conditions are, unfortunately, present in some parts of our region. Such conditions potentially allow these groups to set up and conduct their criminal operations with ease – and with a substantially lower risk of detection than would be the case in a society where robust governance regimes are in place.

Advances in communications and transport technologies now allow these groups to spread easily, and relocate quickly across national borders, potentially undermining the security of the wider region. In recognition of this fact, the protection of vulnerable nations within our own region has become a priority for regional governments.

In Australia, this focus on fighting terrorism and on protecting vulnerable nations from destabilisation arising from criminal elements has led to a significant shift in the AFP crime-fighting emphasis. The result is that even more law enforcement resources are now being directed to offshore operations in co-operation with overseas partner agencies. To support this expansion, in 2005 the Australian government introduced amendments to the Australian Federal Police Act to clarify the functions of the AFP. These amendments confirm that AFP functions include assisting and co-operating with domestic and foreign law enforcement organisations and government regulatory and intelligence bodies in criminal investigations, responses to major disaster situations, international peace and stability operations and capacity-building missions.

Importance of networks in providing assistance

The AFP International Network of liaison officers currently comprises 86 AFP personnel based in 31 cities in 26 countries.[3] Operational AFP deployment missions are underway in the Solomon Islands, Papua New Guinea, East Timor,[4] Nauru, Cyprus[5] and Jordan. Specialist advisory positions have been created throughout the Asia-Pacific region, and a number of newly established regional law enforcement co-operation mechanisms are either underway or being planned. These include setting up Transnational Crime Units[6] in Fiji, Samoa, Tonga, Vanuatu and Papua New Guinea, as well as the Pacific Transnational Crime Co-ordination Centre[7] in Suva, Fiji. Similar institutions are being established in several Asian countries, including Indonesia, Cambodia and the Philippines.

Box 5.1   Locations of the AFP liaison officers in the International Network

Bali (Indonesia)	London (UK)
Bangkok (Thailand)	Manila (Philippines)
Beijing (China)	Phnom Penh (Cambodia)
Beirut (Lebanon)	Pretoria (South Africa)
Belgrade (Serbia & Montenegro)	Pt Moresby (PNG)
Bogotá (Colombia)	Pt Vila (Vanuatu)
Brasilia (Brazil)	Rangoon (Myanmar)
Chiang Mai (Thailand)	Singapore (Singapore)
Dili (East Timor)	Suva (Fiji)
Dubai (United Arab Emirates)	The Hague (Netherlands)
Hanoi (Vietnam)	Washington (USA)
Ho Chi Minh City (Vietnam)	**Secondments**
Hong Kong (China)	United Nations – New York (USA)
Honiara (Solomon Islands)	Interpol – based in Lyon (France)
Islamabad (Pakistan)	Pacific Islands Chiefs of Police
Jakarta (Indonesia)	Conference (PICP) Secretariat (New
Kuala Lumpur (Malaysia)	Zealand)

The central objective for Australia is, through our liaison network and policing engagement activities, to build the capacity of national law enforcement agencies to generate a co-ordinated response to criminal activity in our region. The challenge has been to implement these programs and at the same time ensure that we do not impose our own values and systems on host jurisdictions, but instead customise our approach to take into account cultural and local issues.

Three key current examples of AFP international engagement worthy of exploration in this regard are Indonesia, the Solomon Islands and Papua New Guinea. These have been selected because each presents us with unique lessons about the challenges associated with relationship-building, and formal and informal network formation.[8]

Co-operation with Indonesia

The importance of Indonesia has long been recognised by the AFP, with the establishment of a police liaison officer position in Jakarta in 1979. The police-to-police relationship has been remarkably successful despite significant cultural, social and political differences. The AFP has continued to co-operate closely at all levels with Indonesian law enforcement authorities, to combat transnational crime that impacts upon the security of both Indonesia and Australia. This co-operation was therefore well established, long before the closer relationship that developed following the Bali, Marriott and Australian Embassy terrorist bombings.

The separation of the Indonesian National Police (INP) from the Indonesian military establishment in 1999 has had a positive influence on the INP focus on its key policing capabilities, particularly criminal investigations, and has allowed clearer commonalities of interest and lines of communication with the AFP. The close professional co-operation between our national law enforcement agencies includes:

- continuing regular dialogue and consultation between our respective national law enforcement agencies to improve access to information and our influence with Indonesian law enforcement authorities;
- building the capacity of the INP to enable them to more effectively prevent, respond to and investigate terrorism and transnational crime;
- strengthening links between officers at all levels in both national police services through dialogue, consultation and, where appropriate, the exchange of personnel to ensure high-level access and influence with key Indonesian decision-makers;
- ensuring the regular and ongoing sharing of information through enhancement of legal, political and technical mechanisms that facilitate information exchange; and
- strengthening the capacity of law enforcement agencies throughout the Asia-Pacific region through working closely with Indonesia in multilateral law enforcement forums.

The AFP recognises that the range of transnational criminal threats that may impact on the security of both our countries includes, but is not limited to, terrorism, trafficking in illegal drugs, people-smuggling, arms-smuggling, sea piracy, money-laundering, international economic crime and cyber crime. We have also witnessed extraordinary flexibility demon-strated by transnational crime groups, who shift technologies and com-modities to match the efforts of the more co-ordinated approach by the INP and the AFP.

Our key bilateral means of achieving this is through the AFP liaison officers based throughout Indonesia, and through our funding and advisory support to Indonesia's Transnational Crime Centre (TNCC) and the Jakarta Operations Centre (JOC). This framework of co-operation and the trust built through personal contact has been vital to the rapid and co-oper-ative police responses to events such as the Bali bombings, the Marriott Hotel bombing and Australian Embassy bombing, and the recent 'white powder' incidents, when suspicious material was sent to the Indonesian diplomatic missions in Australia.

The AFP is also working with the Indonesian authorities towards the establishment of more coherent and cohesive regional policing struc-tures for information-sharing and for capacity-building. This includes the further development and consolidation of key regionally focused institu-tions based in Indonesia, such as the Jakarta Centre for Law Enforcement Co-operation (JCLEC).[9] The JCLEC is noteworthy in that while it has Australian funding of $36.8 million over five years, it also has funding support and involvement from European Union countries.[10] The centre is showing all the potential to become a permanent and valu-able contributor to law enforcement in the region at both the practi-tioner and academic levels.

RAMSI (Regional Assistance Mission to the Solomon Islands)

Prior to the request for assistance made by the Solomon Islands govern-ment, ethnic tensions and civil unrest had led to severe economic regression and social disorder there.[11] By early 2003, the Solomon Islands was showing clear signs that without significant change, it risked becoming a failed state. Law and order had broken down and many of the local people were afraid to venture outside their homes or villages. The local police had been rendered ineffective and some were known to be aligning themselves

Box 5.2: Jakarta Centre for Law Enforcement Co-operation (JCLEC)

The JCLEC, based at Semarang, Indonesia, began as a joint Australian/Indonesian training centre to enhance law enforcement skills in the region, particularly in relation to counter-terrorism.

JCLEC received $36.8 million in initial funding from the Australian government.

Opened in July 2004, it now offers a wide range of education and training programs, including the International Management of Serious Crime (IMOSC) course. The first IMOSC course attracted participants from 19 countries.

JCLEC is fast becoming a multinational/global 'centre of excellence' and is a good example of developing international co-operative mechanisms for law enforcement.

The Netherlands government has contributed 5.3 million Euros for the development of accommodation infrastructure and intends to contribute a further 5 million Euros, making it the second-largest contributor to the Centre, behind Australia.

The Danish government has contributed US$500,000 for information technology infrastructure and training.

The Italian government delivers a maritime security training program;

The French government delivers human trafficking and crisis management programs.

The Russian government has expressed interest in delivering a bomb technicians' program in addition to donating related technical equipment.

The European Commission has expressed interest in contributing an initial 300,000 Euros via the Rapid Reaction Mechanism (RRM) to increase the European profile in relation to counter-terrorism in Indonesia.

The British and New Zealand police forces are negotiating to provide for short-term deployments of their staff to JCLEC.

with members of militant groups. Corruption among public officials was rife and extortion was draining already depleted government resources. Industry was faltering badly and debt was spiralling.

To try to reverse this decline before it became even more unmanageable, regional governments forming the Pacific Islands' Forum, led by Australia and New Zealand, were invited by the Solomon Islands government to formulate an assistance package. The largest and most visible element of the package was the Participating Police Force (PPF). The mission of the PPF was to restore safety and order by implementing a three-phase response. This included restoring law and order, then building capacity, trust and confidence in the local police and thus contributing to the creation of an environment conducive to economic reconstruction and human development on a sustained and sustainable basis.

The first and most critical challenge was to restore law and order. The PPF, in concert with military assistance from Australia, New Zealand and several Pacific Island military forces, presented a united show of force in an attempt to deter criminal gangs and militias from continuing their violent actions against each other and within the Solomon Islands community. These measures were important symbolically as well as for their deterrent value. By conducting highly visible patrols, arresting offenders for crimes and removing weapons from the streets, the local communities could see tangible benefits in the presence of the PPF. As is the case in most societies, it became clear once more that if people disobeyed the law, they would be caught and would then suffer the legal consequences of their actions.

An important initial decision was made for the PPF to go unarmed in order to demonstrate that the objective was to reassert the legitimacy of the state to govern with the backing of the rule of law, rather than to do so through compliance based on the threat of an escalation of force.[12] This contrasts with a military, or even a military-led intervention, which may well have created a very different impression and local reaction. This approach proved highly successful, with more than 3700 weapons and 300,000 rounds of ammunition seized, more than 5000 arrests made (including of serving members of the Royal Solomon Islands Police) and more than 7300 charges laid for criminal offences.

As the first police-led assistance mission by Australia in the region outside UN missions, the different strategic role of the military in RAMSI also posed challenges for the Australian Defence Forces (ADF). The ADF built a coalition of contributing countries, as they had done in East Timor, but this time those forces were used in a supporting role for a broader governance and development assistance mission. This mission, for the military, was more akin to a humanitarian emergency role, requiring a modicum of armed protection, but with a possibly longer timeframe.

The Australian and regional military forces assisted greatly in addressing the initial geographical and logistical hurdles over things that we take for granted, including power, telephones and other means of communication. The military forces also provided infantry and maritime patrols, helicopter and ship transport, logistics management, and medical, communications and operational planning assistance.

It was also important that while a stable security environment was maintained by the military and the PPF, complementary efforts began in terms of rejuvenating the Solomon Islands' legal and judicial system to ensure that prosecutions of criminal activity would have a chance of going through an efficient and effective process. This legal and judicial aspect will be critical to all assistance missions: it reaffirms the credibility of the host government, courts and police forces in countries coming out of a period of political turmoil, or difficulty in governing effectively.

Regional co-operation perspective

The early stages of establishing RAMSI involved considerable close co-operation with the governments of New Zealand and the Pacific Islands. The legitimacy of the mission, although it was clearly undertaken at the request of the Solomon Islands' government, was assisted by the Pacific Islands' Forum endorsement of it. With such regional support in place, the next step – 'mission endorsement' by the United Nations – could be taken more easily.

The second aspect of regional co-operation, from the AFP perspective, involved being able to field a police contingent in the PPF drawn from police forces including Australia, New Zealand, Fiji, Vanuatu, Kiribati, Papua New Guinea, Tonga, the Cook Islands and Samoa. The multilateral nature of the force ensured a good mix of professional policing experience and expertise combined with increased Pacific cultural understanding, thanks to the Polynesian and Melanesian contributions. The experience of participating in RAMSI also proved a worthwhile training measure for the police from these countries, and will be something the AFP builds on in the future through the IDG.

State/Territory police contributions

An important facet of the RAMSI mission for the AFP was the relationship with the State and Territory police forces. To co-ordinate and deploy a police contingent offshore on this scale was unprecedented in both Australian and international experience. The IDG is now responsible for the selection and rotation of police personnel for overseas missions. It is the central co-ordination point for State and Territory police services to liaise regarding the participation of their policing personnel on AFP-led overseas missions.

While there is further work to do in bedding down the management and operation of the IDG, the AFP is confident that the State and Territory police contributions to future IDG missions will increase and be seen as a unique developmental experience for the individuals who participate. It will also be seen as an asset to the home police force, on their return.

RAMSI: The way ahead

From a law enforcement perspective, Australian government agencies and regional counterparts are now concentrating on: building capacity within the Royal Solomon Islands Police Force; continuing the work to strengthen the courts and secure the prison system; and updating the criminal statutes to ensure that they list the full range of criminal offences, so that they can deal with the prosecution of all types of crime. The bigger challenge now is a broader one: revitalising all of the Solomon Islands public institutions and kick-starting the economy to ensure that the recovery is permanent and that future development is sustainable. Therefore the work of the RAMSI civilian advisers in the Solomon Islands public sector is now critical to the long-term success of RAMSI, even after the majority of police and military advisers have returned to Australia.

The work of these advisers is helping to restore stability to government finances, balancing the national Budget, helping the Solomon Islands government better manage revenue and expenditure, and improving revenue collection. This work has already paid dividends, with a 40 per cent increase in revenue during the 2003/04 financial year alone.[13] And there are signs that efforts to improve business confidence are yielding results. The Solomon Islands' Gross Domestic Product (GDP) increased by 5.8 per cent, and there were also increased exports and lower inflation.[14]

The difficulty ahead lies in the fact that foreign investment remains minimal and there are still widespread problems attributed to poor infrastructure. The increased revenue collection, if maintained, will gradually be used to provide better health and education services, as well as to improve key areas of infrastructure such as main roads, wharves and bridges. All of these initiatives remain important from a policy perspective, because the youth and workforce need to be provided with alternatives to criminal behaviour and budgets for policing need to be balanced with budgets for competing services such as health and education. A more efficient police and justice regime will return resources for these other critical areas of the public sector.

Lessons from Papua New Guinea

The Enhanced Co-operation Program (ECP) in Papua New Guinea (PNG) followed the RAMSI mission as the next large-scale regional assistance mission for the AFP. The program aimed to deliver assistance in the areas of law and order, justice, economic management, public sector reform, border control and transport security and safety. While the ECP was supported by a treaty between the governments of Australia and PNG that was signed in December 2003, a successful constitutional challenge has caused the ECP mission to be withdrawn from PNG pending resolution of the issues between the governments.

From the law enforcement perspective, the ECP involved up to 210 members of the IDG working within the Royal Papua New Guinean Constabulary (RPNGC). The role of the Australian Assisting Police (AAP) mission was to assist and advise the RPNGC on police operations and administration. This included areas such as general duties, criminal investigations, fraud and anti-corruption, intelligence, prosecutions, executive development, professional standards implementation, and human resource management. The emphasis was on training and mentoring rather than on assuming the responsibilities of the local police personnel. A second aspect of the policing assistance program was to undertake capacity-building projects: these included refurbishing police stations, replacing old police vehicles and providing equipment to assist with training and development courses.

Some of the challenges that faced the ECP mission were similar to those experienced by the RAMSI mission. They included language and cultural differences, a general lack of technology and communications infrastructure, and the concept of applying the rule of law in traditional village communities that may have had either very little exposure to the need for legal compliance or adverse experiences of interaction with police and government officials.

There are also many differences between RAMSI and ECP. This is most apparent in the scale of the task. The population of PNG is approximately 5.7 million people, compared with the approximately 500,000 people in the Solomon Islands. The land area of PNG is nearly twenty times larger than that of the Solomon Islands. The criminal groups are more entrenched than the militia groups were in the Solomon Islands, and the nature of the crimes being perpetrated is generally more serious. For example, much of the crime in Honiara was petty and opportunistic when compared with the activities of the entrenched criminal gangs of Port Moresby, who generate large profits from criminal activities; the rate of acts of violence and murder in Port Moresby puts it in the unenviable position of being one of the most dangerous cities in the world.

While the contingent was only in PNG for approximately nine months, it made some significant practical improvements. These included being instrumental in initiating the upgrade and repair of all police stations in the National Capital District, of RPNGC operational vehicles and of the NCD radio communications network, providing equipment for forensic services, and personal accoutrements, and using force training for the RPNGC. Capacity-building in Bougainville, in addition to AAP operational assistance, included the upgrading of the Buka Police Station, the refurbishment of the Arawa Police Station, planning for the establishment of another station at Buin and the introduction of a vehicle repair program.

It is important to note that the decision to withdraw the AAP contingent on 17 May 2005 centred on the constitutional basis for giving the Australian police immunity from prosecution; it was not a result of local political or community-based complaints against the AAP directly.

Other regional policing assistance programs

As well as the lessons being learned from the RAMSI and ECP experiences, there are smaller, but similar, regional and international policing assistance programs underway. These include the provision of police training and support to East Timor,[15] Jordan, Cyprus and Nauru. With the exception of the Cyprus involvement, which is longstanding, the AFP has established a key role for itself in building the skills and policing capacity of other police forces and their personnel. The two personnel in Jordan are assisting in the training of the Iraqi police. With the transition from the United Nations Mission to Support East Timor (UNMISET) to the United Nations Mission in Timor-Leste (UNOTIL) mission, the AFP involvement reduced to four positions. This is separate from the bilateral program it has in place for the training of the Timorese police forces. In Nauru there is a Director of Policing and an adviser. This assistance is under review and may even expand in future to ensure that Nauru continues to enjoy a stable community-policing environment while other programs address Nauru's long-standing economic and social difficulties.

An issue that is separate from the AFP capacity-building programs is the fact that senior AFP personnel have taken up overseas positions, including that of Police Commissioner in Fiji and, earlier this year, Police Commissioner in the Solomon Islands.[16]

What the future holds

There are three main themes that are pertinent to the future role of the AFP in engaging with regional countries. The first is the AFP's transition to a more prominent role in national and international security matters, primarily with regard to terrorism. The second is the importance of building strong liaison networks and maintaining good relationships with counterpart and regional law enforcement agencies. The final point, as epitomised by the recent decisions on the PNG ECP, is that strategies for capacity and institution-building require the firm political commitment and ongoing support of national governments if they are to be successful over the longer term.

The AFP and national security

Under the twin influences of globalisation and the break-up of the Soviet Union ending the Cold War, transnational crime expanded through the 1990s. As it did so, the increasing impact of its products (including drugs, arms and illegal immigration), its profits and its methodology (corruption of state institutions) on the economic and social well-being of nations increasingly blurred the line between law enforcement and national security. Of all transnational criminal activity, terrorism is the most strongly connected to traditional notions of national security, so the heightened threat of international terrorism following the September 11, 2001 attacks brought law enforcement even further into the national security arena. The addition of security-related priorities, many of which have an international dimension, has had an ongoing impact on the AFP's regional strategies, planning, and operational focus.

The importance of networks and relationships

The key message from the above case studies is that to build, or rebuild, state and community institutions requires significant trust, co-operation and collaboration, underpinned by a political commitment from the host country's government and people. The three stages of this kind of work – stabilising, consolidating and then maturing national institutions and policy frameworks – will continue to be relevant for future planning of similar regional assistance missions.

The particular circumstances and local environment leading up to the establishment of an assistance program clearly indicate that there are only a few areas where generalisations can be used about mission planning and in terms of cultural awareness. Another lesson is the recognition of the long-term nature that such assistance programs represent, if the ultimate objectives are to be achieved. In the Pacific countries, for example, the national police forces will ideally mature in such a way that Australia's relationship with them in the law enforcement arena ends up placing more emphasis on collaboration and liaison than on assistance, training and mentoring.

The future: Institution building with political commitment

The key focus for the AFP in its role of assisting the Australian government is to implement bilateral and regional assistance programs for building the capacity and capability of regional police forces as part of broader Australian government programs designed to assist countries with their governance, security and development needs. The implementation of these initiatives within the AFP will to a large extent fall to its newly formed IDG. As the IDG has only existed as a separate entity within the AFP since February 2004, there is still some way to go in developing the IDG as well as in ensuring that the AFP has the right numbers of suitably qualified and trained personnel ready to deploy on police capacity-building missions as directed by the Australian government. It should be remembered that personnel who deploy on IDG missions are all volunteers; the human resource considerations of such deployments will continue to be a factor in their planning and delivery.

In terms of regional mechanisms, regional security and law enforcement forums and networks will continue to mature and evolve. These groupings could be expected to gradually take on a role more akin to that now being developed by the European Union and African Union, where regional co-ordination is leading to tangible results in terms of establishing frameworks for the planning and operation of regional peacekeeping and policing missions. Australia is in a strong position to work with regional countries in terms of similar future plans for regional institutional development and assistance initiatives.

The lessons learned from RAMSI and ECP by Australia can also provide useful insights for the United Nations and for other countries that are considering either mechanisms for providing assistance in remote provinces, and/or future participation in regional organisations, and/or potential contributions to future UN or regional assistance missions. To this end, the AFP has engaged academic institutions to further investigate the successes and shortfalls of these offshore operations and to identify areas for improvement on future international deployments. A major aspect of this research will focus on the ability of the AFP to develop a strong regional network of relationships with regional governments and with our international law enforcement counterpart agencies.

Notes

1   As detailed in Department of Prime Minister and Cabinet 2004.
2   The AFP International Network refers to diplomatically accredited AFP positions based within High Commissions and Embassies throughout the world. There are also advisory positions based in some countries and major international law enforcement organisations.
3   As of 14 July 2006, this includes personnel based in the Jakarta Operations Centre and the Manila Operations Centre.
4   With the expiration of the UNMISET mandate on 19 May 2005, the new UNITOL mission will have a reduced international policing component, comprising some 45 personnel, of which Australia will have four positions. UNITOL's mandate expired in May 2006.
5   Cyprus is somewhat unique in that Australian police have provided support to the UN Mission (UNFICYP) dating back to 1964. This mission therefore had different underpinnings and the deployment was made in a historical strategic context very different from the circumstances of the other current missions, all of which commenced no earlier than 1999. Cyprus and previous closed missions to Haiti and Somalia are more of the traditional peacekeeping mission that dominated international forms of assistance in the early 1990s in particular.
6   The host country runs the transnational crime units.
7   The Pacific Transnational Crime Co-ordination Centre is a regional facility serving many Pacific countries.
8   I refer here particularly to the different nature of networks that exist between public officials, elected representatives and governments as identified in Slaughter (n.d.).
9   Details of the JCLEC mandate and regional programs are at <http://www.jclec.com> (all websites listed were correct at the time of writing).
10 Europol have also separately agreed to negotiate an information-sharing agreement with Australia. This agreement, combined with European involvement in JCLEC, will strengthen linkages between Europe and the Asia-Pacific region, especially with regard to combating terrorism.
11 Previously the Solomon Islands received support as a result of the Townsville Peace Agreement and the establishment of the International Peace Monitoring Team (IPMT) in 2000/01.
12 This was a decision based also on the experience of previous missions, including the police deployments to East Timor.

13 See Australian Federal Police 2005.
14 See Department of Foreign Affairs and Trade (n.d.), p. xii.
15 A joint AUSAID/AFP program worth $40 million is providing long-term support for the development of the Timorese national police force and for other aspects of the justice system.
16 The Police Commissioner position, previously held by a UK police officer, William Morrell, is separate from the head of the AFP-led RAMSI PPF contingent, who works to the Solomon Islands Police Commissioner in a Deputy Commissioner capacity.

References

Department of Foreign Affairs and Trade (n.d.) *Solomon Islands: Rebuilding an Island Economy* report, at <http://www.dfat.gov.au/publications/rebuilding_solomon/index.html>.

Department of Prime Minister and Cabinet (2004) *Protecting Australia Against Terrorism: Australia's National Counter-terrorism Policy and Arrangements*, at <http://www.dpmc.gov.au/publication/protecting_australia>.

Australian Federal Police (2005) *RAMSI Fact Sheet: Creating a More Prosperous Solomon Islands*, at <http://www/afp.gov.au/afp/page/Publications/Speeches/010405PeaceandJusticeConf.htm>.

Slaughter, Anne-Marie (n.d.) Global government networks, global information agencies, and disaggregated democracy, *Harvard Law School, Public Law Working Paper*, 18, at <http://ssrn.com/abstract=283976>.

INTELLIGENCE-LED POLICING: THE AFP APPROACH | 6

Grant Wardlaw and Jennine Boughton

The pace and scale of change in the modern world – and the resulting need for individuals, organisations and nations to be able to sense and respond to changes that affect their vital interests or competitiveness – have raised the requirement for foresight to an unprecedented level.

In the criminal environment, forces such as globalisation and technological change are driving rapid and significant changes in the nature, extent and impact of crime – locally, nationally and globally. The damage that can be done by individual criminals – particularly those involved in sophisticated financial crime and terrorism – has reached levels never experienced before. In particular, internet technologies enable organised crime to operate in a virtual environment that knows no boundaries, and criminals are able to exploit this technology to transcend jurisdictional borders. Unlike law enforcement, these groups and individuals lack the moral and legal accountability mechanisms by which law enforcement is defined. Globalisation and interconnectivity mean that any particular law enforcement agency – or even individual investigative unit – faces more and different adversaries than they are used to and may be prepared for.

The global organisational configuration of organisations such as Al-Qaeda, the international movement of funds, the travel for planning and logistics purposes, and many other international aspects reveal that only limited parts of the intelligence picture for any terrorist event can be constructed from information obtained solely from local sources.

Even with the revelations regarding 'home-grown' terrorism that emerged from the bombings in London in July 2005 – and hit home in October that same year, with the arrest of 17 men in Sydney and Melbourne on charges of planning terrorist attacks – there is often an international link that needs to be pursued.

For the Australian Federal Police (AFP), this international aspect of modern crime is the core reason for a high level of interaction and engagement with regional and global law enforcement counterparts. Experience has repeatedly demonstrated the vital role played by a collaborative approach to fighting crime, by pooling resources, networking generally and international sharing of criminal intelligence. The importance of these policing networks is widely understood and accepted as an important factor in bringing criminals to justice and averting acts of terror. But a willingness to share is only part of the equation. A common understanding of the threat environment and an appreciation of the respective operating parameters and capabilities is critical to identifying those vital and often elusive pieces of information needed by others.

Integral to the success of any policing network are notions of trust and confidence. Agencies need to trust that operational information can be passed and handled in a secure fashion, and that the information content and source will be safeguarded and not compromised. However, the depth of knowledge needed for efficient interoperability only comes from a continuous level of engagement, and trust, which can only be developed over time – trust is a commodity that is often in short supply during a crisis, when an immediate operational response is required.

Networks: The backbone of intelligence-led policing (ILP)

The concept of intelligence-led policing (ILP) is now widely espoused by police services as a fundamental part of the way they do business. But for such a widely talked about concept, there is remarkably little clarity about its definition and fundamental concepts – and even less evidence that it has moved beyond rhetoric to being truly embedded into police practice.

The core idea in ILP is that police work, from the tactical to the strategic levels – and beyond, to government policy – should be informed by high-quality, relevant and actionable intelligence analysis. It is a model in which intelligence guides and shapes operations, strategy and policy, rather than simply supporting isolated investigations. It is a model in which intelligence underpins proactive police work, rather than merely acting as an adjunct to reactive policing.

The nature and complexity (and the sheer numbers) of criminal challenges require a fundamental shift in the approach to law enforcement. Law enforcement needs to move from a reactive to a proactive strategy if it is ever to gain an advantage over criminals. A truly proactive strategy, however, requires a rethink of many of the ways in which both police and governments deal with crime. And this in effect means adopting a much wider definition of things like 'information', 'intelligence sources', 'partners' and 'clients'.

Part of the challenge is to break down intelligence obstacles and agency competition. In a sense this means being prepared to open the doors to intelligence holdings – although in reality, preparedness does not always translate to action. There will always be limitations on what can be shared, with whom and when, whether they be legal impediments or security requirements. But one of the greatest barriers is that of culture. Intelligence has always been about keeping secrets, but now with so many more network nodes to service, the culture of sharing must move from a default mode of exclusion to one of inclusion.

International engagement and co-operation

The global nature of criminal activity has meant that criminal investigations in Australia have increasingly had an international dimension. Recent experience has repeatedly demonstrated the vital role played by international sharing of criminal information.

The AFP has invested heavily in establishing partnerships with international agencies, and its international liaison network has become an integral element of the investigation of transnational crime. The liaison officer network serves not only as a focal point for co-ordinating joint efforts, but also as an early warning system and a means of taking the fight against crime offshore. The benefits of such networks have been amply demonstrated by the results of the successful relationship between the AFP and the Indonesian National Police in relation to the investigations into the Bali, Marriott Hotel and Jakarta embassy bombings.

AFP collaboration with international law enforcement for multi-agency illicit drug investigations continues to reap significant rewards for the Australian community. It was a multinational team approach that led to the disruption of major heroin-trafficking syndicates, which in turn significantly contributed to the heroin shortage experienced in Australia in late 2000.

The AFP is committed to sustaining and enhancing these relationships. The AFP's Law Enforcement Co-operation Program (LECP) provides an exceptional platform for a number of intelligence-related initiatives in the region. One such initiative that has received LECP funding in the past is the Asia Region Heads of Criminal Intelligence Working Group. This initiative seeks to build partner agency capabilities and foster communities of trust though joint projects on strategic intelligence issues of mutual interest, training opportunities, intelligence practitioner exchanges and agreement on intelligence terminology and procedures.

The AFP Intelligence Function is also a driving force behind the Transnational Targeting Network (TTN), which includes the US Drug Enforcement Administration, HM Customs and Excise, the UK's Metropolitan Police Service National Crime Squad and National Criminal Intelligence Service, the New Zealand Police, and the Royal Canadian Mounted Police, and aims to develop joint strategies to disrupt major drug traffickers who target these countries. The TTN, as a collective, allows a broader range of transnational resources to be allocated across jurisdictions to combat major organised crime groups. The effectiveness of the network is measured by its ability to add value above that which can be achieved through the standard individual and ad hoc bilateral or multilateral investigations.

One thing that the AFP is particularly cognisant of is the need to prioritise its investment in international networks and undertakings to ensure that the joint operations engaged in have the greatest impact possible on the criminal threat level to Australia. The AFP constantly reviews its overseas network to make certain that resources are positioned in the most relevant and appropriate locations from an operational and a criminal intelligence perspective. The AFP is only a small force, relatively speaking, with finite resources at its disposal, and it must make well-informed decisions about its international involvement. AFP Intelligence aims to drive this process by providing ongoing predictive descriptions of the international operating environment for the AFP out to 2–5 years. This management-initiated assessment is a substantial undertaking that endeavours to capture and reflect all aspects of AFP interests.

Getting intelligence to a wider audience

If one of the consequences of the changing nature of the threat environment is the recognition that nations cannot act alone, then an obvious extension of this is the need to engage a much wider range of agencies on a domestic level. Talk of bioterrorism, or agri-terrorism, immediately moves both the prevention of, and the response to, terrorism outside the traditional national security/law enforcement agency arena. These forms of terrorism mean a direct and comprehensive involvement of fire and rescue services, health services, disease surveillance systems, Departments of Agriculture, Natural Resources Departments and others. Sharing intelligence with this wider group has now become imperative, both to inform their own response planning and to alert them to impending events. This clearly produces major problems for law enforcement and the Australian intelligence community in terms of releasing sensitive information to an ever-wider group.

The trend so far has been to release information in a greatly declassified form to protect collection sources and methods. But the result has often been such sanitised product that the clients sometimes complain that they would be better informed by reading any of the respected news magazines or commercially available intelligence services.

Initiatives such as the Business–Government Ministerial Forum on National Security are part of a range of measures designed to overcome such problems by strengthening the partnerships between business and government in countering terrorism and by building the relationships and systems of trusted communication that will allow a greater flow of more detailed terrorism-related intelligence to the private sector. The AFP has a number of measures in hand with key members of the private sector to enhance the effective flow of intelligence to them.

Embracing the private sector

The use of the term 'private sector' relates not only to business and industry, but also to academic and research organisations and non-government organisations (NGOs). Much of the information needed – particularly in fields such as counter-terrorism or transnational sexual servitude and trafficking – is held by these organisations. Major corporations, especially those with international reach, are a potential source of information about terrorists because of their use of the infrastructures that terrorists must use in planning and executing attacks. The travel industry is a vital source of information about terrorist travel plans. The banking and financial sector is vital in attempts to choke terrorist finances, and is also the repository of a wealth of information on, for example, fraud and identity crimes – important facilitators of terrorist activity. As well, NGOs know a lot about what is going on in quite remote parts of the globe that are difficult to cover officially, but are often important locations for terrorist networks.

Increasingly, it is becoming obvious that it is not enough to see these organisations as just sources of information that can be obtained through liaison; they are critical nodes within the intelligence network. A number of countries are examining proposals to link industry databases to intelligence systems – especially watch lists. Also, intelligence often needs to be passed to the private sector so they can protect their own assets against criminal or terrorist attack. This implies a quite different relationship from that of the past, a relationship that has significant implications for how classified information is handled, how privacy is protected, and so on. And undoubtedly, there is much more that criminal intelligence can gain from the private sector that will prove crucial in the prevention of terrorism and the investigation of transnational crime.

Enlisting community participation

Although not a new concept, the role of the community in safeguarding the nation has been given new consideration in the post-September 11 environment. Expanding on existing national initiatives such as Crime Stoppers, the National Security Hotline was established on 27 December 2002 as both a mechanism to increase public understanding and reassurance and a means of eliciting information on possible terrorist activity. As the virtual 'eyes and ears' of the nation, the community itself therefore becomes an integral element in the Australian counter-terrorism policing network. While this adds another layer to the whole-of-government response to protecting Australian interests, it also adds additional challenges for police and intelligence analysts who need to find those critical pieces of the puzzle that will avert a potential terrorist event or criminal activity.

In terms of community policing, law enforcement intelligence must also be more attuned to the fact that there are thousands of police officers on the streets who are in effect intelligence collectors. Greater effort needs to be put into providing education and guidance so that we can more fully exploit this capability explicitly for counter-terrorism purposes.

Finding the balance between policing and security networks

While there is an obvious and real need for sharing, the distinction between criminal intelligence and security intelligence is becoming increasingly blurred. The challenge for the AFP, as for other law enforcement bodies, is to make sure those who need to know *do* know, and yet still remain focused on its core role as a law enforcement agency.

The convergence of criminal and security intelligence has other potential ramifications for policing networks. During 1996–97, the AFP made a decision to abandon the use of rank titles in favour of the designation 'federal agent' and adopted a flexible, team-based approach to its activities. However, many of the agencies with which the AFP deals are still organised along more traditional hierarchical lines. The nature of the threat environment, particularly the prospect of a terrorist incident on domestic soil, dictates a much closer relationship with the Australian Defence Force and an imperative for clear lines of command, control and communication. Similarly, liaison and engagement with many regional police is assisted by unambiguous chains of command and strict hierarchical structures.

This situation does not necessarily fit well with other ILP initiatives, such as developing intelligence networks with other government departments and the private sector, where a rigid bureaucratic approach can in fact hamper meaningful exchanges. However, AFP officers are fast adapting to this multidisciplinary environment, and effective communication, liaison and negotiation skills are now decisive factors not only when it comes to representative posts but also in relation to general career progression.

What is also becoming increasingly evident is that this new security environment carries hidden dangers for police. In attempting to be all things to all people, police risk being drawn too closely into the wider intelligence community and losing their neutrality in terms of being perceived as intelligence collectors – particularly with regard to international law enforcement networks. International partners need to have confidence that information and intelligence exchanges with the AFP are about crime prevention.

In any interaction there is always a measure of 'sizing up' the other party. From the law enforcement – as opposed to security – perspective, any assessment of capability is based on determining what actions may be needed to ensure a mutually beneficial exchange rather than maintaining or gaining a knowledge or technological edge. So while policing and security are predicated on vastly different objectives, the intersecting of the two networks, brought about by the new global threat environment, is also having wider implications for security agencies, which now find themselves, by necessity, in a much more co-operative, collaborative arena.

A prime example of an attempt to resolve this is the creation of the National Threat Assessment Centre (NTAC) within the Australian Security Intelligence Organisation, to ensure that all relevant intelligence holdings relating to terrorist threats are factored into the national intelligence picture. The creation of the NTAC – to which the AFP seconds two officers – is a leading example of a successful whole-of-government initiative to integrate information from a range of agencies. This centre is based along the 'collective identity' lines of the United Kingdom's Joint Terrorism Analysis Centre, which is based on the premise that involvement of staff from participating agencies helps 'remove barriers to inter-agency intelligence sharing' (ESRC 2005: 20).

On the one hand, AFP involvement in this initiative may heighten perceptions that the AFP has dual roles: as a policing and an intelligence entity. On the other, no law enforcement agency, regardless of charter or nation, would turn a blind eye to information that had even a vague chance of stopping a terrorist attack. For the AFP, there is therefore often a fine balancing act required between responsibilities within Australian policing and security networks in terms of a whole-of-government response to threats to Australian interests and the management of international partner and stakeholder expectations.

Issues in intelligence sharing

If intelligence networks are to have maximum impact, the intelligence problem must be attacked from a number of angles. The first problem is the perennial one of sharing intelligence among relevant agencies and integrating intelligence from all sources. The purpose of information sharing is to enable the best use to be made of all the sources available, to link data and detect emerging patterns and critical associations and to produce warnings that can be used to plan preventive actions wherever possible.

To be optimally useful, both the analysed product and the raw data on which it is based must be appropriately shared. The raw data must be shared to enable the collation, comparison and analysis of information from multiple sources, which in turn enables the identification of relevant links and patterns of behaviour. The finished product must be shared with the right people at the right time for it to serve a useful operational purpose – especially when it is intended for warning and prevention.

The sharing, or lack of sharing, of intelligence is always a number one issue in debates about the reasons for intelligence success or failure. There is a growing realisation – to say nothing of a pressing political imperative – of the need to find ways of disseminating intelligence without compromising security. One of the primary barriers is a lack of confidence in the security of the information systems and practices across the growing number of organisations that need to be included in contemporary counterterrorism responses. So information assurance and the development of trusted systems are integral to building the networks that are vital to the prevention of terrorism and crime.

To address this issue between national law enforcement agencies, the Australian Crime Commission is substantially upgrading the data capture, security and analytical capabilities of the Australian Criminal Intelligence Database via a 4-year project named ALERT, which was funded in the 2002–03 federal Budget. This will enable the sharing and analysis of sensitive intelligence in ways that have not been possible before.

Developing the internal mechanisms for success

Consumer education – directing intelligence activities

If intelligence is going to drive proactive policing, then it too must evolve – as must its organisational context. Intelligence needs to be seen as critical to decision-making within law enforcement. This means going beyond merely seeing intelligence as certain pieces of *information* that are critical to preventing *specific* criminal acts or solving *specific* crimes. *Information* has always been critical to successful policing. But clearly *intelligence* – if what is meant by intelligence is value-added analysis for decision-making – has not been.

A limited understanding of how to use intelligence, largely resulting from an inability to differentiate between intelligence and information, has long been a dilemma for law enforcement. In the law enforcement environment there are also embedded misperceptions and biases, not only over the value of intelligence but also in terms of the field of intelligence as a whole, that need to be overcome. To a certain extent then, what is needed is a degree of internal marketing to turn around organisational cultures and place intelligence squarely where it belongs: at the heart of all strategic organisational decisions.

The AFP has had a significant criminal intelligence capability for many years. However, the decision to make it an organisational priority to increase both the scope and quality of that capability led to the creation of a separate Intelligence Function – a critical turning point for AFP Intelligence. What essentially has been created is an internal intelligence network dedicated to integrating intelligence into all major organisation decisions at the tactical, operational and, importantly, strategic levels of decision-making.

In late 2004, the AFP Intelligence Function underwent a major rework, aimed at bringing it into closer alignment with other operational functions within the organisation and thus making it better placed to address the dynamics of the criminal environment. Crucial to this redesign was an examination of information flows within the Intelligence Function, and outward to the rest of the organisation, to detect inefficiencies, gaps and potential choke points. These flows need to be constantly maintained and adjusted as new client and provider nodes emerge within the network, bringing with them new requirements and capabilities. Therefore, equally crucial was the factoring in of strategies to develop the skills of analysts, so that they can address the new class of problems and identify appropriate services and products that enable their results to be conveyed to those who need them.

The AFP has designed its intelligence product suite to directly influence AFP strategic planning and policy development by providing regular analysis of the criminal environment and effectiveness of the law enforcement response. But strategic analysts cannot operate in a vacuum, and therefore a certain amount of interplay needs to, and does, take place between the analysts and the policy-makers to ensure that analysts have a sound understanding of organisational policy contexts and directions. The key to success is making sure that these organisational directives do not in turn become the drivers of intelligence outcomes.

To ensure that intelligence is not prejudiced by internal policy agendas or external political influences, the AFP has put into place a number of checks and balances, such as: aligning information flows to ensure that strategic analysis is fed and supported by real-time operational data; developing an auditable national electronic collection management system; centralising editorial and quality control mechanisms; and peer reviewing all intelligence product.

Success or failure of an intelligence-led approach to policing rests not only with the application and integration of intelligence into the organisation's overall mission, but also with the organisation's ability to get the intelligence to those who need it. This is not always a simple undertaking. Dissemination and sharing mechanisms must be responsive to the ever-changing internal organisational and political imperatives as well as to the number and types of external partners and clients that need to be serviced — all of which are ultimately dictated by the dynamics of the criminal environment.

Bringing together the various pieces of the puzzle

Police need to make some significant strategic investment decisions about information management systems to ensure that intelligence is properly fed by all the relevant information held by the organisation, that the information is analysed using the most advanced analytical software, and that the system is capable of disseminating the resultant intelligence to the right people at the right time. Most importantly, the organisational linkages need to be right, otherwise the end result is a series of disparate outcomes.

The events of September 11 were quickly dubbed an intelligence failure. The US Congressional Committee that examined the intelligence response revealed that there were warnings about the use of aircraft as weapons, about the suspicious activities of the hijackers at flight schools and about the methods of entry of the terrorists into the United States, among other things. Certainly the post-incident investigations turned up a large volume of information about the terrorists' methods of communication, travel, spending patterns, lifestyle and sources of income. While these terrorists were well organised, resourced and co-ordinated, they left a lot of evidence about their planning, their identities and their activities.

One of the central challenges of the information society is how to adequately analyse all the incoming data. Although these issues are not unique to law enforcement, there are substantial information technology and knowledge management questions to be resolved before the huge amounts of data can be sorted and patterns or key items of information that might indicate an impending crime or terrorist attack can be identified. And even then, often the warning is not specific enough to prevent a particular act at a particular time and place. Getting to this level of sophistication is a major priority of intelligence organisations worldwide.

Developing cutting-edge technologies and analytical techniques

Law enforcement intelligence needs to place greater focus on developing cutting-edge technologies and analytical techniques that can meet the challenges of the analytical problems surrounding criminal activity, and process, link and make sense of huge amounts of information in real time. The problem of information overload is a common one – but it is particularly acute in the counter-terrorism field, where the imperative is to analyse the information very quickly to get intelligence out to prevent terrorist attacks, but at the same time to ensure that relevant data that is already contained with information systems is not discounted or missed.

There is significant technical development being undertaken in Australia on intelligence processing and display, especially within the defence environment, and there is recognition of the need to factor law enforcement requirements into this work. Considerable work is being undertaken by the AFP to further develop existing systems so that they can better enable previously undetected patterns within data holdings to be uncovered. In late 2004, the AFP received Proceeds of Crime funding for a project to improve the ability of intelligence staff to link, display and analyse the information held in the AFP's major intelligence and case management system, PROMIS. Significant progress on this project has already been made, and new funding has ensured continuing work in this field over the next two years.

Although it is difficult to secure funding for the development of analytical tools for law enforcement intelligence, it is exactly such work that has the potential to help us better understand, for example, the psychology of terrorists, terrorist group dynamics, terrorist decision pattern analysis, etc – all of which are required to advance the ability of intelligence to better contribute to terrorism prevention.

Apart from the data management issues, analysis is often constrained by the techniques used. There needs to be a much more open approach to a range of analytical techniques, many of which are relatively unfamiliar in law enforcement intelligence: for example, to gain foresight about where terrorist tactics may go, both generally and with respect to particular groups. Various modelling and scenario-generation techniques are now being used to expand our thinking about terrorism.

Scenarios in particular can be very useful in thinking about prevention strategies and in constructing indicators for specific lines of terrorist activity that can form part of a strategic warning system. The AFP has developed a sophisticated capability in the area of scenario generation which is now routinely used as a major input to our strategic planning. The production of scenarios in the terrorist area has been very useful in helping design a strategic approach to counter-terrorism.

Strategic positioning for future planning

One of the most significant drivers of every sphere of human activity is the pace of change. But paying lip service to this assertion is not enough. If strategy must factor in change of a type or speed that has not been the norm, then the intelligence networks that support that strategy must be equally dynamic. This underscores the need for intelligence systems that can scan and monitor the environment to continually update assessments and provide early warnings. Such systems must also identify emerging issues for new analytical work in areas that will be of concern to police in the future – areas that may not yet be on the radar of strategists.

Strategy is all about situating oneself in the environment for long-term advantage. In the past, planning assumed that the wider environment was either relatively stable or relatively predictable. So faith was placed in forecasts, and strategic thinking became ossified into plans and budgets and rigid structures. But the world has ceased to operate that way. In fact, it never actually did, but the changes that occurred were often of such a nature or speed that they could be coped with by relatively slow and large changes to the plan. The world is now characterised much more by discontinuities and sudden changes; the environment is extremely dynamic and uncertain. Plans of the old style are rapidly overtaken by events, rendering them useless as strategic navigation aids.

In the law enforcement context, this need to be 'one step ahead of the game' has been at the heart of the ILP approach to addressing crime. ILP has made a major contribution to enabling police services to have the maximum impact possible at all levels from the tactical to the strategic, and it remains particularly relevant in positioning agencies for strategic advantage.

But having said this, no matter how true law enforcement tries to be to the doctrine of being intelligence led, an ever-present challenge will always be the widening sphere of influence of global events on daily activities. International events that, even as little as five years ago, would not have made much of an impact, now require immediate intelligence responses – thereby placing the law enforcement community squarely back into the realm of being reactive rather than proactive. The art is to be aware that this is happening and make sure that environmental scanning and threat monitoring continues to take place.

The AFP's threat monitoring function aims to do just that – provide an all-source fusion capability that acts as both an alert system for emerging threats and a safety net for analysts during times of peak activity or staff absences. Admittedly, the AFP has a way to go in further developing and refining this capability, but with time and maturity, this process will be a critical component of a value-added data repository and collection management system.

The professionalisation of intelligence

Although ILP requires major changes in police organisations – in the way they view intelligence – the driving force for these changes will be the quality and relevance of the service provided by intelligence professionals. The onus therefore is on police managers to ensure the continuing development of the profession of intelligence.

The intelligence profession needs to be a leading example of the information edge. Surviving and contributing to the new era of policing requires significant investment in the development of competencies for intelligence officers, new training and education options, and a major push for the continuous development of new analytical techniques.

What is needed is not just more intelligence, but better, more relevant intelligence that can drive decision-making. It is decision-making that is actually crucial. But for the decision-maker to have confidence in the intelligence, there must be an undertaking to match analytical tools to the nature of the problems that confront the organisation. This implies a continuous development of more sophisticated techniques and an increasingly skilled workforce able to apply them.

For the AFP this has meant increasing analysis skill levels through the complete redesign of its intelligence training program, and aligning courses with the new operational needs. This has included a multilayered analytical course and ongoing examination and review of the latest international research and experience to continuously refine AFP intelligence doctrine and analytical techniques.

One AFP initiative seeks to bring together national and regional heads of law enforcement intelligence to: look at the conceptual aspects of 'joining the dots'; define the parameters that each agency operates under; and gain an understanding of just what expectations each agency has of its intelligence functions. The learning and relationships that will emerge from this type of initiative will provide a greater degree of longevity and robustness to domestic and international policing co-operative networks. Importantly, this project aims to complement and leverage off other initiatives being undertaken by other AFP areas, such as the International Network, the International Deployment Group and the LECP.

There is also an increasing demand for suitably language-qualified analysts – particularly in the field of counter-terrorism intelligence – who know the societies in which terrorist ideology flourishes. Foreign language skills are vital not only to efforts to interview people or process terrorist documents, but also to the ability to more fully exploit the vast array of foreign language open source information that is of relevance to terrorist intelligence analysts. And, of course, a deep knowledge of the cultural context of the terrorists will be crucial to trying to understand their mindsets and motivations.

The AFP has been active in addressing this challenge. It has substantially expanded its language training program, and implementation of this program – across a number of key languages – is well advanced. The AFP is also paying more attention to recruiting analysts with a wider range of language and cultural abilities. It maintains ongoing dialogue with Islamic community leaders in all capital cities and has an active cultural awareness program as part of counter-terrorism and other investigations training.

Conclusion

Efforts to ameliorate the threat of transnational organised crime and terrorism have increasingly drawn law enforcement agencies into the international realm and resulted in the building of relationships and linkages with a much broader partner base than was envisioned as little as a decade ago.

Globally, police services are seeing ILP as a fundamental approach to the daily business of fighting crime. This approach is heavily dependent on forging new and dynamic relationships – domestically and internationally – and drawing these entities into the wider policing network.

This is not always a simple task; even with broad agreement about the necessity to share and work collaboratively, there are many impediments. Security restrictions such as the classification of information or the caveats on its use are one example. Others include organisational cultures, levels of trust, and the actual physical means to enable it to happen.

In the AFP, major efforts are underway to address the information management issues through the introduction of more secure systems, and attention being paid to the problem of assuring the quality of data entered onto systems and secure connections to relevant partner agencies. Relationship issues such as trust form the foundation of any partnership-based sharing mechanism, and to a certain degree these relationships rely on the level of return on the efforts involved. As with any relationship or confidence-building endeavour, there need to be considerable investments of time and resources before positive results can be expected.

There is much more that can be said about the ways in which intelligence-led policing can develop to better support the mission of preventing crime and terrorism. For example, we need to work on better exploitation of open source information and integration of this information with sensitive holdings, inclusion of local law enforcement to build more effective local-level intelligence collection, and the development of robust indications and warning systems for terrorism. However, this chapter aims to provide just a flavour of both the challenges faced by law enforcement and the measures that the AFP has in place, in collaboration with other parts of government, the private sector and international partners, to make a major contribution to the protection of Australian communities.

Reference

Economic & Social Research Council (ESRC) (2005) *Report of St Andrews/Southampton ESRC Project on the UK's Preparedness for Future Terrorist Attack*. Swindon: ESRC, Centre for the Study of Terrorism and Political Violence.

7 | POLICE UNIONS AS NETWORK PARTICIPANTS

Mark Burgess

Introduction

Australia's police unions[1] are 'high-profile insiders' (Fleming & Marks 2004). By this I mean that through their well-developed networks, they are important players in the complex Australasian policing environment — they are key bodies involved in the shaping of police workplace conditions and policing policy. Given this, it is almost unnecessary to state that police officers make a vital contribution to the safety, wellbeing and cohesion of our communities. In a recent study looking at social attitudes towards a range of Australian organisations (Wilson et al. 2005), 72 per cent of Australians had a 'great deal of trust' in the police, second only to the Defence Forces, and well ahead of charities (61 per cent), major companies (42 per cent), and churches (35 per cent). Police unions are aware of the trust that the community places in its police forces, and are conscious of not betraying that trust in their dealings on behalf of their members. The unions have a vested interest in ensuring that Australian police conduct themselves as professionals with a unique set of skills and ethics.

The formation of the Police Federation of Australia in 1998 created a two-tiered structure to represent Australia's 50,000 police officers (99 per cent of whom are members of Australia's police unions). These unions have well-developed relationships across the representational landscape: with the wider union movement in Australia; with international police unions; with Police Commissioners and police departments; with state, territory and federal governments; with the media, and with many community groupings and other public interest advocates. Given this web of associations, Fleming, Marks and Wood (2006) posit that police unions are part of a growing network of stakeholders in policing that contributes greatly to the way in which policing is shaped and determined.

This paper provides an account of the role the state, territory and federal police unions, and the Police Federation of Australia (PFA), play in representing Australia's police. It examines the effectiveness of the police unions as 'networkers' who represent the professional and industrial interests of police officers, and provides background information about the membership base of Australia's police unions, and about their organisational features. It also outlines the objectives of these organisations and how they make use of networks to achieve these objectives, both inside and outside traditional policing and political circles. The paper also evaluates the effectiveness that police unions have had in delivering outcomes for their members and for policing in general.

This paper adopts a critical approach and acknowledges the gaps in the current networking profile and agenda of the police unions. It concludes by identifying the challenges that confront police unions if they hope to contribute to innovations in, and the democratisation of, policing in Australia. Some of these challenges are: federal constitutional arrangements; state and federal legislation; oversight and accountability mechanisms; external political agendas; the move to policing as a profession in the context of member expectations; and a changing national industrial environment.

The role of police unions

Australia's police unions are democratic member-owned and member-driven entities. With the exception of the Australian Federal Police Association (AFPA), which represents both sworn and unsworn members of the Australian Federal Police (AFP), to be a police officer is the main membership requirement. With the exception of a limited number of functions, all members of police unions are sworn police officers: that is, they hold the Office of Constable. The leaders of Australia's police unions are elected, and all elections are conducted by the Australian Electoral Commission in accordance with federal legislation.

With the creation of the PFA, the police unions created a two-tier structure. The state, territory and federal police unions take responsibility for the day-to-day member issues occurring in their respective jurisdictions. When these 'branches' unite under the banner of the PFA, they are able to expand their areas of responsibility and address issues that cross jurisdictional boundaries, particularly issues of a political, industrial and professional nature.

At all levels, the police unions view their primary role as enhancing the professional and industrial interests of their members – that is, Australia's police.

Networks and policing

Policing is about networks. Policing operates on a 24/7, 52 weeks a year basis. Few other agencies do likewise. For police organisations to operate effectively, they must develop intricate networks at the local, jurisdictional, national, and importantly in today's world, international level. The police are aware that they are not alone in attempting to meet the many needs of the community. Effective policing requires the mobilisation of a wide range of state and non-state bodies also concerned with public safety.

Rhodes and Fleming (2005) suggest that networks are about creating partnerships. Working in partnership with other service organisations is embedded in policing operations, and the police unions are keen advocates of 'partnership policing'. Hence, for example, in the PFA submission to the Senate Select Committee on Mental Health (2005), we argued that all police jurisdictions should develop Memorandums of Understanding (MOUs) with their respective Health Departments regarding the provision of mental health care. The submission suggested:

> Their [MOUs'] general aims are to develop and formalise local working relationships between Police and Health services by providing guidelines for the handling of situations which involve both services, ensuring standards of care for the mentally ill and agreeing on procedures for management of crisis and high risk situations (Senate Select Committee on Mental Health 2005).

MOUs, and other such agreements, are common in policing when working in partnership with agencies providing services to local communities. There is a plethora of MOUs at various levels of policing across Australia and internationally, and police officers are aware of the importance of these and other partnership mechanisms when addressing issues. It is only natural that such thinking is also duplicated by the police unions.

Fleming and Rhodes (2005) suggest that networks are characterised by diplomacy, trust and reciprocity. In the past, police officers may not have been judged positively in terms of these attributes, yet these kinds of characteristics fundamentally underpin police operations, especially those carried out in conjunction with other agencies (such as other emergency services). Australian police unionists believe that these qualities are actually the strength of Australia's police unions, and it is on the basis of these very characteristics that the police unions operate, both internally and in their dealings with each other. These intra-relationships are, we believe, mirrored in our dealings with external agencies and organisations. Later in this paper I will discuss the structure of Australia's police unions and their relationship to the PFA to show how the PFA needs to operate on consensus, goodwill and trust.

Networks and police unions

While networks are 'en vogue' in the policing literature, the establishment of networks per se is not novel for police unionists. Police unions have been establishing networks since the formation of the first police union in Australia, the Police Association of South Australia, in 1911. As historian Mark Finnane points out:

> Having won their battle for recognition, the Australian police unions spent most of the succeeding years of the inter-war period consolidating and extending their reach. The achievements were substantial. Recognition was not only formal – increasingly it meant that police union conferences were places where government ministers and even premiers should be seen. With their status rising, the unions found doors open for discussion on key issues in police administration and even law reform (Finnane 2002: 57).

Little appears to have changed in the intervening years, except that even more doors have opened, and the unions' influence has widened. The PFA's Strategic Plan in 2000 highlighted the importance of networks to what was then a recently formed organisation. In discussing its program, the PFA clearly indicated that networking (particularly with government bodies) is an essential strategy in broadening the reach of the police unions:

> The PFA requires a strategy to increase its influence with the Federal Parliamentary and Government Process and thereby raise the profile and influence of affiliates within their own jurisdictions. In this context the 'process' includes all elements of the Government, including the Opposition and the parties and individuals of the cross-benches, the Commonwealth bureaucracy, and extends to key members of the media and influential party figures external to the parliamentary process.
>
> The range of issues will include workplace relations, matters of a professional nature and broader community concerns of specific interest to policing.
>
> The long-term objective is to ensure that when any matter of interest to the profession is under consideration by Government or policy makers at the Federal level, the Federation is included in the consultative process (PFA 2000).

Since then the PFA has focused on both the *development* of networks and working *within* networks to achieve the outcomes identified in the Strategic Plan.

The most misunderstood aspect of policing is that of 'police culture'. Police culture has become the target of the media, the judiciary and sometimes even academia. However, the existence of a separate and identifiable culture is in itself a good indication that its participants share values and possess a commonality of purpose. Like other large professional bodies, such as the Australian Defence Force, a strong sense of cohesiveness and identity is encouraged and embedded within police forces.

But it is not just the police unions who seek to network with other organisations. Police unions are also sought by other sectors to become involved in their respective networks, in pursuit of these other agendas. We believe this is due to the credibility and strength of purpose that police unions can demonstrate, and their ability to reach out to the general public. For example, following the PFA's submission to the Senate Select Committee on Mental Health, a range of mental health advocacy groups contacted the PFA to seek our assistance in lobbying for various resources to improve the plight of the mentally ill. The PFA has been asked to write opinion pieces on the impact on police of dealing with the mentally ill. Not only did the PFA's submission receive significant media exposure, but in the eyes of many mental health advocates, the public support of the PFA went a long way to legitimising their claims.

The recent partnership between the PFA and the organisations involved in the International Day for the Elimination of Violence Against Women (White Ribbon Day) has also proven beneficial to both parties. Beneficial for the PFA because its members are at the forefront of handling the damaging effects of domestic violence and our members see their national union reinforcing measures to eliminate this serious offence, and positive for White Ribbon Day because the intricate network that the PFA has with police agencies and political leaders right across the country provides an efficient and effective method of communication and information dissemination.

There are, however, areas in which police unions need to be more aggressive in developing networks, and these will be described later in this chapter.

Australia's police unions

There are nine police unions in Australia (including the PFA, to which all others are affiliated as branches).[2] The New Zealand Police Association (NZPA), whilst not formally part of the PFA, has a close relationship with Australia's police unions, contributes an annual subscription, and attends meetings held under the auspices of the PFA. This relationship with the NZPA goes back many years, to when the two organisations were combined as the Police Federation of Australia and New Zealand. Federal registration of the PFA in 1998 resulted in the NZPA ceasing to be a formal member, but the relationship between the PFA and the NZPA remains strong.

It is also important to understand that the PFA, as the name implies, is a *federation* of police unions. It is not the peak national decision-making body for all police unions. The PFA exists in addition to the other police unions, not instead of them. Affiliated member unions of the PFA operate under an 'autonomy' rule which gives them the ability to manage and control their own organisations. The relevant PFA rule states:

> Any Branch so established shall be completely and absolutely autonomous in matters affecting members of that Branch or its property and funds and shall be responsible for its own govern-

ment and administration. It shall possess full and adequate powers to conduct its own affairs and to seek its objectives under the Rules. The control of the Branch shall reside exclusively in the members of the Branch. This rule can never be altered except by a ballot of all financial members of the Federation conducted under Rule 33, Clause (d).[3]

The autonomy rule is entrenched within the PFA rules of registration. A plebiscite of all PFA members is required to change it. This rule was created deliberately, to ensure that affiliates could be part of a national federation, and that larger affiliates could not interfere with the operations of other affiliates. By creating this rule, the founders of the Federation showed a fundamental desire for the organisation to work on a consensus basis in relation to decision-making processes. To date the founders' philosophy has proved successful.

Australia's police unions as network participants

Given that networks are comprised of organisations and individuals who share a common purpose and set of values, the autonomy rule itself demonstrates that Australia's police unions, despite forming independently and operating autonomously, also operate in reality as a network. And as previously mentioned, police unions in Australia operate on the basis of consensus, goodwill and trust: the PFA's structure, and in particular the autonomy rule, underpin these attributes.

The environment in which these interactions occur can be described as vigorous and multilateral, consisting of overlapping 'internal' and 'external' networks. Within these internal networks participants are affiliated with the PFA; the external networks are those in which the PFA operates outside its membership boundaries.

The important point in differentiating between these two types of networks is that for the PFA to operate effectively in its external network, its internal network must be operating efficiently. Strong internal relationships are vital to Australia's police unions, and as previously suggested, they are one of our greatest strengths; the unions have learned to work well together and their achievements bear testament to that.

Internal networks

In the jurisdictional context, all police unions have similar objectives. This means that desired outcomes at the national level are shared by the constituent police unions at a state and territory level. Decisions made at the PFA level are based on consensus, as opposed to majority votes. As the autonomy rule implies, the PFA Executive cannot make a binding decision that impinges on the rights of any individual union.

It is also only natural that police who are drawn to seek elected positions within these affiliated unions have similar values to their counterparts in other states and territories, and are motivated to act in the overall best interests of their membership: Australia's police officers.

The practical application of the networks available to police unions in the context of the autonomy rule has been evident in negotiations around wages and other terms and conditions of employment for police officers. In one example, an affiliate garnered the support of all other affiliates to pursue a statewide program of regional meetings, with associated media attention, in support of a pay claim. In this particular instance, affiliates were able to talk to the attending members about a range of issues, including the ideology of unionism in the context of the salary claim of that particular union.

In this case, the network application was used simply in a spirit of fraternalism, fulfilling the core functions of the particular police union. What it also demonstrated was the capability for all police unions in the country to mobilise and deploy together. It demonstrated a willingness of Australian police officers to become involved in a state-based issue. This had a profound effect on the state union in question, and it also demonstrated the value of strategic alliances for all other PFA affiliates.

It is simplistic, however, to suggest that this sense of mutuality is confined to core issues such as wage negotiations. The real test of the police union networks will probably arise not as a result of the industrial issues for which their members contribute their fees, but from police union engagement in issues such as the professionalisation debate, the policing ideology debate, and the rights of state-based police officers in an increasingly federalist policing environment.

There is a dilemma in that decisions of the governing elected officers are not binding. There are similarities here between police unions and other national employer groups, such as the Australasian Police Ministers' Council (APMC), the Senior Officers' Group, and the Commissioners'

Conference, in that the governing officers of these groups also do not have a capacity to make decisions that are binding on the group's constituent members.

Each police jurisdiction is represented on these bodies as an independent member, and no decisions of the national group can be forced on any jurisdiction. There is therefore also a necessity for those groups to work on a basis of diplomacy, trust and reciprocity. Their key challenge lies in operating with the extra layer of governance, administration and policy imposed by state, territory and federal governments.

The APMC is the peak group of the abovementioned bodies, but in respect to policy decisions (particularly in relation to legislation), the respective governments must, of course, agree to the decisions taken for them to be enacted. There have been a number of occasions over the years where an agreed APMC position has been reached on model legislation, and yet each jurisdiction has ultimately introduced variations to that legislation. Any potentially political decisions at the APMC level also have implications for the Senior Officers' Group and the Commissioners' Conference, as these groups both report to the APMC. As such, the challenge for a group such as the APMC is to be apolitical in its decision-making processes.

The PFA structure also allows for standing subcommittees to be formed, where the participants are 'subject matter experts' from each the jurisdictions and the NZPA. Whilst these committees ultimately report to the PFA Executive, committee members do have common and specific shared values which create a relationship that has a range of wider network characteristics.

The utilisation of these internal networks has a number of advantages to both the operational and strategic perspectives of the police unions of Australia and New Zealand. Some argue that policing is a unique profession — no other profession/occupation has a legislated obligation which prevents the officeholder from walking away from a set of circumstances which require a policing response. This uniqueness is shared by police across western democracies.

One ingredient missing in the cohesiveness of police unions is a commitment to a stronger research capacity. While there are several organisations and individuals undertaking research on a range of policing issues, the challenge is for police unions to bolster their internal network capacity by engaging in more research. As unions have traditionally focused on 'nuts and bolts' industrial concerns, the question is how this should be achieved, and how this can be linked to research being undertaken in other countries, and by other police unions around the world.

External networks

The PFA is closely aligned to a range of external networks, which in turn are also interconnected.

International Law Enforcement Council (ILEC)

ILEC was formed in Canada in 1996 following an international police union forum held to discuss issues of relevance to police officers across the western world. Membership of this network, to date, has been constrained to unions from Australia, New Zealand, England and Wales, Scotland, Northern Ireland, Canada, the United States and Denmark. However, there are moves to broaden this grouping by including, for example, police unions from South Africa and police associations from the South Pacific.

ILEC has been described by its founders as a gathering of 'like-minded people'. Whilst I agree with this description, I also suggest that it is a network of police unions which exhibits all the characteristics of networks (including diplomacy, trust and reciprocity), as well as a community of purpose and shared values. Like the PFA, decisions taken at ILEC are consensus-based, with unions representing as many as 250,000 members sitting side by side with others representing only several thousand police officers.

ILEC has been slowly evolving since its initial meeting. At its 2004 meeting, ILEC members agreed to develop a discussion paper for future ILEC programs. It is anticipated that a more formal structure will bolster a cohesive international police union voice. This will entail ongoing work on the part of all participants to maintain a cohesive framework.

ILEC will no doubt become one of the most important networks for the PFA in coming years. There are many policy developments being imposed on police forces as politicians across the western world engage with policing for political advantage. This is occurring with little, if any, consultation with either the profession or the practitioners, and is often based on matters totally unrelated to the provision of a professional policing service. ILEC provides an opportunity for police unions, representing more than a million police officers, to take an international position on those matters.

Police unions in the South Pacific

The PFA has formed a close bond with the Police Association of Papua New Guinea (PNG) and is conscious of its obligation to assist, where possible, other police unions in the region. The relationship between the PFA and the PNG Association is based on fraternal bonds; it is not the kind of paternalistic or post-colonial relationship that has been experienced by some Pacific nations in their dealings with dominant nations.

The PFA is currently developing a network that includes not only the PNG Association, but also the Australian Council of Trade Unions (ACTU), the Trade Union Congress (TUC) in PNG, and the South Pacific and Oceanic Council of Trade Unions (SPOCTU).

It is important in such a partnership that the larger organisations (including the PFA and groups like the ACTU) do not try to impose outcomes on the PNG Association. The PFA believes that whilst it is apposite to offer some guidance arising from our own experiences, it is not appropriate to tell an organisation how to conduct its business. We aim to listen to their concerns and needs and do what we can to assist, but only at their request and only on their terms.

So far this budding partnership has resulted in two PFA visits to PNG; assistance with organisational structures and rules; financial advice; and participation in annual conferences. In relation to the provision of financial advice, the PFA was able to successfully activate our networking assets by using the resources of the Queensland Police Credit Union to help not only the PNG Association, but other credit unions in PNG, with training and support.

Australian Council of Trade Unions and the various Labor Councils/Trades Hall organisations

The PFA (through our wider constituency), and various local police unions, have had varying degrees of affiliation with the ACTU since the early 1950s. Some state police unions are also affiliated with their respective Labor Councils or Trades Halls. In this context, police unions are seen as an integral part of the wider union movement. The PFA's relationship with the ACTU has allowed us to make initial links with police forces in the Pacific region – our introduction to the issues facing the PNG Association was made under the auspices of the ACTU, as part of an official visit to PNG in early 2005.

Ericson (1982), in Fleming, Marks and Wood (2006), argues that there is a tension between, on one hand, the police identifying with the broader labour movement, and on the other, being required to function as 'reproducers of order'. This tension also exists within the Australian police union network, as is illustrated in research work undertaken by Fleming and Marks (2004), who conducted interviews with Australian police unionists.

Over the years, liaison between the various police unions and the wider union movement has ensured that protests, picket lines and other campaigns in which public rallies have occurred as legitimate forms of protest, have been conducted in accordance with a negotiated set of protocols agreed to by the union movement, police unions and police departments. The links between police unions and the wider union movement have greatly assisted in the policing of these types of events. These networked relationships have allowed for an operational response which considers civil rights as well as appropriate policing responses. Much of this co-operation has been achieved through the work of police union networks flowing through to operational policing responses.

Individual police officers may find the conflicting nature of their role typified by industrial action policing, where police unions identify with the objectives of the trade union movements. While conducting themselves professionally at a protest or picket line, police officers may simultaneously be in ideological agreement with the protesters.

Police officers often play an important role in the aftermath of major industrial disputation. There have been a number of instances where major disputes have seen towns divided along lines of union and non-union labour. When these disputes are finally settled, often it is the police who play a key role in rebuilding the 'community'. The valuable grass roots networks that police have been able to develop in those situations provide a basis for that rebuilding. Police unions have often also played a vital part in this process due to their ability to deal directly with the other unions involved. This enables them to garner the support of those unions for the work of the local officers.

These links with the broad labour movement could prove important in coming months as the Howard government's new federal industrial relations changes come into effect. This potential conflict, both material and ideological, between union and non-union labour could leave police in a difficult moral position. The strength and resilience of the relationship between police unions, the ACTU, and other trades unions will be tested during this time, and it remains to be seen exactly how the tensions between the required functions of police officers and their own status in the government's 'new workplace' will be resolved.

Australasian Police Professional Standards Council (APPSC)

APPSC is an incorporated body consisting of the Police Commissioners of Australia and New Zealand, the PFA and the NZPA. APPSC is the only entity in which Australia's and New Zealand's police unions participate with their Commissioners on an equal basis, and with equal voting rights. APPSC's key role is to progress the police occupation towards full professional status. However, like most national arrangements in policing, decisions of APPSC are not binding on individual jurisdictions. This has particular challenges, given that there are not only nine police unions but also nine employers of public police in Australia and New Zealand, not to mention those seeking to gain admittance to policing through private security and second-tier policing agendas.

Although the APPSC work has been proceeding relatively smoothly, there is a potential for Police Commissioners to treat APPSC as 'their' body. If this imbalance of power eventuated and became an issue, APPSC would not be operating effectively as a network (a network, I would argue, that is possibly one of the most important in Australasian policing at the current time). The challenge for APPSC is to make the best use of its potential as a professional policing voice. If APPSC fails to get traction on this issue, the void is likely to be filled by police unions, who at least have some measure of co-ordinated national structure and opinion.

Commissioners and Ministers

Groups affiliated with Commissioners (government-appointed heads of state, territory and federal police forces) and with state and federal government Ministers include:

- Australasian Police Ministers' Council (APMC);
- Senior Officers' Group (SOG);
- Police Commissioners' Conference (PCC); and
- Common Police Services.

These groups have been established over time to promote and co-ordinate national responses to law enforcement issues, and to maximise the efficient

use of police resources. The PFA is, on occasion, invited to make presentations to these groups (sometimes as a result of the PFA approaching the
respective committee and seeking to be placed on their agenda to report on
and discuss specific issues).

I referred earlier to the decision-making process of the APMC, SOG,
Commissioners' Conference and Common Police Service agencies, and the
fact that their decisions are not binding on their constituent membership.
There is, therefore, a strong need for these groups to operate on goodwill
and consensus wherever possible, as they have no power to compel a jurisdiction to enact an agreed outcome from the groups. As mentioned previously, there are many examples of agreements having been reached at these
levels, only to be changed when implemented at jurisdictional level.

Should the PFA and the NZPA, as vital police insiders, be invited to
participate in more of the above forums? Just as importantly, does the PFA
or the NZPA feel the need to fully participate in these bodies?

Dupont (2003) discusses the issue of different types of capital – economic, cultural, political and symbolic. The relationship between police
unions, politicians and Commissioners is an intimate intertwining of these
four types of capital. Dupont argues that from time to time, police unions
have a 'love/hate relationship' with politicians and Commissioners and that
police unions have sometimes been successful in achieving their aims by
bypassing Commissioners and dealing directly with politicians. Police
unions have also become very astute at using the media to force favourable
political outcomes. However, more often than not the working relationship
between police unions, politicians and Commissioners is constructive, as
shown by positive outcomes from those relationships for police officers, the
profession and the community.[4]

The media

Police unions have well-established networks throughout the media sector,
and police unionists' opinions are regularly sought by all types of media.
This is because a perception exists (in the eyes of the media) that governments and police departments push political lines, whereas the unions are
the 'real McCoy': they have access to information from a wide variety of
sources, and an ability to canvass both sides of the story. Although the
validity of this view is debated amongst commentators, media exposure continues to play an important role in increasing public awareness of the relevance of police unions. This exposure, whilst demonstrating the significant

contribution to policing made by police unions, also helps the wider community understand that police themselves have a view on social issues; police are members of the public as well as professional officers. The media are likewise an important forum in which police unions can communicate with their members.

The wider police family

The PFA and state police unions also have intricate networks with a range of groups commonly termed 'the wider police family'. The list includes (but is not restricted to):

- Police Credit Unions
- Police Legacy networks
- Retired Police Associations
- United Nations Police Association of Australia (UNPAA)
- International Police Association (IPA)
- Police sporting organisations
- Police charity organisations:
  - Blue Ribbon
  - Bluey Day
  - National Police Memorial.

Although some of these facilities and events are well known and others may be not so familiar, they nevertheless show that police union networks are entrenched in an array of police activities. Most of the organisations listed above are made up of police officers, retired officers, the families of police, and other supporters of police. It is interesting to note that within individual police jurisdictions, representatives of these organisations are also often members of the police union, forming yet another layer within the mesh of networks within which the unions operate. Again, this helps union members and the police profession achieve constructive outcomes.

Universities

Australia's police unions have taken a long time to engage with the tertiary sector. At a time when an increasing number of their members are undertaking tertiary studies, the challenge for police unions is to develop stronger networks with these institutions. Despite this delayed engagement, universities and the various police unions have collaborated over the years on matters relating to police education and training, as well as on specific topics of research being carried out by universities that are also of interest to police unions (such as work currently being undertaken by Flinders University on aspects of the International Deployment Group and the Australian Federal Police). The PFA also has a good working relationship with Security 21 at the Australian National University. The ability to work collaboratively with universities in the pursuit of research grants is an area requiring further exploration.

The tertiary sector is likely to become a key participant in the debate on the future of the police profession. Whilst it is vital that the members of the police profession drive the debate, it is equally important that academics are engaged in it. This will obviously be difficult to achieve if collaboration between police practitioners and academia is not undertaken in an open and trusting environment. The challenge for the police profession is to activate this debate and use the resources and expertise available within the tertiary sector, rather than leaving the field open to all comers. A stronger network between the police and the tertiary sector will do much to address any concerns relating to the validity of groups or individuals seeking to join the policing debate purely in order to further their own purposes, and will help guarantee the authenticity of work being undertaken on and statements made about the policing sector by these groups.

Gaps and challenges for police union networks

Whilst police organisations and members have strong links within the general community through their work and personal interests, police unions have yet to establish formal ties with the community sector. Although police unions have run successful campaigns which have had significant community input, these campaigns have often centred on internal industrial issues such as staffing resources within police organisations. The challenge for police unions is to develop community relationships around a more comprehensive set of issues, issues of mutual concern to the police and to community groups.

In this regard, the PFA has been advocating that for too long the federal government has considered community policing a purely state government issue. The PFA has challenged this by arguing that there needs to be a more integrated approach to the issues, and acceptance that all levels of government have a responsibility for local law enforcement and crime reduction. In this respect the PFA's key objective is to encourage the federal government to accept that crime is a national problem deserving national responsibility, attention and resourcing. This objective will not be achieved without input from local communities, and this input will not be forthcoming unless police unions can establish effective community networks.

Police unions are also conscious that many other groups looking to establish stronger networks are seeking police union participation. There needs to be an awareness that some networks are driven by politics, budgets, or other vested interests, rather than by more altruistic concerns, and this awareness must then inform future decisions about participating in such forums. Police unions must continually evaluate what the respective network participants are trying to achieve, in order to determine whether it is or is not in their best interests to be involved.

Finnane (2002) notes that, historically, state police unions have developed sophisticated methods of lobbying their respective governments on matters affecting police and policing. A major challenge for the PFA is to develop this same ability at the national level. For this to occur, the unions will need to embrace a more strategic approach to lobbying federally. They should also identify strategies for engaging federal politicians on local law and order issues as they apply to their electorates, as has been done successfully with state and local politicians. Programs such as the Australian Defence Force Parliamentary Program[5] would give federal politicians a direct insight into issues affecting their local communities, and identify mechanisms, such as federal government networks, through which they might be able to contribute.

Our ability to meet many of the challenges outlined above will be determined by our research capacity; this is one area that has been clearly identified by ANU researchers as needing improvement (Fleming & Marks 2004). Police unions must determine how best to develop such a capacity to further both the interests of their members and the interests of policing more generally.

For police union leaders, the biggest challenge is how to meet these needs while at the same time responding to the more immediate daily expectations of members. In a discussion with police union leaders from the United States, Canada, Australia and New Zealand in August 2003, Professor Marty Linsky, from the Kennedy School of Government at Harvard University, described this challenge. In his presentation

'Leadership on the line: Staying alive through the dangers of leading', Linsky outlined what he called the profound differences between 'authority' and 'leadership' in the context of running a police union. He described the authority given to police union leaders as a contract for service. Those that had been given the authority by their membership were in turn expected to provide direction, protection and order for their members.[6]

For Linsky, leadership can be described (amongst other things) in terms of disappointing your own people, if unavoidable, only at the rate they can absorb, and helping them to accept these losses. Professor Linsky argued that in order to bring about change, police union leaders must bring their members with them at a rate they can take on board, or they will face the consequences of being rejected by their membership. One could justifiably argue that Police Commissioners may face the same dilemma if they move without the support of their police officers.

Conclusion

The police operate in a complex political environment – an environment structured by networks and strategic alliances. Australian police unions have traditionally been important participants in such alliances. Police unions in Australia display many of the characteristics of network actors and have a robust community of purpose and shared values. The national structure of the police union movement in Australia promotes networking values in its quest for goodwill and consensus.

Since their formation in the early 1900s, police unions have developed strong networks which address both the 'internal' and 'external' aspects of policing, particularly at the political level. These networks have paid large dividends for police officers in terms of their influence over public policy matters, as well as in terms of specific industrial issues such as employment terms and conditions. Over the years these networks have grown, and today Australian police unions are at the forefront of forging and maintaining links with international police unions.

The strong lobbying base of police unions has been consolidated at the national level through the PFA/affiliate two-tiered representation arrangement. This has allowed for a more focused national approach on a range of issues affecting policing, and the array of network partners that police unions have developed over the years has allowed such an approach to flourish. Whilst police unions, and the wider policing sector, would benefit from measures to strengthen the role of police officers in community networks, much progress has been made in other areas, such as meeting the government's continually expanding national security concerns with minimal additional resources, particularly at the state and territory level. Just how long these extra demands can be met remains to be seen.

In September 2003, when the Prime Minister, John Howard, opened the then newly purchased PFA premises in Canberra, he said:

> [I]n declaring this building open ... I'm sure that it will be the hive and the launching pad of much lobbying of the federal government and I'm sure my colleagues will get very used to, over the years, the staff who work here.[7]

The Prime Minister, in his own words, had recognised what the PFA's 2000 Strategic Plan had foreshadowed on behalf of its 50,000 members. The PFA had arrived, and was accepted as a legitimate lobbying arm of Australian police and policing by the highest officeholder in the country.

Notes

1 I will use the generic term 'union' when referring to police associations and police unions throughout this chapter, as there are six (6) police associations and two (2) police unions in Australia as well as the one (1) police federation.

2 Queensland Police Union, New South Wales Police Association, Australian Federal Police Association, The Police Association of Victoria, Police Association of Tasmania, Police Association of South Australia, Northern Territory Police Association, West Australian Police Union, Police Federation of Australia.

3 From Registered Rules of the Police Federation of Australia.

4 In particular, agreement to and advancement of police education and training.

5 Parliamentarians are able to undertake an ADF attachment for one week during parliamentary recess.

6 The author was present at Marty Linsky's presentation on 9 August 2003.

7 The author was present at John Howard's speech on 16 September 2003.

References

Dupont, B. (2003) Public entrepreneurs in the field of security: An oral history of Australian Police Commissioners, paper delivered at In Search of Security: An International Conference on Policing and Security, Montreal, Canada.

Finnane, M. (2002) When Police Unionise: The Politics of Law and Order in Australia. Sydney: Institute of Criminology, University of Sydney.

Fleming, J. and Marks, M. (2004) Reformers or resisters? The state of police unionism in Australia, Employment Relations Record, 4(1): 1–14.

Fleming, J., Marks, M. and Wood, J. (2006) Standing on the inside looking out: The significance of unions in networks of police governance, The Australian and New Zealand Journal of Criminology, 39(1).

Fleming, J. and Rhodes, R.A.W. (2005) Bureaucracy, contracts and networks: The unholy trinity and the police, The Australian and New Zealand Journal of Criminology, 38(2).

Police Federation of Australia (2000) Strategic Plan.

Senate Select Committee on Mental Health (Federation of Australia) (2005) at <http://www.aph.gov.au/senate/committee/mentalhealth_ctte/submissions/sublist.htm> (all websites listed were correct at the time of writing).

Wilson, S. et al. (eds) (2005) Australian Social Attitudes: The First Report. Sydney: UNSW Press.

8 | WHAT WORKS, WHAT DOESN'T WORK AND WHAT LOOKS PROMISING IN POLICE RESEARCH NETWORKS

David Bradley, Christine Nixon and Monique Marks

Introduction

Recommending the use of the handbook on policing he has edited, Tim Newburn observes that 'for an increasing number of highly educated and reflective officers working within an increasingly professionalised service ... there is no comprehensive and authoritative source on policing they can turn to' (2003: 7). Today, more than ever, such guides are much needed. Research-based knowledge of, and for, policing has increased significantly in volume over the last two decades, in the United States, the United Kingdom and Australia. For example, in a recent review of evidence about American police effectiveness and fairness, it was observed that 'before publication of the President's Commission on Law Enforcement and the Administration of Justice ... there was hardly any scientific research on the police. Today, there is so much that scholars and police find it difficult to keep up, let alone evaluate its qualitative merits and practical utility' (Skogan & Frydl 2004: 20).

In what follows, and drawing upon examples from the United States, the United Kingdom and Australia, we explore this growing volume of police research, and its particular location within an institutional network populated by public police agencies, universities, subject disciplines and learned societies, research-funding bodies, policy communities and governments. Viewed from our various perspectives – as police leader, police educator and police researcher – our interest is in the complex and problematic relationships between the generation, validation, dissemination and use of the major kinds of police research-based knowledge. In particular, we want to explore issues concerning the current impact of this knowledge on the capability of the public police to pursue and realise their aims and objectives, including crime control.

The final section of the paper explores what changes to policing research networks are required to significantly affect the intellectual formation of the public police and to promote evidence-based police organisational change. We examine, as an example, the research approach taken up in a joint research project between the Victoria Police and the Australian National University. The paper concludes by pointing out the considerable challenges these changes will pose for governments, universities and police agencies.

The critical police research tradition

Police research does not just happen. 'Police studies, like policing itself, [are] based on material, political and cultural interests that pattern the production and distribution of knowledge' (Manning 2005). Police research is knowledge-generating work conducted by workers whose activities are regulated within particular governance arrangements and who operate in networks linking them in different ways with governmental, police, educational and other organisations. These arrangements help shape the subject matter, nature, quantity and quality of knowledge generation and use. Specialist organisational forms – universities – play a central role in these arrangements, state-licensed and regulated as they are to generate knowledge through research and to disseminate it through publication and teaching. Within universities, academic knowledge workers are usually organised through subject-based groups called disciplines and their associated learned societies, institutes and journals. The latter are the vehicles through which the quality of knowledge work is assessed and the reputation and status of knowledge workers is conferred. For example, when referring to key police scholars in the United Kingdom and North America, Manning notes that they:

form something of a network of relations. Through these networks flow rewards and sanctions – invitations to write, to visit, to serve on PhD committees in several countries, and the gossip, competition, and envy that stabilize rankings within the network. Most of the senior figures in the policing drama have known each other since the 1970s; attended many police-oriented conferences in the United States, United Kingdom, Canada and on the continent; and appeared in, reviewed, and praised each other's books (Manning 2005: 25–26).

This group and its Australian counterpart, together with contributors from other university disciplines, began, and continue to sustain, what we refer to as the critical tradition of police research. Within this tradition the public police constitute part of the subject matter of many university-based academic disciplines, including, inter alia, political science, public administration, law, history, sociology and criminology. It valorises 'theorizing and organizing, proposition-generating research' (Manning 2005: 34). At least in contrast to the so-called applied disciplines in universities, it is 'pure' to the extent that it is free from any formal obligation to meet the research and educational needs of the public police. It is not pure in the sense of constituting study conducted for its own sake, to the extent that in value terms its agenda is informed by a range of normative and political issues and concerns about the public police.

Given the social and political significance of the public police's role and the turbulence of social and political change from the 1960s onwards, the emergence of such a research tradition is unsurprising. The public police's public order role made it inevitable that as they became caught up in fierce and often bitter politically contested issues such as civil rights, race relations, anti-war protests and industrial conflict, they would attract scholarly attention (Skogan & Frydl 2004: 24). Early ethnographic studies of police patrol revealed the nature and extent of police discretion and the latitude for discrimination this allowed (Banton 1964; Reiss 1971; Cain 1973; Skolnick 1977). In the United Kingdom, in particular, with the tension created between the competing claims of constabulary independence and police accountability both to central government and local government, the problem of democratic control over policing has continued to attract academic attention (Brogden 1982; Jefferson & Grimshaw 1984; Patten Report 1999; Reiner 2002). In all three countries, police scholars have continued to provide critical accounts and explanations of police occupational culture, police violence, and the problem of police corruption (Skolnick & Fyfe 1994; Chan 1997; Coady et al. 2000).

The critical police research tradition has been normatively shaped by public interest values and concerns, and in that sense has made, and continues to make, a significant and important contribution to the political agenda of policing reform (Reiner 1992; Brogden & Shearing 1993; Loader & Mulcahy 2003). However, its direct impact upon the police is difficult to measure. Apart from acting as gatekeepers with regard to research access into their organisations, police have not been required to play a formal role in setting the critical research agenda, shaping its development or engaging in critical dialogue with those who produce it (Blair 2005). What can be said with certainty is that the findings of the critical police research tradition have often caused police leaders to be highly defensive about their organisations and their officers, and deeply wary of attracting further critical academic attention (Young 1991; Reiner 2000; Brodeur 2003). From the inception of the new police, the worlds of the public police and the public university have been very separate, with little if any formal interchange occurring between them (MacDonald 1986; Brown & Waters 1993; Shaftoe 2004). Practically oriented, reactive, control oriented and generally conservative in values, police have found it difficult to engage with the agenda and the language of the critical police research tradition (Ackroyd et al. 1992).

The policy police research tradition in the United States

Since the early to mid-1980s, in the United Kingdom, the United States and Australia, police agencies have become the subject of another form of expert academic attention. To varying degrees, but driven by the same values and ideas associated with changes in public management, the police have become increasingly the subject of a research agenda designed to generate knowledge to be used in enhancing their policies and practices. Still largely conducted by university-based academics, many of whom find they are bestriding both the critical and the policy police research traditions, this evidence-based policy and practice police research tradition has grown significantly over the last twenty years, nourished by streams of government funding (Skogan & Frydl 2004; Bullock & Tilley 2003; Manning 2005).

It might be expected that this new police research tradition, in contrast to the critical research one, would bring police and academia together and create positive and collaborative relationships of a kind that would lead to enhancement of police policies and practices. As we shall see, there is some evidence that this has happened, more so perhaps in the United States and Australia than in the United Kingdom. There is also the prospect that this new form of alliance between police and researchers may significantly contribute towards a deepening of the democratic control of the public police, for example through providing more transparent and accurate measures of their achievements (Skogan & Fydl 2004). As we shall also see, though, the nature of the networks underpinning and shaping this new police research tradition, together with the organisation of the public police, have features that limit the extent to which the public police can adopt and effectively use the new knowledge and evidence available to them. Interesting and sometimes highly effective results have been achieved, but progress has not been as rapid and straightforward as some had hoped (Knutsson 2004; Laycock 2001).

In the United States, early university-based policy police research was largely funded through bodies set up through private philanthropy, such as the Police Foundation. Now things are different, with government dominating the funding of police research (Skogan & Frydl 2004: 34). This funding has been mandated through federal legislation. The Omnibus Crime Control and Safe Streets Act of 1968 led to the creation of the National Institute of Justice, the major sponsor of police research in the United States. In 1994 the Violent Crime Control and Law Enforcement Act, which funded increased numbers of police officers at state and local levels as long as they were deployed to community policing programs, also 'included a mandate to evaluate programs already under way or to be sponsored by funds from the legislation itself' (Skogan & Frydl 2004: 1). The result has been that 'police research has become a substantial industry in 35 years, with a dedicated core of scholars, a large body of published work, several specialised journals, many accessible data sets, and regular professional meetings' (Skogan & Frydl 2004: 22).

What has been the impact of this substantial industry of knowledge generation upon the public police? In 2002, the United States' National Research Council was asked by the federal Department of Justice's National Institute of Justice and the Community Oriented Policing

Services Office to assess police research and its influence on policing (Skogan & Frydl 2004: 1–2). The council established a Committee to Review Research on Police Policy and Practices. The committee limited its examination to research evidence based on American scientific, peer-reviewed publications. This committee was able to point to a large body of police policies and practices about which there was no contemporary scientific evidence of effectiveness. The provision of substantial non-crime related services, crime prevention and policing road safety had all escaped scientific attention. According to Skogan and Frydl, despite recent developments in forensic science and technology, scientific research on the effectiveness of criminal investigation is limited to a small number of crime types, such as residential burglary and car theft, and is largely 30 years out of date. Overall, the committee's review revealed a serious and significant scientific knowledge deficit in American policing, particularly when seen in the context of lives lost to crime, the costs and benefits of government expenditure on law enforcement, and the moral obligation embedded in the use of coercive authority (Skogan & Frydl 2004).

The committee maintained that this scientific knowledge deficit could not be blamed upon the police. The growth and size of the published research, much of which required access by academic researchers to police agencies, was treated as strong evidence of the extent to which American police agencies had become open to the policy research tradition. Few other American institutions, public or private, allow 'outsiders' to observe routine operations or share in-house information as freely as the police do (Skogan & Frydl 2004: 35). It is no surprise, then, that the committee (all of whose members were leading members of the American police research tradition) suggested that the remedy was for the federal government to provide more substantial and continuous support to the university sector for police research.

While endorsing the desirability of a sustainable funding base for police research, we would argue that this 'more of the same' recommendation is, from a police reform perspective, problematical. The methodology and terms of reference of the Committee to Review Research on Police Policy and Practices did not enable it to explore the issue of knowledge generation, diffusion and use within police agencies. The committee acknowledged that there were industry-wide features that may work to retard the diffusion of scientific innovations within American policing, but lamented that 'there is no systematic evidence on what industry structure best promotes effectiveness, innovation, and experimentation' (Skogan & Frydl 2004: 2). It is interesting, too, that the committee did not look for a deeper explanation of the absence of research it had discovered in so many areas of American policing, but simply cited lack of sufficient research funding by government.

The committee also avoided reflection upon the nature of the organisation of the policy police research industry. It simply noted and endorsed the fact that 'in the United States there is a division of labour between those who do policing and those who study it. This is often deplored, because it deprives police of in-house research capacity but it has helped to ensure more independent inquiry' (Skogan & Frydl 2004: 34). That position is predicated on a false dichotomy, assuming as it does that research work must either be conducted by university academics or by police-based researchers. This simplistic approach avoids exploration of more sophisticated and complex ways of combining police and academia, ways that may better set the police research agenda's issues and priorities, improve ways that research is conducted and, crucially, enhance the interface between researchers', practitioners' and policy-makers' knowledge and expertise.

David Bayley, perhaps one of the most eminent of the scholars associated with the policy police research tradition, has observed that despite its volume, and despite the police openness to research policy, police research has not led to 'widespread operational changes even when it has been accepted as true' (Bayley 1998: 5). Yet Bayley is impressed by the amount of innovation that has occurred in American policing since the 1960s. There is, Bayley believes, a new appreciation of the importance of evaluation and the timely availability of information, which he attributes to the indirect rather than direct influence of academic police research.

Overall, it would seem that the nature of the impact of the American policy police research tradition on actual police policies and practices has been equivocal. A significant reason for this is that it is a research tradition that firmly embraces a particular paradigm about how scientific knowledge must be validated, one that generally discounts or neglects the morally complex and sociologically embedded nature of police practices and their contexts (Thacher 2001). The great majority of police research publications remain 'thought' pieces, while outcome evaluations of operational programs and practices remain very much in the minority (Beckman et al. 2003, 2005). The scientific validity of police innovations does not appear to be a significant factor in the way innovations have spread in American policing (Weiss 1997).

While policy-driven research now dominates the American scene, the critical police research tradition also continues there. While many of its members remain resolutely critical of what they regard as the significant weaknesses of the policy tradition, it seems that there has been some conflu- ence between the two traditions. Manning (2005), for example, contrasts research that asks low-level, policy-shaped questions rather than theoretical ones. He claims that policy-driven police research pays little attention to normative questions. At the same time, he is concerned that police researchers from the critical tradition are now more dependent on funding and more inclined to 'a theoretical study of any current fashionable question without theorising it' (Manning 2005: 38).

What Manning alerts us to is that the applied study of police policies and practices can and should be theoretically informed, and that when it is, it carries substantial practical relevance. Two examples provide strong evi- dence for this. Tilley (2004) has examined in rich depth the theoretical com- plexity and practical weight of the effectiveness of various forms of focused policing operations. Homel has fully articulated the theoretical basis of the highly successful general deterrence impact of random breath-testing in reducing road trauma (Homel 1988). As Manning suggests, it may be true that the quality of useful police research is threatened by demands to meet short timeframes, but this is a factor that needs to be engaged with and, where possible, changed. As we shall show later, it is certainly not necessary that practically driven police research be restricted to short timeframes. And while Manning claims that the contemporary policy police research tradition is empty of normative concerns, we believe that this statement is excessive. There is in fact a growing theoretically significant and pragmatically grounded research interest in the ethical dimensions of the police role (Kleinig 1996; Miller et al. 1997; Neyroud & Beckley 2001).

The policy police research tradition in the United Kingdom

Reiner (2000), reviewing the recent history of British police research, links changes in the overall research agenda in that country to the changing poli- tics of criminal justice. Arguably, though, the British critical police research tradition, rich in theoretical diversity, has continued to grow and prosper, sustained not least by the expanding size of higher education. From its early beginnings with the work of scholars such as Banton and Cain, to the recent body of work illustrated by the writings of those such as Reiner, Newburn and Loader, the public police have been subjected to a level of academic attention that has produced a robust ongoing understanding and critique of their roles and relationships.

In contrast to its American counterpart, and although much progress has been made, there are still significant problems in the police–academic relationships that have developed within the policy police research tradition in the United Kingdom. These, and some of their possible causes, were fore-seen by one of the British pioneers of police research, Michael Banton. In his foreword to a collection of papers on police effectiveness edited by two Home Office-based government administrative criminologists, he wrote that:

> in Great Britain at present there is no shared understanding about who is to accumulate new knowledge on various aspects of policing, how they are to be rewarded for it, and how that knowl-edge can best be passed on ... police research cannot fit snugly within any single institution. It must relate to police forces, gov-ernmental bodies and to the universities. It must draw upon several specialisms. Its main problems are not those of money, but of building a community of imaginative and enthusiastic research workers who can collaborate in developing the potentialities of a body of good ideas (cited in Clarke & Hough 1980: 6–7).

What prompted these thoughts as a number of instances (cited within the collection) of police resistance to practical research findings.

A few years later, Molly Weatheritt, deputy director of the newly estab-lished Police Foundation of England and Wales, also reported that police often found the message that research had for them to be 'unpalatable' in the sense that it claimed to find so many policing policies and practices bereft of evidence of effectiveness (Weatheritt 1986: 20). She claimed that 'many aspects of policing have remained immune from critical scrutiny and the police service has been able to discourage and rebuff the attentions of research with ease' (Weatheritt 1986: 18). She did concede, though, that 'research deals in a language which is very different from that used in everyday policing; and that it operates at a level of generality which is simply unconvincing to those whose experience derives from having to deal with the immediate and particular' (Weatheritt 1986: 20). Consequently, in her view, academic police researchers have had great difficulty in gaining access to the police and in finding a receptive audience in the police.

Ten years later, the intellectual landscape of policing in the United Kingdom had changed considerably. These changes were largely driven by central government, combining its growing policy research capacity with a strong inspectorate and audit capability over the police service. The cumulative results emerging from the latter two functions had convinced government that large parts of the police service were under-performing (Neyroud & Beckley 2001). The police service found itself being subjected to a growing regime of performance indicators and measures. In response, it expanded its own capacity to conduct policy and practice research, not just through a growing collection of training and research organisations within its headquarters at the Bramshill Police College, but also through building research capacity within organisations such as the Association of Chief Police Officers.

In 1999 the government announced its intention to spend £400 million on a three-year 'what works in crime reduction' research program. One of the program's funding streams was called the Targeted Police Initiative (TPI), making available some £30 million for funding police-based research designed to advance problem-oriented policing. Problem-oriented policing entails 'identifying and analysing community problems and developing more effective responses to them' (Goldstein 1990: 3). A move towards this style of policing requires new ways of thinking and has implications for the entire police organisation in terms of its personnel and its practices. Problem-oriented policing requires all police, regardless of rank, to be problem solvers since the solutions to crimes are often very tied to local conditions and local knowledge. While the wide range of problems that the police deal with are often linked, what is required are different responses to particular problems, not a generic response to all crimes and policing problems. Problem-oriented policing incorporates prior analysis of problems and a recognition on the part of the police that they need to draw on other agencies in resolving crime and disorder problems (Goldstein 1990).

Individual police forces were required to draw upon the extant body of problem-oriented policing knowledge, develop comprehensive and innovative plans for crime analysis and prevention, and then competitively apply to the Home Office for funds with which they could pay for the expertise and resources needed to conduct the projects. To ensure that the program made a contribution to the policing body of knowledge, the government insisted that 10 per cent of the fund's monies be spent on rigorous evaluation of the police projects.

Accounts of nineteen of these projects, collectively costing over £8 million, were published (Bullock & Tilley 2003b). The evaluations revealed widespread failure of the projects, caused not just by poor management of the program by government, but also by poor implementation by the participating police forces. The police appeared to have serious deficits in knowledge and skills, particularly in regard to their ability to grasp problem-oriented policing principles (Bullock & Tilley 2003a).

In another edited collection of academic articles exploring why problem-oriented policing has for so long remained a marginal innovation in the public police rather than a mainstream manner of doing business, a similar explanation is offered: the police need to be provided with more enlightened long-term police leadership; projects should be less rushed and better planned; academics should be more closely involved in leading the projects; and participating police need much better training and crime-reduction kits (Knutson 2004). These crime-reduction kits could include a range of tools for identifying and analysing problems and for fostering a teamwork approach within police organisations.

The view of both of these collections is that the current networks supporting the policy police research tradition are adequate to the task of reforming policing, but only if the relationships between the key parties – government policy-makers, police management and university academics – are improved. It is hard to disagree with this. However, we would want to go further. Our view is that significant progress will also require a much deeper reflective engagement on the part of the academic expert community about the nature of the public police as an organised body of practitioners. The same is required of police policy-makers and managers with regard to the research community. Indeed, we maintain that there is a general problem within the public services generally, and not just within the police. It is the problem of how academic expert knowledge can effectively engage with practitioner expert knowledge in the search for enhanced effectiveness.

From knowledge generation to knowledge use

In 1980, MacDonald and his colleagues at the Centre for Applied Research in Education (CARE) brought democratic program evaluation and curriculum theory together in their critical engagement with the task of achieving police reform through improved training (CARE 1986, 1990; Interim Police Education Training Advisory Council 1986). To appreciate the nature of this approach, it is worth quoting from MacDonald at length:

> [The academics] negotiate with their sponsors and with their subjects, seeking an accommodation between the interests of those responsible for programmes and the interests of those the programmes are intended to serve. They seek access to all levels of decision-making relevant to programme origin and action, so as to get a grasp of how and why the programme came about, and what the consequences of changing, continuing or abandoning it might be ... They are case-oriented ... working on actor frames of reference and value commitments. They work within the language of those they seek to influence ... They depend upon persuasive and educative interaction to achieve impact rather than authority ... and they insist upon their obligation to represent the views of those who hold neither power nor office (CARE 1986: 42).

This was the approach the CARE team brought to bear upon its evaluation of police recruit training in New South Wales (CARE 1990). CARE's strengths stem, first, from the way it engages with policy-makers, practitioners and their organisational contexts. It is highly sensitive to the politics of place, to the organisationally and culturally embedded nature of extant policy and practices (Nutley & Davies 2000). It respects practitioner knowledge and judgment, recognising that practitioners, through engagement with their everyday world, learn solutions to the problems they face, and cumulatively build up tacit knowledge. If evidence-based research is to help improve practices, the nature of those practices must be understood from the point of view of practitioners.

Second, this approach avoids a top-down linear treatment of knowledge generation, validation, diffusion and use, in which knowledge is seen as coming from expert knowledge generators who hand it over to program managers who then implement evidence-based change through management of practitioners. With CARE, researchers and the police meet each other as partners in a shared enterprise.

Third, this approach is built on an understanding of the multiple pressures and influences that shape practitioner behaviour. These include routines, craft knowledge, procedural knowledge, peer pressures and values,
organisational resources, organisational structures and cultural norms,
service user demand and pressure from other stakeholders, and, possibly,
research evidence and formal, declarative knowledge (Nutley & Davies
2000: 337). This is a way of engaging with policy and practising evidence-
based change that requires a full collaborative partnership between academics and their clients throughout the whole process of knowledge
generation, validation, diffusion and use.

It is worth observing that the critical police research tradition has long
acknowledged and understood the deeply embedded nature of police practices, and in that respect it has much to teach the police policy and practice
reform project. Muir, for example, in his study of an American police patrol,
was able to trace the complex ways in which the normative dimensions of
passion and perspective informed varieties of good and bad policing (Muir
1977). Recently, Reiner drew attention to Muir's much neglected work and
identified a contemporary need to engage in sustained, detailed observa-
tional studies of police operations if we wish to identify and understand
good policing (Reiner 1998).

An ethnographic approach requires a researcher's immersion in a milieu
(such as a police organisation), and the employment of a range of methods,
such as conversations, formal and informal interviews and participant observation. Ethnographic studies allow the researcher to gain insight into deep-
level culture through continuous engagement with respondents and their
environment. Police researchers using this approach are able to appreciate
the complexity of the fine detail of activities that take place within police
organisations and the various technologies that are employed in getting
tasks done. Sustained interactions with and observations of the police in
their own natural settings provide researchers with invaluable information
about the power relations that exist between members of the police organisation; the effectiveness of new policies, training and recruitment practices
in changing behaviour and values; and the nature of the micro-relationships
between police and community members (Marks 2004).

Ethnographic studies, carried out as a partnership between researchers
and practitioners, are, we believe, the best way to derive knowledge that can
be used to bring about change in work practices and relations. These ethno-

graphies should be jointly designed with the overall aim of engaging police about their current practices (both good and bad) and ways of improving these, while taking into account organisational constraints and traditions.

An Australian case study

How are current police research networks to be managed and changed to take on such challenging police research? To address this question we turn our attention to policing in Australia. Australia has its share of both the contemporary police research traditions. Critical police research is conducted across a range of academic disciplines within the universities, while through the federally funded Australian Criminology Council, with an annual budget of around $7 million, Australian governments are provided with practical studies, advice and links to knowledge networks. Australian police agencies contribute proportionately to the modestly funded Australasian Centre for Police Research. To augment this policy police research, and in the context of its commitment to the professionalisation of policing, the Australian Police Commissioners have created a Police Professional Standards Council. The council examines, as one of its focus areas, how police may best develop strategic educational partnerships with universities (Police Commissioners' Conference 2005).

In the past fifteen years, some significant changes have taken place in regard to building stronger relations between the police and tertiary education institutions. The NSW Police, for the last fourteen years, have required their recruits and constables to complete university-based associate degrees in policing practice (Dobson 2004). The Tasmanian Police have established a partnership to conduct police research with the state university through the Tasmanian Institute for Law Enforcement Studies. And across Australia, and with great success in Victoria, Australian Police Commissioners, in partnership with university groups, have applied for and been awarded funding for applied research through the Australian Research Council's (ARC's) Linkage Grant scheme.

Victoria Police have made research-informed policy and practices and intelligence-led policing central elements of their strategic direction (Victoria Police 2003). If this commitment to research-informed policy and practice is not to remain a rhetorical statement, then practically, it requires Victoria Police not just to draw upon, adapt and use relevant published evi-

dence and ideas about policing, but also to actually *do* research. This presents a considerable problem. In common with other police agencies, Victoria
Police have a limited research capability. Currently, unlike occupations whose
members are required to be trained within universities, the public police in
Australia do not have a university-based group of workers whose teaching
and research agenda centres on good policing policies and practices.

One answer has been found through a form of networked policing. The
ARC has a significant biannual research funding stream for applied
research conducted through partnerships between 'industry' and university
groups. Over the last five years Victoria Police, with a range of partnering
university research units, have received funding by the ARC for eight
applied research projects. Typically, the projects are of between four and
five years' duration. The problems they address include child abuse, organisational behaviour, corporate citizenship in policing, counter-terrorism and
policing multi-faith communities.

Success in applying for ARC funds has required considerable effort by
Victoria Police. For example, selecting suitable university partners requires
knowledge of the relevant academic community. Crucial, too is the commitment to, and ownership of, the projects by various senior police managers
and their police teams. All the projects were initiated by senior police, aware
that their realisation of the goals of their strategic plan depended on successful outcomes of such research. The cumulative impact of all the various
projects is monitored by Victoria Police's corporate committee. The police
union, too, has taken the program seriously, requesting and getting periodic
briefings and participating in some of the research program steering groups.

The program steering groups are composed of academic staff, police
staff and, in some cases, members of the community, such as faith leaders
and journalists. This joint management of the research projects is essential
if the long-term commitment of Victoria Police is to be maintained – this is
always a risk given the turnover of middle and senior police managers. Each
of the projects constitutes an empirical test of what is required for successful knowledge generation, validation, diffusion and use within a public
police context. Each aims, by its completion, to have achieved alterations in
the way Victoria Police conduct their services. They constitute a test of the
advice of MacDonald to the Police Foundation and of the action research
approach as the means through which strategic changes in police thinking
and action can be achieved.

The challenge of action research

As we have shown, the current policy police research tradition has encountered problems of knowledge diffusion and adoption across the public police. In the United States the tradition has produced a growing scientific body of material about what works and what doesn't work in policing. However, the spread and use of this knowledge is inhibited by the absence of a sustained interface between researchers and practitioners throughout all the phases required to ensure that change occurs: knowledge generation, validation, diffusion and adoption. In contrast to the United States, in the United Kingdom, policy researchers are employed by or located within government; this brings them closer to the police service. However, as was demonstrated in the Targeted Police Initiative, significant implementation failure was encountered, in part because of a lack of clarity about the role of the external experts and their relationship to police managers and practitioners (Townsley & Pease 2003; Matassa & Newburn 2003). In Australia, applied research partnerships between police and university academics are beginning to flourish, but they rely on a funding base that is uncertain.

Australian police services and academics are beginning to explore more participatory and action-oriented research approaches. University-based researchers (particularly at the Australian National University [ANU]) and the Victoria Police have searched for a model that promotes police/researcher partnerships that are based on mutual trust, respect and an appreciation of one another's skills and knowledge bases. The Victoria Police and the ANU in their joint ARC research project have adopted the participatory action research (PAR) approach as the best model currently available.

In essence, the PAR model is centred on notions of collaboration. It is an approach that tries to overcome the traditional gap between research and practice (Whyte 1991; Ainscow, Booth & Dyson 2004; Lynch 1999) through a two-way ongoing involvement of researchers and research subjects (Geva & Shem-Tov 2002: 192). Practitioners, in this case the police, are directly involved in the research process from problem identification to research design to data collection and analysis, and thereafter to dissemination and uptake of research findings and recommendations. The action research encounter is one where 'equal partners meet, enter into dialogue and share different kinds of knowledge and expertise' (Jordan 2003: 190).

Rather than the traditional research model, where there is a rigid distinction between researcher and subjects and a quest for objectivity, PAR
focuses on a 'dialogical relationship between theory and practice' (Jordan
2003: 188), where knowledge is generated within the everyday world of
participants.

There is little written evidence of the PAR approach being adopted
within a police research context. The reason for this is not hard to find.
PAR came into being in less developed countries in the 1960s, inspired by
political events such as anti-colonial struggles. It has traditionally been
viewed as 'a methodology at the margins' (Jordan 2003: 186), geared
towards advancing agency among the marginalised, poor and disenfran-
chised and thus creating more just and democratic societies (Jordan
2003).

Is PAR appropriate, then, to the study of the police? While academic
researchers may engage the police in research projects aimed at more just
and democratic policing with better safety outcomes for all, the police themselves cannot be viewed as a marginalised group. On the contrary, the police
are a powerful organisation in society (Bent 1974). Their power emanates
from laws and conventions, from the fact that they are armed, and from the
symbolic capital in social ordering that individual police members embody.

Despite, or perhaps because of, their authoritative position in society,
police have typically not been viewed as partners (let alone equal partners)
in academic research endeavours. Academic researchers have always
written *about* the police, not *with* them. Policing scholars have written at
length of the difficulties of 'gaining access' to police organisations in the
first instance (Brewer 1991; Greenhill 1981; Punch 1975). The
object/subject distinction in such research endeavours has always been
very stark. When it comes to knowledge production, the police as a community could be regarded as 'disempowered'. Disempowering such an otherwise powerful grouping from knowledge production that affects the very
security of all societal groupings is potentially very damaging. This fact
alone is an impetus to rethinking current police research traditions to allow
police (at all levels) to be included in the process of the generation and validation of research.

While the idea of PAR with the police may sit uncomfortably with
some methodologists – given the philosophical and historical framing of this
approach – there have been moves to mainstream PAR. Indeed, in recent

years, PAR has been journeying from the borders to the centre, as organisations such as the World Bank, government agencies and major NGOs are
now promoting this approach. However, those who are critical of the
'colonisation' argue that an empowering research methodology may serve to
reinforce dominant power relations (Jordan 2003). As noted above, PAR
was developed by researchers working in the third world, who wanted to
use the research process not simply as a means for understanding social conditions but also as a way of creating agency among marginalised people.
According to Jordan, though, when PAR has been adopted by mainstream
private consultants, government bodies and international development
bodies, it has led to a reinforcing of dominant social relations and practices.
Jordan gives the example of industrial relations consultants who use PAR
'to co-opt workers' knowledge and understandings of the labour process in
order to effect "paradigm shifts" on how to boost productivity and competitiveness' (Jordan 2003: 191).

We believe that rather than discounting this methodology as 'unusable'
with the non-marginal groups, it is important to think of ways to use this
approach wisely. This, we believe, means incorporating the following questions into the research design: To what end are people (in this case the
police) being 'empowered'? Who will benefit from this 'empowerment'
process? How can this research approach be used to promote democracy and
social justice?

The Victoria Police/ANU research project on networked policing is a
good example of how such questions have been used to frame a research
project. The basic aim is to engage the police directly in a research project
whose goal is to mobilise the capacities and knowledge of a range of civic
and state groups, and create security institutions that are more just and
more apposite. The point of this research is not to strengthen the Victoria
Police organisation. Rather, the point is to engage the police in developing
innovative models that support policing partnerships with a host of state
and non-state agencies, with the aim of achieving important police objectives such as reducing crime and enhancing feelings of safety (Victoria
Police 2003).

The Victoria Police are engaged in this networked policing research
project as active partners at all stages of the research process. Police
members (particularly at the local level) have mapped out focus areas and
existing safety providers. Where possible, police members at all levels of the

organisation are supported in conducting data collection and analysis. Police, together with researchers and other stakeholder groups, have devised pilot models for testing new policing networks and practices. Through engaging in this research process, police are, often for the first time, provided with the tools and the space to think critically about their role and to question their familiar 'tried and tested' practices. It has also provided the momentum for reaching out to a range of agencies and individuals within policing networks and discovering how local groups define and shape security arrangements.

There are, however, a number of challenges to the effective implementation of PAR. In the first instance, the organisational features of policing make it difficult to provide scope and support for sustained applied research. For example, the daily demands of policing often result in research being viewed as a secondary activity. Second, police are pragmatists (Bayley 1994), and are generally concerned with short-term gains rather than with long-term strategic interests. Third, police organisational priorities and indicators of performance do not (at least directly) refer to research engagement. Fourth, police organisations have accountabilities and communication approaches that are vastly different from those of academic researchers.

Successful PAR therefore requires institutionalising new ways of working and learning within the public police bureaucracy. For this to occur, space at all levels of the police organisation needs to be created for research engagement. Such engagement needs to be widely viewed as central to improving police practice. Police organisations committed to such an engagement would have to value long-term strategic visions as highly as short-term interventions.

One way of ensuring that a space for critical thinking and engagement is opened up is to build the intellectual capacity of the organisation through revising current training and educational arrangements. This could involve developing stronger links between police training and higher education. That development has commenced in Australia, and there are signs of it emerging in the United Kingdom (Dobson 2005; Kent Police 2005). In New South Wales, all currently employed 14,000 sworn officers have undertaken a training course leading to the award of a university associate degree in policing practice (Dobson 2005). The police–university partnership has developed strong practicum sites within local area police commands. The long-term strategic importance of the partnership between universities and police organisations lies not just with the greater content and higher standard of the police curriculum. The promise is the development of a police faculty whose members will engage in applied research into better policing practices. As foundational police education for general practitioners is established, it will provide the basis on which higher-order policing knowledge and skills can be built into postgraduate courses. It will also potentially provide a publicly accessible institutional base for a cumulatively evolving body of police knowledge and skills.

The emergence of an applied discipline of policing also invites the possibility of new and more democratic ways of regulating police performance and standards. Australian police are currently exploring the possibility of creating police registration boards similar to those in nursing and other university-based occupations (Australian Police Commissioners' Conference 2005). Such bodies extend the regulation of practitioners beyond their employers to include organisations such as police unions in a regulatory network. Finally, enabling as it will a break between training and employment, the emergence of a new applied discipline of policing could come to encompass all professional policing, both public and private. This would bring not only higher standards of capability to networked policing, but also more open and democratic forms of regulating it.

The opening up of the universities to the police and actively involving the police as research partners also presents real challenges to academic researchers and their institutions. Academics will need to seriously engage with practitioner knowledge and expertise. This may require innovation in regard to research methodologies and approaches in order for researchers to fully grasp the daily rigours of policing and police organisational cultures (Perez & Shtull 2002). An uptake in the use of ethnographic approaches is one important way of committing to such understandings. At the institutional level, universities may need to reconfigure academic measures of performance to include innovative research and teaching methodologies, direct engagement with practitioner groups, and fieldwork. It will also require a rethink on the part of academic administrators and sponsors about what constitute 'valuable' academic outputs for evidence-based change programs among practitioner groups and about the dissemination of research findings in a range of forums and publications (not simply those that are peer reviewed).

Conclusion

The current approaches (both critical and policy oriented) to police research have had limited direct impact on actual police programs and practice. This is because there has been a serious deficiency in regard to a sustained interface between researchers and practitioners throughout all the phases of change: knowledge generation, validation, diffusion and adoption. For this to be remedied, police and researchers need to come together in a policing research network whose objective is forging 'a system of policing practices which promotes the security of citizens and communities, and does so in a fair and efficient way' (Marenin 2004: 299). Within this research network, the relationship between police practitioners and researchers will need to be based on equal partnership and a dialogic engagement, as proposed by those who are committed to a PAR approach.

Creating such a network, enacting a PAR approach, and generating strategic police reform all present numerous challenges to the institutions of the police, academia and government in Australia and elsewhere. Universities will have to include policing in their profiles. The federal government must agree that through its funding of the universities it will effectively subsidise the training of state-based policing. State governments will need to understand that police capability is just as important as police numbers. Police leaders will have to be prepared to relinquish their monopoly of control over police education. These challenges have been met by these institutions to varying degrees in Australia already. Police unions will also need to rethink their role and identity. In so doing, they need to enlarge their range of responsibilities to their occupation beyond the traditional industrial ones. All Australian police unions and their national union have committed to this path (Fleming, Marks & Wood 2006).

The capacities, standpoints and structural constraints of both the police and academic researchers will probably always present challenges to collaborative research partnerships. Notions of professionalism and ways of evaluating performance and success will have to be revisited on an ongoing basis. Police and academics need to climb out of their boxes and enter the labyrinth of research and modelling programs together. Academic researchers will have to pay attention to what the police say and tune in to their everyday world. They need to realise that police are not analogous to disempowered and marginalised groups. Rather, they operate within structural and cultural constraints which sometimes limit their capacity to be visionaries and innovators in public safety research networks. Successful participation in collaborative research networks promises liberation from those constraints.

References

Ackroyd S., Harper, R., Hughes, J., Shapiro, D. and Soothill, K. (1992) *New Technology and Practical Police Work*. Buckingham: Open University Press.

Association of Chief Police Officers of England, Wales and Northern Ireland (2001) *Blueprint for Policing in the 21st Century*, at <http://acpo.police.uk/policies.asp> (all websites listed were correct at the time of writing).

Australian Police Professional Standards Council. <http://www.appsc.com.au/index2.php>.

Australian Police Commissioners' Conference (2005) *Discussion Paper on Professionalisation*. Melbourne.

Banton, M. (1964) *The Policeman in the Community*. London: Routledge & Kegan Paul.

Bayley, M. (1994) *Police for the Future*. New York: Oxford University Press.

Bayley, D. (1998) *Policing in America: Assessment and Prospects*, Washington DC: Police Foundation.

Beckman, K., Lum, C., Wyckoff, L. and Wall, L. (2003) Trends in police research: A cross-sectional analysis of the 2000 literature, *Police Practice and Research: An International Journal*, 5(2): 79–96.

Beckman, K., Gibbs, J., Beatty P. and Caigiani, M. (2005) Trends in police research: A cross-sectional analysis of the 2002 literature, *Police Practice and Research: An International Journal*, 6(3): 295–320.

Bent, A. (1974) *The Politics of Law Enforcement*. London: Lexington Books.

Blair, I. (2005) The Richard Dimbleby Lecture, *Guardian Unlimited*, 16 November, at <http://www.guardian.co.uk/crime/article/0,2763,1643995,00.html>.

Brewer, J. (1991) *Inside the RUC: Routine Policing in a Divided Society*. Oxford: Clarendon Press.

Brogden, M. (1982) *The Police: Autonomy and Consent*. London and New York: Academic Press.

Brogden, M. and Shearing, C. (1993) *Policing for New South Africa*. London: Routledge.

Broudeur, J.P. (ed.) (1998) *How To Recognize Good Policing*. London: Sage Publications.

Brown, J. (1996) Police research: Some critical issues, in F. Leishman, B. Loveday and S. Savage, *Core Issues in Policing*. London: Sage Publications.

Brown, J. and Waters, I. (1993) Professional police research, *Policing*, 9: 323–334.

Bullock, S. and Tilley, N. (2003a) From strategy to action: The development of problem-oriented projects, in S. Bullock and N. Tilley (eds), *Crime Reduction and Problem-oriented Policing*. Devon: Willan Publishing.

Bullock, S. and Tilley, N. (eds) (2003b) Crime Reduction and Problem-oriented Policing. Devon: Willan Publishing.

Cain, M. (1973) Society and the Policeman's Role. London: Routledge & Kegan Paul.

CARE (1986) The Police Probationers' Program: Stage Two. Norwich: University of East Anglia.

—— (1990) PREP Evaluation. Sydney: NSW Police Board.

Chan, J. (1997) Changing Police Culture: Policing in a Multicultural Society. Cambridge: Cambridge University Press.

—— (2003) Fair Cop: Learning the Art of Policing. Toronto: University of Toronto Press.

Clarke, R. and Hough, J. (eds) (1980) The Effectiveness of Policing. Aldershot: Gower Publishing.

Coady, T., James, S., Miller, S. and O'Keefe, M. (eds) (2000) Violence and Police Culture. Melbourne: Melbourne University Press.

Davies, H., Nutley, S. and Smith, P. (eds) (2000) What Works? Evidence-based Policy and Practice in Public Services. Bristol: The Policy Press.

Dobson, G. (2005) Police Education. Sydney: NSW Police Service.

Royal Commission into the New South Wales Police Service (1997) Final Report (The Wood Report). Sydney.

Fleming, J., Marks, M. and Wood, J. (2006) Standing on the inside looking out: The significance of unions in networks of police governance, The Australian and New Zealand Journal of Criminology, 39(1).

Goldstein, H. (1990) Problem-oriented Policing. New York: McGraw-Hill.

Homel, R. (1988) Policing and Punishing the Drinking Driver: A Study of General and Specific Deterrence. New York: Springer-Verlag.

Geva, R. and Shem-Tov, O. (2002) Setting up community policing centres: Participatory action research in decentralised policing services, Police Practice and Research: An International Journal, 3(3): 189–200.

Greenhill, N. (1981) The value of sociology in policing, in C. Pope and N. Weiner (eds), Modern Policing. London: Croom Held.

Irving, B. and Bourne, D. (2002, unpublished) Enhancing performance in basic command units: The appropriateness of the strategic approach outlined in 'Policing a new century: A blueprint for reform', proof of evidence to the Home Affairs Select Committee Conducting pre-legislative scrutiny of the Police Reform Bill, Police Foundation of England and Wales.

Jefferson, T. and Grimshaw, R. (1984) Controlling the Constable: Police Accountability in England and Wales. London: Frederick Muller.

Jordan, S. (2003) Who stole my methodology? Co-opting PAR, Globalisation, Societies and Education, 1(2): 185–200.

Kent Police (2005) The Student Police Program. Ashford: Kent Police.

Kleinig, J. (1996) The Ethics of Policing. Cambridge: Cambridge University Press.

King, R. and Wincup, E. (2000) Doing Research on Crime and Justice. Oxford: Oxford University Press.

Knutsson, J. (ed.) (2004) Problem-oriented Policing: From Innovation to Mainstream. Devon: Willan Publishing.

Laycock, G. (2002) Methodological issues in working with policy advisers and prac-titioners, in N. Tilley, (ed.), *Analysis for Crime Prevention*, Crime Prevention Studies Series, Vol. 13: 205–237. New York: Criminal Justice Press.

Laycock, G. and Webb, B. (2003) Conclusions: The role of the centre, in K. Bullock and N. Tilley (eds), *Crime Reduction and Problem-oriented Policing*. Devon: Willan Publishing.

Leishman, F., Loveday, B. and Savage, S. (eds) (1996) *Core Issues in Policing*. London: Longman.

Loader, I. (2000) Plural policing and democratic governance, *Social and Legal Studies*, 9(3): 373–45.

Loader, I. and Mulcahy, A. (2003) *Policing and the Condition of England: Memory, politics and culture*. Oxford: Oxford University Press.

Lusher, E. (1981) Lusher Report of the Commission to Enquire into NSW Police Administration. Sydney: NSW Government Press.

Manning, P. (2005) The study of policing, *Police Quarterly*, 8(1): 23–43.

MacDonald, B. (1986, unpublished) Research and action in the context of policing: An analysis of the problem and a programme proposal, Police Foundation of England and Wales, London.

Matassa, M. and Newburn, T. (2003) Problem-oriented evaluation? Evaluating problem-oriented policing initiatives, in S. Bullock and N. Tilley (eds), *Crime Reduction and Problem-oriented Policing*. Devon: Willan Publishing.

Marks, M. (2004) Researching police transformation: The ethnographic imperative, *British Journal of Criminology*, 44: 866–88.

Miller, S., Blackler, J. and Alexandra, A. (eds) (1997) *Police Ethics*. Sydney: Allen & Unwin.

Muir, W. Ker, Jr (1977) *Police: Street Corner Politicians*. Chicago: University of Chicago Press.

Newburn, T. (2003a) Introduction: Understanding policing, in T. Newburn (ed.), *The Handbook of Policing*. Devon: Willan Publishing.

—— (ed.) (2003b) *The Handbook of Policing*. Devon: Willan Publishing.

Neyroud, P. and Beckley, A. (2001) *Policing, Human Rights and Police Ethics*. Devon: Willan Publishing.

Nutley, S. and Davies, H. (2000) Making a reality of evidence-based practice, in H. Davies, S. Nutley and P. Smith (eds), *Evidence-based policy and practice in public services*. Bristol: The Policy Press.

Punch, M. (1986). *The Police and the Ethics of Fieldwork*. Los Angeles CA: Sage Publications.

Reiner, R. (1998) Process or product? Problems of assessing individual performance, in J.P. Broudeur (ed.), *How To Recognize Good Policing*. London: Sage Publications.

—— (2000) *The Politics of the Police*. Oxford: Oxford University Press.

—— (2000) Police research, in R. King and E. Wincup (eds), *Doing Research on Crime and Justice*. Oxford: Oxford University Press.

Reiss, A. (1971) *The Police and the Public*. New Haven CT: Yale University Press.

Report of Inquiry pursuant to orders in Council (The Fitzgerald Report) (1987). Brisbane: Queensland Government Printer.

Savage, S., Charman, S. and Cope, S. (2000) *Policing and the Power of Persuasion: The Changing Role of the Association of Chief Police Officers.* London: Blackstone Press.

Shaftoe, H. (2004) *Crime Prevention.* Basingstoke: Palgrave Macmillan.

Sherman, L., Gottfredson, D., MacKenzie, D., Eck, J., Reuter, P. and Bushway, S. (1998) *Preventing Crime: What Works, What Doesn't, What's Promising: A Report to the United States Congress.* Washington DC: National Institute of Justice.

Skogan, W. and Frydl, K. (eds) (2004) *Fairness and Effectiveness in Policing: The evidence.* Washington DC: The National Academies Press.

Skolnick, J. (1966) *Justice Without Trial: Law Enforcement in Democratic Society.* New York: Wiley.

Skolnick, J. and Fyfe, J. (1993) *Above the Law: Police and the Excessive Use of Force.* New York: Free Press.

Smith, C. (2005) Confronting crime control – crime control under New Labour, *British Journal of Forensic Practice*, 7(4).

Thacher, D. (2001) Policing is not a treatment: Alternatives to the medical model, *Journal of Research In Crime And Delinquency*, 38(4): 387–415.

The Independent Commission on Policing in Northern Ireland (1999) *A New Beginning : Policing For Northern Ireland* (The Patten Report).

Tilley, N. (2004) Using crackdowns constructively, in R. Burke-Hopkins (ed.), *Hard Cop Soft Cop.* Devon: Willan Publishing.

Townsley, M. and Pease, K. (2003) Two go wild in Knowsley: Analysis for evidence-led crime reduction, in S. Bullock and N. Tilley (eds), *Crime Reduction and Problem-oriented Policing.* Devon: Willan Publishing.

UK Audit Commission. <http://www.audit-commission.gov.uk/policeandcrime/index.asp?CategoryID=english%5E573&page=index.asp&area=hpsector>.

Victoria Police (2003) *The Way Ahead: Strategic Plan 2003–2008.* Melbourne: Victoria Police.

—— (2006) *A Fit-For-Purpose Service Delivery Model for Victoria Police.* Melbourne: Victoria Police.

Weiss, A. (1997) The communication of innovation in American policing, *Policing: An International Journal of Police Strategies & Management*, 20(2): 293–310.

Weatherburn, D. (2004) *Law And Order in Australia: Rhetoric and Reality.* Sydney: Federation Press.

Weatheritt, M. (ed.) (1986) *Innovations in Policing.* London: Croom Helm/Police Foundation.

Whyte, W. (1991) *Participatory Action Research.* Newbury Park CA: Sage Publications.

Young, M. (1991) *An Inside Job: Policing and Police Culture in Britain.* Oxford: Clarendon Press.

PEACEMAKING NETWORKS AND RESTORATIVE JUSTICE 9

John Braithwaite

Policing peace

This chapter argues that police peacekeepers have an important role in building peace in nations that have been racked by armed conflict. Their role is conceived as sustaining networks for the governance of peace and being part of such networks. Because peacebuilders are vulnerable to assassination by actors with a stake in the war, I will argue that the crucial role for the police is to protect such peacebuilders. The case of the civil war in Bougainville is used to illustrate the potential of restorative justice in peacebuilding. Circles of reconciliation in one pacified space can be networked out through to victims and perpetrators from unpacified spaces. Police can help identify combatants who might join peacebuilding circles and thus forge crucial links between war-making and peacebuilding networks. When combatants give up their weapons, the objective is to reintegrate them into a democratic society by providing legitimate opportunities for a productive future. They need to be given a stake in peace. Peacekeepers are conceived as supplying a responsive regulatory capability to escalate up a regulatory pyramid of progressively more coercive strategies to motivate peacebuilding at the base of the pyramid. Democracy-building is then conceived as accomplishing multiple separations of semi-autonomous powers in civil society. The ideal for sustained peace is seen as a plethora of civil society actors, all with their own capacity to regulate one another (and the state) by escalating from more deliberative to more deterrent political strategies that stop short of violence.

New wars

From the time of the rise of strong states in the Middle Ages until 1989, the way to understand war and how to prevent it was to grasp shifts in the balance of power among major states. From 1945 to 1989, the key thing to understand about the maintenance of peace between major states was the relationship of those states to the two superpowers. When war broke out in minor states – in Cuba, Korea, Vietnam, Angola, Vietnam, Afghanistan – it had to be understood in terms of superpower rivalries in the periphery. Of course there were many other schisms. It is not as if ancient divides such as that between Islam and Christendom had disappeared; it was just that it was clear which was by far the most consequential schism between 1945 and 1989 in shaping the outbreak of wars. This meant that to be effective, diplomacy had to engage superpower elites – negotiating diplomacy was something Kissinger and Gromyko did. Such men are no longer the principal architects of war and peace:

> Who are the architects of postmodern war, the paramilitaries, guerrillas, militias, and warlords who are tearing up the failed states of the 1990s? War used to be fought by soldiers; it is now fought by irregulars. This may be one reason why postmodern war is so savage, why war crimes and atrocities are now integral to the very prosecution of war (Ignatieff 1999: 5–6).

Contemporary wars, Keen (1998) points out, are numerous (51 nations were involved in internal armed conflict between 1994 and 1998), and in many cases seem intractable, with hostilities resurfacing repeatedly after they seem to be resolved. The problem, according to Keen, is that in many of the most crippled states in the contemporary world, war is more an economic opportunity than a problem to the protagonists. Securing control of some weak states has less to offer than do pillage, collection of protection money (Mafia style), monopolising trade of key commodities such as oil through violence, forced labour, appropriating depopulated land and mineral resources, selling off the forests or the ivory, stealing foreign aid and/or simply setting up road-blocks and making people pay 'taxes' to be allowed through.

Persistence of conflict can therefore in part be understood by armies on both sides having an interest in keeping the war going, at least at some points during complex shifts in alliances. Relations between warlords can be cordial in such circumstances of co-operative conflict. Keen's analysis (1998: 18–19) can make sense of practices such as avoiding pitched battles (for example, in Liberia) and selling arms and ammunition to the other side (for example, in Cambodia, Chechnya, Sierra Leone, Sri Lanka). 1993 was the first year since the recording of conflicts when armed conflicts over autonomy or independence markedly outnumbered conflicts over the type of political system or government composition (Australian Department of Foreign Affairs and Trade 1999: 74). A connected statistic is that between 1975 and 1995, unregulated population movements – forced movement or movement across borders unsanctioned by governments – increased over 1000 per cent; most of these people were trans-border refugees, internally displaced as a result of war or persecution (Dupont 1999: 162).

However collaborative warlords are, hatred and fear across the schisms of dominated populations are necessary to keep these wars going. Accomplished warlords have cruel skills in exacerbating the fissures in contemporary weak states. Part of our analysis of what is therefore needed in the contemporary world is grass-roots peacemaking skills for healing these fissures, so that power-hungry, money-hungry, rape-hungry warlords have less fear and division to work with. What late-modern warlords need is a situation where terrified citizens are saying, 'Who is to protect us now?', so that they can say, 'I will protect you.' Yugoslavia since Tito is an example of ethnic political–military elites filling a power vacuum in a disintegrating state by offering protection from other ethnic groups, thereby furthering the disintegration of the state and driving other ethnicities into the arms of warlords.

At the same time as globalisation increased the interests of developed economies in a peace that secured their trade networks, it also increased the rewards of warlordship in weak states. Warlords establish linkages with organised criminal elements in wealthy states: they sell drugs into affluent markets out of the Golden Triangle, Afghanistan, Tajikistan, Peru or Colombia and through states like Nigeria; they profit from global markets in arms; they hold western business executives or tourists hostage for ransom payments; they do dirty work for a fee for western security agencies; they dump toxic wastes on the land of their people in return for large payments from western business; they plunder foreign aid supplies; they hire themselves out as enforcers of western intellectual property rights against pirate manufacturers in the periphery, while themselves replacing real and expensive medicines with valueless counterfeits. The drugs situation in AIDS-ravaged nations says something of the ruthlessness of the criminal exploitation of the people of Africa that is occurring. Pharmaciens Sans Frontières estimates that 60 per cent of Cameroon's national market in medical drugs is pirated products, sometimes just capsules filled with flour (Hibou 1999: 107).

Hence the globalisation of markets simultaneously increases the costs of warfare to major states and increases the rewards of warlordship and state crime within weak states. To understand contemporary African wars, we need to recognise the process of the criminalisation of the state in Africa, which has both required and produced symbiotic relationships among official controllers of state and military power, international organised crime and local warlords (Bayart, Ellis & Hibou 1999). One of the reasons restorative justice notions developed in criminal justice systems are relevant to late-modern wars is that war and state crime are part of the same phenomenon. They co-exist in processes of using violence to acquire power for purposes of plunder.

The networked governance of peace

Kaldor (1999) concluded that islands of civility always survive, even in countries ravaged by the worst of wars. Her peacebuilding strategy is to link those islands of civility to support from transnational institutions – aid organisations, human rights non-government organisations (NGOs), pro bono lawyers, the Red Cross, peacekeepers. I would add that these islands of civility in the war-torn civil society should also be linked to support from restorative justice initiatives and an International Monetary Fund (IMF) and World Bank that have been reformed and now follow a strategy of bottom-up consent. Regional experts from specialist institutions such as the IMF should be important participants in high-quality deliberation for peacebuilding, not only because they are indispensable stakeholders, but because they have an expert competence that should not be dismissed by their political critics.

As UN Secretary-General Kofi Annan is fond of saying, 'We can't impose peace.' But the United Nations must be adequately funded to support peacemakers and their democratic institution-building. The evidence from Doyle and Sambanis's (2000) multivariate analysis of 124 wars of the late 20th century is that international peace operations are more likely to end violence and increase prospects of postwar democratisation when the United Nations is involved and when the operation involves a more holistic commitment to peacebuilding through multidimensional development of institutions (as opposed to just peacekeeping, as in patrolling borders and monitoring ceasefires). An objective of peacebuilding becomes to shift states out of the category where plunder is the best strategy for the acquisition of wealth and power to the category where development through peaceful trade creates the most lucrative paths to wealth and power.

Of course the worse the war has been, the more decimated the islands of civility will be and the more outside support they will need. Yet Kaldor (1999: 121) argues that there were many cases of locally negotiated peace accords between factions in South Africa, Northern Ireland, Central America and West Africa and even Somalia. They are zones of peace that can be expanded outwards into the zone of war; they are repositories of local knowledge about how to heal the conflicts at issue. The appealing thing about Kaldor's approach is that it transcends the barren stand-off between those who favour a truce and top-down structural adjustment versus defenders of humanitarianism and neutrality.

Sadly, criminalised governance in war-torn societies often appropriates humanitarianism to line its pockets. Neutrality – studiously avoiding taking sides on any controversial issue – is fine for the Red Cross, according to Kaldor, but impartiality is the principle she suggests peacemakers should follow. Impartiality means an absence of discrimination on the basis of nationality, race, religion, political party and the like, but impartiality is not neutral on the law. It stands for justice and protecting the victims of human rights abuses, for being clear that abuses of human rights are wrong and must stop.

This mirrors the distinction in the restorative justice literature between neutrality in mediation of 'conflicts' and restorative justice to right 'wrongs' of injustice. In the worst wars, islands of civility need courage and protection from outside – police protection, lawyers promising to launch war crimes prosecutions against anyone who liquidates them, perhaps regular video reports to sister NGOs outside, peacekeeper patrols around their homes. If all we promise is neutrality, then we promise them death. The United Nations ran when members of the exemplary human rights community in Rwanda were systematically assassinated after they predicted 'massive atrocities unless named perpetrators were called to account' (de Waal 1997).

That story needs to be told across international civil society, so that such desertion of human rights advocates is constituted as shameful. Kaldor (1999: 124–25) also argues that peacekeeping is not enough. What is needed is capability to enforce international humanitarian and human rights law. In the theoretical frame of responsive regulation (Ayres & Braithwaite 1992), what is needed is a capability to escalate up an enforcement pyramid from non-intervention to dialogue and preventive diplomacy, to peacekeeping, to peace enforcement (see Figure 9.1). This means mostly policing with consent rather than soldiering with force. It is what the British peacekeeping manuals describe as 'minimum necessary force', contrasted with the Weinberger/Powell doctrine of 'overwhelming force', which failed so spectacularly when applied in Somalia (Kaldor 1999: 129). It implies adopting the Brahimi Report (2000) recommendation about shifting the balance of peacekeeping personnel from military to police. The role of such police is to secure islands of civility as nodes from which peacebuilding networks are built outwards.

We don't need to stretch our imagination even as far as the troubles of failed states to understand this need. What happened after the New Orleans hurricane of 2005 was a failure of initial policing capability to secure nodes such as hospitals from which humanitarian assistance could be networked. Once the breakdown of policing allowed the gangs and the looters to take over the city, security faced an enforcement swamping problem as well as swamping by water. Humanitarian workers were kept out for want of secure nodes from which to network their assistance.

Where there are injustices in terms of breaches of international law and injustices that are root causes of a war, the difference between a restorative justice philosophy and a philosophy of peacekeeping (as in simply ending the conflict) is that the restorative justice approach demands best efforts to right the wrongs, to heal the injustices. If amnesty of a war criminal is necessary to end a war, to begin reconstruction and to right structural injustices, then such an amnesty can be justified according to a responsive theory of restorative justice. Granting amnesty to specific rapists can be necessary to preventing further rape in war; equally, promising war crimes prosecution of rapists if they walk away from the peace negotiations can deter rape. The objectives are healing survivors, prevention of rape and communication in a morally clear way that rape is never acceptable in war; the restorative justice objective is not the consistent punishment of rape.

Figure 9.1: A responsive regulatory pyramid of international diplomacy

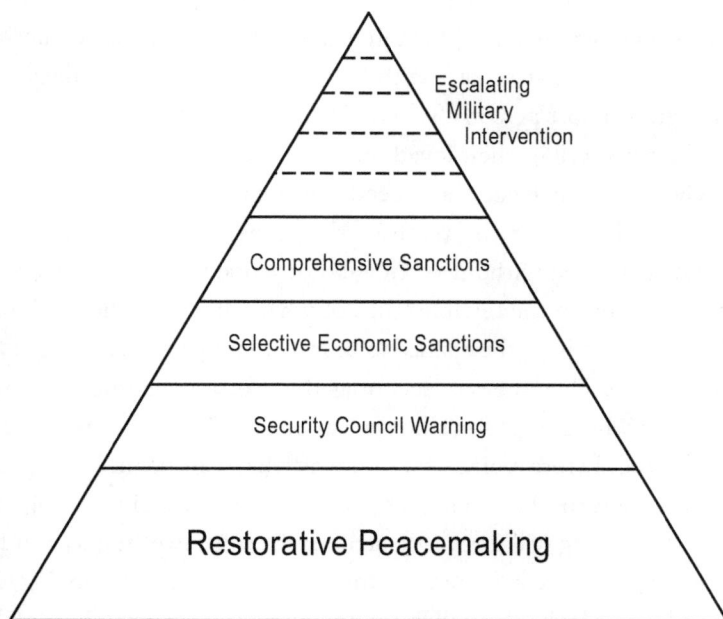

Starting up restorative justice in islands of civility

Restorative justice is a strengths-based approach. When children from a particular family are constantly in trouble with the law, the key question is not, 'What are the problems of that family and those children and how can we fix them?' It is, 'What are their strengths and how can we build upon them?' Typically, we build upon them by mobilising networks of support from the extended family, from a school community, a neighbourhood, a church community, a sporting club, who sit in the circle of a restorative justice conference. Equally, Kaldor's islands of civility strategy is a strengths-based approach. Her key question is, 'What are the locales where civil society is surviving as a foundation from which the development of peace, human rights and democratic governance can be networked? Those islands of civility might also be the locales from which restorative justice can be networked.'

Restorative justice is a process where all the stakeholders affected by an injustice have an opportunity to discuss who has been hurt by the injustice, how those harms might be repaired and how the needs of those affected might be met (Zehr 1990; Van Ness & Strong 1997; Howley 2002). With a war crime, it can mean a process like the South African Truth and Reconciliation Commission. Or it can mean restorative justice conferences conducted in ways that accord with local custom, where the alleged war criminal, with support persons from their family or tribe, sit in a circle with victims of the war crime, their loved ones, other community supporters and others who can help meet their needs through, for example, providing trauma counselling. First the truth of the crime must be confronted. In general, reconciliation without truth will not work. Once there is a certain level of agreement on the terrible truth of what happened, those who have been damaged by it have the chance to bear testimony to the nature of their family's suffering. Then they are encouraged to express their needs. Do they need to know where their son's bones can be found? Do they want him to be remembered before voices for 'putting the war behind us' prevail? Perhaps someone in the circle suggests renaming his old school in his memory so the young will forever remember the tragedy of the war and this particular victim's place in it. Perhaps they just want to hear an apology from their son's killer. Maybe that killer, for her part, wants to give them a gift in hope of healing. Perhaps they want support from the community to pay for the education of the dead man's children and the rebuilding of the house burnt down during the conflict. They might want assurances from political leaders that the political project in whose name their son was murdered is a political project that will be forever defeated in a new democracy with a new rule of law. Sometimes none of this would be enough, and the victim's family asks for support from a circle to persuade a war crimes prosecutor to mount a criminal case against one or more of the perpetrators.

Mostly, perpetrators and their supporters will come from a different community than victims and their loved ones. So a conference convened in an island of civility, where some perpetrators live, would invite victims and their families from surrounding communities to hear the terrible truth uttered in hope of reconciliation. When that reconciliation happens, a bridge is built from the island of civility to the neighbouring community. If that neighbouring community's citizens believe they benefit from the ritual of healing, their perpetrators might be persuaded to offer up their truth, apology and gifts of repair to a third community. This is the restorative justice ideal: ripples of peacebuilding moving out from islands of civility. Local creativity, and familiarity with local custom, are crucial to turning ripples into waves of peace that wash across a nation. In the Bougainville case study of such a restorative justice process discussed in the next section, music delivered by police peacekeepers was culturally important to creating pacified spaces for restorative justice; leadership from women's NGOs was also critical, as this is a matriarchal society where much of the conflict was over land, and women are the traditional custodians of the inheritance of land.

Civil war and restorative justice in Bougainville

The civil war on Bougainville concerned secession of this island from Papua New Guinea and fighting between different local factions. It has been a testing ground for a restorative justice approach to peacemaking. From the mid-1990s, women's NGOs joined hands to create ever-wider spaces for peace. They organised women's peace marches winding across long distances of the island, networking together so many women who had never met before in their shared aspirations for peace. They were a driving force for reconciliation at the crucial peace talks of the late 1990s (Sirivi & Havini 2004). Bougainville women on both sides of the conflict worked together at the Global Conference on Women in Beijing, in 1995, attracting considerable international attention with their pleas for peaceful intervention (Spriggs 2004: 122). Sirivi explains the role of reconciliation in Bougainville society very clearly:

> Reconciliation has been the mainstay of the strength of the Bougainville peace process. Ten years of war, suffering, numerous failed negotiations and peace agreements from 1989 to 1997 were more than we, the mothers of Bougainville, could bear ...
>
> Because the reconciliation process is a tried and true part of Bougainvillean culture and is integral to who we are as a people, it has come to form part of our political process. This process mends and heals, restores peace and harmony and puts relationships back in their rightful place ... Traditional processes represent a holistic approach for conflict resolution, restorative justice and reconciliation. The clan looks after its own. No matter how gross the offence, the clan will represent the offender – but the clan will also make them address their behaviour. The individual is always accountable to their family and clan. Very often, the clan will ask for some act of good faith from their erring member before they will agree to stand for the guilty and act for them in the reconciliation ...

Humility is an essential part of the process. Forgiveness must be accompanied by an acceptance of truth by all parties to create a meeting point where an agreement on compensation or atonement can be negotiated. In traditional culture, as in Christian teachings, for forgiveness to be genuine, the feelings need to be real and deeply felt from the heart. There would be no point proceeding with a ceremony if there was any doubt that one party was genuine (Sirivi & Havini 2004).

The PEACE Foundation Melanesia, funded by Caritas, the New Zealand Overseas Development Agency and the Princess Diana Fund, has given basic restorative justice training to 10,000 people on Bougainville, including 500 as facilitators (this group includes many traditional chiefs), and 50–70 as trainers (Howley 1999, 2002). Out of this, the PEACE Foundation Melanesia produced some 800 active village-based mediators to deal with the conflicts that have arisen in the aftermath of a civil war, from petty instances of ethnic abuse up to rape and political killings. The Bougainvilleans are discovering their own ways of doing restorative justice, consistent with their Melanesian principle of 'wan bel' (literally one belly), or reconciliation.

Former PEACE Foundation Director Brother Patrick Howley points out that civil war becomes an opportunity for old grievances between people that have nothing to do with the war to be acted out. Unless these conflicts are healed when the shooting stops, they may lay dormant, waiting to contribute to or escalate the next outbreak of hostilities. For example, men used the war to win old disputes over land by making allegations that their adversary was a spy, in an effort to have them killed so the land could be seized. Howley believes that the new hatreds that are most damaging for long-term peace, the hatreds that must be healed, are in the hearts of traumatised children who witnessed their parents being tortured in sadistic and degrading ways – sodomised by a rifle barrel, for example. These children need help to heal so that they do not become the avengers who cause the next war. Remarkably, Howley reports that there were cases of the civil war being used to even scores from World War II, when some Bougainvilleans helped the Japanese and others the Americans. In Bosnia such failures to heal after World War II atrocities are even more important to understanding the violence of the 1990s (Shawcross 2000: 47).

Realist international relations theorists might look at a case like 'Now Buin is moving again' and say this is not the stuff of war; this is the settling

Now Buin is moving again

Reprinted from PEACE Foundation (1999b)

In October 1998, Paul Bobby the BRA [Bougainville Revolutionary Army] Commander for Buin was shot dead in his village Kararu in Buin District. Since this incident the situation in Buin had been tense. The peace process not only halted but several ambushes and shoot-outs threatened to return Buin to the conditions of the crisis. In a wave of reprisals and counter reprisals, the ensuing 8 months saw armed clashes between the relatives, soldiers and supporters of Paul Bobby and the followers of Thomas Tarii (the other main BRA Commander in Buin). During this period the BRA splintered into factions and all efforts by the higher BRA commanders to resolve the conflict failed.

The conflict resulted in restrictions of movement especially on the Buin highway to Arawa and the strategic road to Kangu where ships are unloaded. Consequently there was a disruption to the delivery of services to the district ... Incidents of lawlessness increased especially in Buin town and a general feeling of fear and uncertainty prevailed. The conflict threatened to spread into neighbouring Siwai and Kieta districts as incidents spread ... [I]t was generally acknowledged throughout the island that this conflict represented the gravest threat to the peace process ...

[A]s the number of incidents escalated, individuals and organisations from outside the BRA became more active in trying to begin the process of reconciliation. Enormous credit should be given to the various women's groups in Buin who initiated discreet dialogue between the factions. Their efforts gradually restored a sufficient level of trust between the factions to allow them to come together for the first time to try to resolve the conflict through discussions rather than violence. With the initiative of the Telei District Peace Committee Chairman (Steven Kopana) and with the support of the [UN-backed] International Peace Monitoring Group (PMG) based in Buin, Francis Kauman and Joe Nakota were requested to mediate in the reconciliation. These two experienced PEACE Foundation Conflict Resolution trainers were recognised both for their skills and neutrality as key people in the meeting.

The reconciliation took place at the 'PMG Haus Garamut' (meeting house) in Buin High School on 21/5/99. The meeting started at 9.30 am and concluded at 4.30 pm and was witnessed by hundreds of people who had gathered from the east and the west ... After moving speeches, tears and the shaking of hands, the reconciliation concluded with the signing of a Memorandum of Understanding by the eleven BRA Company and Platoon commanders involved in the conflict. The seven points agreed to in the Memorandum of Understanding (written in Tok Pisin) state clearly the common desired goal, i.e., 'Bai yumi lusim pasin bilong fait na kirapim bek bel sis na trust namel long yumi yet' (We will reject violence and initiate again peace and trust between ourselves). The other points agreed are brief but poignant. Upon close examination they reflect a deep understanding of the root causes of the conflict and possible obstacles in implementing the agreement. This indicates that the Memorandum of Understanding was clearly agreed to after a great deal of honest and assiduous discussion ...

Whilst time will be the ultimate test of the Agreement, there is now a general feeling of relief that an encumbrance has been lifted from the people of Buin. Freedom of movement has been restored and the path has now been cleared for the establishment of a Buin Joint Police Force consisting of ex-BRA and resistance [pro-PNG] soldiers ... In his closing speech at the reconciliation Col. Edgar (CO PMT Buin) remarked that had Francis and Joe not gained these skills there couldn't have been reconciliation. In thanking Francis for his efforts, Linus Konukun, the newly elected Speaker of the recently established Bougainville Constituent Assembly, remarked 'Now Buin is moving again'.

of an insignificant factional conflict. But perhaps this perception of what is an insignificant conflict juxtaposed against real structural conflicts between a reified Bougainville Revolutionary Army and a reified Papua New Guinean state which is attributed unitary interests is the problem with realist diplomacy that occurs in places such as the White House.

This is Shearing's (1995, 1997, 2001) Hayekian critique of state plan-ning to control violence. The social engineers of statist diplomacy don't have enough local knowledge to understand the real conflicts that are touching people's lives. The conflicts on the ground are always more complex than their reifications, more rapidly changing than the intelligence reports from diplomats in air-conditioned offices can keep up with. Only indigenous ordering in a Buin schoolhouse to define the cross-cutting con-flicts in local terms will deal with the local drivers of a war. Equally, there may be geo-political dimensions of the conflict that can only be understood in the language that is spoken in a meeting between major and minor state powers in the Office of the Secretary-General of the United Nations in New York. If they want to be effective in making peace, the big-men of Buin and of New York both must learn when to defer to the local knowl-edge of the other.

The New Zealand, Australian and South Pacific military and police peacekeepers on Bougainville played a complementary role here as well. Their commanders rewarded them not so much for military accomplish-ments, such as completing patrols, but for building relationships with the people through sporting and musical events where good food and fellow-ship were provided.[1] This means a military and police presence that com-plements a restorative approach to peacekeeping, as illustrated by the role of the Peace Monitoring Group in 'Now Buin is moving again'. The peace-keepers were unarmed, a symbolism that seems to have impressed local warriors (see Keelty, Chapter 5). It is the symbolism of a pyramid of restorative and responsive regulation: 'Yes we are warriors who can call upon the firepower required to put down challenges to the peace. But we do not need it; we can do the job with good food, good music, good rela-tionships and goodwill.' Australian Foreign Affairs Minister Alexander Downer has reported how on visiting Bougainville he was moved by the reciprocal gestures of breaking of spears by warriors and spontaneous singing by women. This signifies the difference between realist elite diplo-macy and idealist peacemaking with reconciliation that touches the hearts of ordinary men and women.

Motivating the networking of democratic governance with restorative justice

There is quite a deal of evidence that top-down elite mediations initiated by presidents and foreign ministers of powerful states frequently work in brokering ceasefires. However, Touval and Zartman's research (1985, 1989) shows that top-down peacemaking is much less successful in building permanent peace, because it mostly fails to heal the hearts of people who have been pitted against one another. When there is escalation to dominated mediation in which a major power bangs the parties' heads together and the prospect of escalation beyond this is displayed, we create conditions for the de-escalation of disputing to democratised restorative justice. Co-operative peacemaking should normally be rewarded by de-escalation down the responsive enforcement pyramid. Power-based mediation can sometimes create a temporary peace that opens an opportunity for a restorative justice process to struggle for an enduring peace based on justice, healing and an ongoing commitment to preventive diplomacy. Arguably, the foreign troops and police of the Peace Monitoring Group in Bougainville did just that – they created pacified spaces, with guitars rather than guns (as documented in the film *Bougainville Sky*) so the Bougainvillean factions could meet and discover for themselves the terms of their reconciliation.

While ethnic hatreds, war and plunder are recurrently characteristic of dozens of weak contemporary states, according to my analysis they are consequences of weak institutions of governance that are denied legitimacy by their people. A peace process is actually a historic opportunity to fix institutions. Germany, Japan, Italy and Austria seized this opportunity for democratic institution-building help (with a lot of reconstruction) between 1945 and 1950. The Marshall Plan was costly to the United States, but through trade and collective security it was one of the best investments US taxpayers ever made in their own peace and prosperity.

Restorative justice may have the elements needed to transform a crisis of war into an opportunity for institutional renewal, a potential South Africa may have realised. The main reason for this is that it involves a bottom-up process that seeks to engage civil society in a discussion of the institutional renewal required to make the peace just and permanent. Working together to put the institutional problems in the centre of the circle is a good start to transcending ethnic hatreds. Global financial institutions need to be in the circle as well – listening. When asked to speak, their obligation is to say that lending and investment will not flow unless bankers see fiscal balance, an independent central bank that resists printing money to pay for private armies and like criminalisations of the state. Ultimately, structural adjustment is inevitable, but imposed structural adjustment is not. It can be explained that the new policy of the global financial institutions is for a war-wearied civil society to commit to institutions that will prevent the return of the kleptocratic state, that will replace forever the rule of armies with the rule of law. To get an excellent education system for the new generation, commitment in civil society to this goal and to a legitimate tax system to pay for it, is essential. Understanding is also essential, understanding among the people that the alternative is an inexorable slide down the slippery slope of a structural adjustment package that will cause retrenchment of teachers.

Just as we think the family crisis of arrest for a serious crime can be a resource in a restorative justice conference for finding the motivation to kick a heroin habit, so we propose that the crisis of war can be a resource for restorative justice conferences to motivate institutional renewal that transcends reliance on tyrants for protection from the ethnic other.

Finally, restorative justice may supply a valuable philosophy of diplomacy because late-modern war is a criminal matter much more than modern and early modern war was, waged more against civilian populations than against other armies. Most contemporary wars are systemically criminal and many of their root causes lie in the criminalisation of the state – the use of the institutions of the state as an apparatus of plunder, impoverishing the people and causing them to withdraw legitimacy from the state. It follows that peace is unlikely unless the people can come to terms with their anger and hatred over those crimes. Rituals are needed to heal the damaged souls of the people, to help them find ways to transform hatred into sorrow or forgiveness, to be able to move forward with hope rather than wallow in the evil of the past. Restorative traditions have been developed through the ages in all the world's cultures to help with that transition. The global social movement for restorative justice is now a rich collective memory file for retrieving bits and pieces of those traditions and putting them to use in helping people deal with their most difficult conflicts in a way that is culturally meaningful to them. Desmond Tutu (1999) is probably right that in a society torn by ethnic war there can be *No Future without Forgiveness*.

Rituals of a funeral character have a place in helping survivors put hatred aside to grieve for their people and then resolve to push on in the way their loved ones would have wanted. But if the shame of the survivors' degrada-tions is not acknowledged and discharged, if the hatred festers below the surface, when the next national crisis comes along the political niche will still be there for the demagogue to seek power by blaming the nation's woes on the evil other.

Forgiveness cannot be forced; it can only come when survivors are emo-tionally ready for it. What we can do, what the great global project for peace must do, is provide ordinary citizens with rituals which expose us personally to the sorrows and suffering of the other, and expose them to ours; rituals that create spaces where apology and forgiveness have a chance to be expressed. That is why the PEACE Foundation Melanesia is on the right track in training a thousand Bougainvillean facilitators to move around their villages convening restorative justice conferences to heal the emotional wounds of their war.

Police, security and democracy

The special competence of police in enabling restorative and responsive justice for peacebuilding is in securing pacified spaces. If necessary, though they hope force will not be needed, police stand ready to mobilise coercion to that end, up to calling in military peacekeepers with heavy weaponry. The crucial role of the police is not to create circles of reconciliation, but to secure the perimeters of such circles when they bubble up from civil society with support from outside NGOs, from the World Bank and others with the resources that count for peace. When the Bougainville Women for Peace and Freedom lead peace marches and summits, the job of the police is to ensure they are not killed. In Kaldor's broader terms, it is to ensure that islands of civility are not crushed. In responsive regulatory terms, police peacekeepers are not the primary agents of capacity-building and restorative justice at the base of a regulatory pyramid. Where they become more impor-tant is in escalating to the deterrence and ultimately the incapacitation of those who wish to mobilise violence against capacity-building and restora-tive justice. That in turn creates the conditions where warlords who fear deterrence or incapacitation decide that they can accomplish more by peace-fully joining the circle. Of course a form of capacity-building for which police peacekeepers must be more directly responsible is developing indige-nous policing to take over from them the roles discussed in this chapter.

Peace does require that sympathetic combatants be drawn into reconcil-iation processes. These key combatants who first step in to the circle can then become translators of the mentalities of the peacemakers to the mentalities of the warmakers, and vice versa. The warmakers then learn that, for example, the peacemakers have proposals for them to hand in their weapons; the peacemakers learn that the warmakers will not do that until there are certain guarantees that their voice will be heard in new political institutions that are an alternative to their guns being heard. Once the initial link has been estab-lished between peacemaking and warmaking networks, new nodes of gover-nance can be established – a working group of both peacemakers and warmakers here on weapons surrender, another there on constitutional revi-sion, another somewhere else on preparing for an election, another on food and safe transit back to their homes for hungry refugees.

As in networking islands of civility into surrounding regions of inci-vility, confidence-building is possible by acts of generosity to individuals with the courage to cross over into a peace process. That can be the gen-erosity of forgiveness, of a compensation payment, of an empathic speech, or return of land appropriated during the war. Police have an intelligence role in this confidence-building process. Their contacts with and knowledge of the warlord camps may allow them to suggest to the peacemakers who might be the individuals in the warlord camps who are ready to be the first movers across to reconciliation. If requested to assist in setting up direct peace talks between antagonistic factions, they can provide the food, the venue and the logistics for such an event. They can even provide the music!

Democratic state control of the war of all against all

States control armed conflict when they have an effective monopoly on the use of the most sophisticated armed force. But to be effective in regulating violence, the state needs more than guns. It needs a pyramid of regulatory escalation (Ayres & Braithwaite 1992). At the base of the pyramid it needs the capacity to regulate conversationally (Black 1998). To be effective at this, the state needs legitimacy in the eyes of its people (and the interna-tional community). It also needs an image of invincibility – a belief on the part of regulated actors that if they walk out on dialogue, the state will be sure to escalate its regulatory response. The state needs to be able to esca- late through various more potent forms of deterrence, until ultimately it incapacitates insurgents through imprisoning or killing them.

An invincible state will still be vulnerable to externally funded armed malcontents, however, if those malcontents do not have any capability to influence the state. It is such an ability to influence the state, especially through dialogue and elections, that constitutes state legitimacy. Actors in a differentiated civil society need access to their own regulatory pyramids, so they can regulate the state and other elements in civil society, such as a religious group that vilifies them. If the only weapon they have is to nego- tiate, if they have only a base to their enforcement pyramid without any bar- gaining chips above it, they are vulnerable to predation. If they have no base to their pyramid, only guns that give them the one big bargaining chip of war, they are liable to be predators. Indeed, the more factions there are with a capacity for armed force and without ability to influence deliberation and power-sharing, the less likely peace is (Doyle & Sambanis 2000: 789). It follows that peace is more in prospect when a rich plurality of constituen- cies in civil society, including all vulnerable ones, have an escalated set of deliberative and deterrent regulatory tools available to them, but not the tools of violence (see a dynamic powerpoint of this model at <http: //www.anu.edu.au/fellows/jbraithwaite> [all websites listed were correct at the time of writing]). Second, peace is more likely when a state with legit- imacy has available to it an escalated set of deliberative, deterrent and inca- pacitation tools.

The police and military must also be effectively regulated by the execu- tive of an elected government, by courts that are not intimidated by them, and by the consent of the people who they perceive themselves as serving. Peacebuilding is achieved by constituting a complex separation of powers in a society where each separated power has enough independence of action to regulate other powers and not so much unregulated power that it can dom- inate all other sources of power in the society. An all-powerful presidency is conductive to dictatorship, an all-powerful army to military coups, and all- conquering multinational business to economic dependency. None of these circumstances is conducive to long-run peace. Semi-autonomous police that are institutionally separate from the military are an important ingredient of such a complex separation of powers. States where power is too unitary are especially vulnerable in societies divided into two or more major ethnic groups (Maley 1995). If a unitary presidency controls all power that matters, as in Rwanda, for instance, when the Hutus control that power and exploit it for the benefit of Hutus, legitimate opportunities are blocked for others – in this instance, for Tutsis. Tutsis will then be tempted to remedy this by seeking illegitimate opportunities to seize that unitary power. State structures thus must disperse powers responsively to historical context so as to give all nations, religions and peoples within the state some meaningful sense of self-determination.

Peacebuilding in a failing state without these governance capabilities

A state can fail so badly to regulate armed violence that international intervention becomes legitimate in the eyes of its citizens, and internationally, to establish supra-national authority to prevent war. It is hypothesised that legitimacy is especially likely if the intervention is sanctioned by the United Nations. Peacekeepers only maintain that legitimacy if they are procedurally just (Tyler 1990), administratively efficient (Fishel 1998; Manwaring & Joes 2000), enabling of humanitarian assistance and long-term development, and if they eschew predation themselves (especially crimes such as rape and corruption).

Peacebuilders depend on the same capabilities to secure peace as a competent state – legitimacy, leadership, effective monopoly of armed force, responsive regulatory capability to escalate from conversational to deterrent to incapacitative regulation, professional competence and training, non-corruption, commitment to a rights culture, rule of law and procedural justice (Brahimi 2000), commitment to pluralising governance, to separations of powers, to building collective efficacy in civil society so that even formerly excluded fractions of civil society have a range of responsive capabilities to regulate the polity without armed force. The starting theory posits that peacebuilders will be effective to the extent that they enable an opening of legitimate opportunities to all sections of society and the closing to all of illegitimate opportunities to deploy armed violence. Peacebuilders can work with NGOs and UN agencies that provide humanitarian assistance with competence and in ways that do not sustain the domination of warlords (Andersen 1996).

They must work with the IMF and the World Bank, domestic econocrats, business and civil society to stabilise the economy and rebuild investment confidence. Institutional rebuilding need not be 'one-size-fits-all' (Stiglitz 2002); it can be diagnostic, identifying the bottlenecks that chill investment (Rodrik 2004). It is most likely to sustain peace when collaboratively designed by the emerging separated powers that are nurtured by the peacekeepers. The separated powers with the capacity to responsively regulate one another can be developed contextually and nodally (Shearing & Wood 2003; Drahos, Burris & Shearing 2004). This might be done by networking nodes of conversational regulation of the emerging democracy. For example, the responsive regulatory capability of local human rights NGOs can be enhanced by creating spaces where workers are safe to network with Human Rights Watch, with UN human rights officials, with journalists and women's groups sympathetic to building a rights culture.

Reintegration of combatants

Peacekeepers typically face an enforcement swamping problem. There is too much murder, rape and pillaging going on for enforcement action to be taken against even a tiny fraction of perpetrators. A clear, contextually attuned strategy is needed to resolve enforcement swamping. Usually, this will include negotiating ceasefire terms that are likely to involve qualified amnesties and protection for those who put down their guns, ignoring in the first instance enforcement against atrocities that preceded the ceasefire. This is so that enforcement can be concentrated on guaranteeing escalated action against any combatants who cross the lines in the sand drawn in the ceasefire agreement. Confidence-building is then needed, trust that peace-builders keep their guarantees, so that decommissioning of private armies can proceed. All this means a deep peace process, not one-day meetings but multiple iterations of living and negotiating together for long periods, tackling root causes of conflict in depth.

Humiliation of combatants sets back peace processes (Kennedy 1969); it is important to save face while backing down from armed confrontation (Ting-Toomey & Cole 1990). Integration with development assistance helps when it includes retraining and creating new life opportunities for combatants (Brahimi Report 2000: 8). As illegitimate opportunities to survive through violence are closed off, opportunities to survive through legitimate means need to be opened up to combatants. Trauma counselling, medical and financial help are needed for victims on all sides. This is not only important in itself; it is also vital to trust and reconciliation. Availability of restorative justice to victims and combatants may help with this (Lederach 1997). If truce agreements deliver amnesties, they can be qualified by perpetrator obligations to speak truth, listen to victims, answer their questions (Gibson 2004). Peacebuilders can deal with refusal to co-operate with reconciliation by widening the circle – progressively inviting more senior bosses of war criminals into the circle until undertakings of restorative justice, even at the price of amnesty, are secured. Without truth, testimony, memorialising loss, a hearing that takes seriously the ideas of victims for permanently suppressing the political project that vic- timised them, space for micro acts of apology and repair in local communities, national reconciliation and reconstruction, short-term ceasefires may not be consolidated into permanent peace (Braithwaite 2002: 170).

Conclusion

That is the responsive regulatory theory of how to build peace through justice. Doubtless any explanatory power it has is very partial. Doubtless systematic empirical enquiry will prove it wrong in fundamental and contex- tual ways. The above is the sketch of a starting theory that is laid out in tabular form at < http://www.anu.edu.au/fellows/jbraithwaite>.

The expectation is that the above explanatory framework for moving into this program of empirical research will be found to be wrong in some ways, in need of revision in others, and less illuminating than utterly dif- ferent frameworks for some kinds of understandings. Nevertheless, the thoughts in this chapter offer a starting framework that has some significant empirical grounding and that points towards a more evidence-based approach to building permanent peace. As it happens, police who secure networks that ripple democratic governance outwards from islands of civility are central to its vision.

Note

1   Here and in the following sentences I rely on remarks by Brigadier Bruce Oxborn, Colonel Bob Breen and Australian Foreign Minister Alexander Downer at a seminar, Monitoring Peace in Bougainville, organised by the State, Society and Governance in Melanesia Project, Australian National University, Canberra, 8 September 1999.

References

Andersen, M. (1996) *Do No Harm: Supporting Local Capacities for Peace Through Aid*. Cambridge MA: Development for Collaborative Action, Inc.

Australian Department of Foreign Affairs and Trade (1999) Approaches to peace-building and preventive diplomacy in the Asia-Pacific region, in D. Ball and A. Acharya (eds), *The Next Stage: Preventive Diplomacy and Security Co-operation in the Asia-Pacific Region*. Canberra: Australian National University.

Ayres, I. and Braithwaite, J. (1992) *Responsive Regulation: Transcending the Deregulation Debate*. New York: Oxford University Press.

Bayart, J-F., Ellis, S. and Hibou. B. (1999) *The Criminalization of the State in Africa*. Bloomington IN: Indiana University Press.

Black, J. (1998) Talking about regulation. *Public Law*, 77–105.

Brahimi, L. (2000) Comprehensive review of peacekeeping operations, UN General Assembly Security Council, 55th Sess., Agenda item 87 (provisional agenda).

Braithwaite, J. (2002) *Restorative Justice and Responsive Regulation*. New York: Oxford University Press.

de Waal, Alex (1997). *Times Literary Supplement*, 21 February.

Doyle, M.W. and Sambanis, N. (2000) International peacebuilding: A theoretical and quantitative analysis, *The American Political Science Review*, 94: 779.

Drahos, P, Burris, S. and Shearing, C. (2003, unpublished) Nodal governance as an approach to regulation.

Dupont, A. (1999) Preventive diplomacy and transnational security issues, in D. Ball and A. Acharya (eds), *The Next Stage: Preventive Diplomacy and Security Co-operation in the Asia-Pacific Region*. Canberra: Australian National University.

Fishel, J.T. (1998) 'The Savage Wars of Peace': Toward a New Paradigm of Peace Operations. Boulder CO: Westview Press.

Gibson, J.L. (2004) *Overcoming Apartheid*. New York: Russell Sage Publications.

Hampson, F.O. (1996) *Nurturing Peace: Why Peace Settlements Succeed Or Fail*. Washington DC: US Institute of Peace Press.

Hibou, B. (1999) The 'social capital' of the state as an agent of deception, in J-F. Bayart, S. Ellis and B. Hibou (eds), *The Criminalization of the State in Africa*. Bloomington IN: Indiana University Press.

Howley, P. (1999) *Report on Bougainville for the Year 1999*. Melbourne: PEACE Foundation Melanesia.

—— (2002) *Breaking Spears and Mending Hearts*. Sydney: Federation Press.

Ignatieff, M. (1999) *The Warrior's Honour: Ethnic War and the Modern Conscience*. London: Vintage Books.

Kaldor, M. (1999) *New and Old Wars: Organized Violence in a Global Era*. Cambridge: Polity Press.

Keen, D. (1998) *The Economic Functions of Violence in Civil Wars*, Adelphi Paper 320. Oxford: Oxford University Press.

Kennedy, R. (1969) *Thirteen Days: A Memoir of the Cuban Missile Crisis*. New York: W.W. Norton & Co.

Lederach, J.P. (1997) *Building Peace: Sustainable Reconciliation in Divided*

Societies. Washington DC: US Institute of Peace Press.

Maley, W. (1995) Peacekeeping and peacemaking, in R. Thakur and C.A. Thayer, *A Crisis of Expectations: UN Peacekeeping in the 1990s.* Boulder CO: Westview Press.

Manwaring, M.G. and Joes, A.J. (eds) (2000) *Beyond Declaring Victory and Coming Home: The Challenges of Peace and Stability Operations.* Westport CT & London: Praeger.

PEACE Foundation (1999a) *Report on Bougainville for the Year 1999.* Port Moresby, Papua New Guinea: PEACE Foundation Melanesia.

PEACE Foundation (1999b) *PEACE Foundation's Involvement in the Reconciliation of BRA Factions in Buin.* Port Moresby, Papua New Guinea: PEACE Foundation Melanesia.

Rodrik, D. (2004) *Rethinking Growth Policies in the Developing World.* Cambridge: Harvard University Press.

Shawcross, W. (2000) *Deliver Us from Evil: Warlords and Peacekeepers in a World of Endless Conflict.* London: Bloomsbury.

Shearing, C. (1995) Reinventing policing: Policing as governance, in Privatisierung staatlicher Kontrolle: Befunde, Konzepte, Tendenzen, *Interdisziplinare Studien zu Recht und Staat,* 3: 69–88.

—— (1997) *Violence and the Changing Face of Governance: Privatization and Its Implications.* Cape Town: Community Peace Foundation.

—— (2001) Transforming security: A South African experiment, in H. Strang and J. Braithwaite (eds), *Restorative Justice and Civil Society.* Melbourne: Cambridge University Press.

Shearing C. and Wood, J. (2003) Nodal governance, democracy and the new denizens: Challenging the Westphalian ideal, *Journal of Law and Society,* 30: 400–419.

Sirivi, Josephine Tankunani and Havini, Marilyn Taleo (eds) (2004) *...As Mothers of the Land: The Birth of the Bougainville Women for Peace and Freedom.* Canberra: Pandanus Books.

Spriggs, Ruth Saovanna (2004) Prologue: Unity in the peace process, in Josephine Tankunani Sirivi and Marilyn Taleo Havini (eds), *... As Mothers of the Land: The birth of the Bougainville Women for Peace and Freedom.* Canberra: Pandanus Books.

Stiglitz, J.E. (2002) *Globalization and Its Discontents.* New York: W.W. Norton & Co.

Ting-Toomey, S. and Cole, M. (1990) Intergroup diplomatic communication: A face-negotiation perspective, in F. Korzenny and S. Ting-Toomey (eds), *Communicating for Peace: Diplomacy and Negotiation.* Newbury Park CA: Sage Publications.

Touval, S. and Zartman, I.W. (1985) *International Mediation in Theory and Practice.* Boulder CO: Westview Press.

—— (1989) Mediation in international conflicts, in K. Kressel, D.G. Pruitt et al. (eds), *Mediation Research.* San Francisco CA: Jossey-Bass.

Tutu, D. (1999) *No Future without Forgiveness.* London: Rider.

Tyler, T. (1990) *Why People Obey the Law.* New Haven CT: Yale University Press.

UN High-Level Panel on Threats, Challenges and Change (2004) *A More Secure World: Our Shared Responsibility*. New York: United Nations (A/59/565).

Van Ness, D. and Heetderks Strong, K. (1997) *Restoring Justice*. Cinncinnati OH: Anderson Publishing.

Zehr, H. (1990) *Changing Lenses: A New Focus for Criminal Justice*. Scottsdale PA: Herald Press.

10 | THE GOVERNANCE OF POLICING AND SECURITY PROVISION

Colleen Lewis and Jennifer Wood

Introduction

The reaction by Australian governments to terrorist attacks in New York, London, Madrid and Indonesia has resulted in the granting of extraordinary powers to public police. They vary across jurisdictions, but include: preventive detention for up to 14 days; covert search warrants for police approved by a member of the executive (the courts having been removed from the process) (Hocking 2004, 2005; McSherry 2004); and the power for police to demand information in relation to a person's place of residence, telephone calls, travel and financial transactions. The person subject to such a demand is not allowed to warn others about the nature of the request for information or even that such a request has been made. Professional privilege does not apply and it can be an offence for a person to divulge that documents have been requested and obtained (Anti-Terrorism Act 2005 [Cth]). At both the state and federal level, citizens have been assured that these powers are necessary to keep Australia safe. But as Pue reminds us, 'Even law abiding citizens of democratic states need to be wary of police power' (Pue 2000: 8). The reason for this is well documented in royal commissions and commissions of inquiry in Australia and beyond.

Current debates about police powers and their governance remain central to more general discussions about ways in which to promote, and ideally guarantee, *democratic* policing in Australia and other advanced industrial nations. The reasons for this are obvious. Fear of crime and terrorism can generate all manner of practical responses from governments that may be seen as knee-jerk and populist and, in the long term, threatening to the very principles underlying liberal democratic institutions. Although there is freedom in security, there is also 'security in freedom' (Daniels, Macklem et al. 2001), and at its core, analyses of the 'war on terror' grapple with the question of how to both conceptualise and measure the security–freedom (or liberty) trade-off.

Whilst the governance of the public police and other state security agencies is perhaps now, more than ever, an issue that requires sustained attention and rigorous critique, it is equally important, we argue, to make sense of a rather more complex problem of governing the field of policing and security delivery generally; this is a field consisting of diverse formal institutions and less formal collectivities devoted to outcomes ranging from the reduction of disorder to the minimisation of terrorist threats across national borders. The preceding chapters have contributed significantly to our understanding of how policing and security are provided in 'nodal' or 'networked' environments. Although there is still much we do not know about this field, including the complex interactions between nodes and their effects, we contend, drawing on the observations of Loader (2000), Shearing (2001) and Jones (2003), that the problem of democratic governance must shift from a narrow focus on the functions of the public police to the activities and outcomes of diverse security providers, of which the public police and other state agencies (such as military institutions) are undoubtedly central players. This chapter attempts to contribute to this conceptual move from the governance of the public police to the governance of policing and security provision.[1]

Precisely how nodes and networks of security delivery are held accountable for their actions does not appear to have been subjected to rigorous scrutiny by policy-makers and law-makers (Joh 2005). Issues such as who is accountable when something goes wrong, and what level of accountability attaches to misconduct by private entities which are in effect undertaking a public function, are unclear. More fundamentally, questions pertaining to who should direct and oversee nodal policing remain under-analysed.

Central to such an analysis is a study of current forms or 'modalities' (Scott 2006) of governance as they pertain to existing security providers, be they formal or informal in an institutional sense. Scholars of policing and regulation have looked beyond traditional mechanisms of state-centred command and control governance in examining mechanisms such as con-tracts and other market-based techniques that shape the behaviour of both state and non-state service providers (Vincent-Jones 2000; Crawford 2003). They have also examined other techniques, for example the use of reputational sanctions (Gunningham, Kagan et al. 2004) or shame (Makkai & Braithwaite 1994; Braithwaite 2003) in inducing service providers to comply with particular standards of conduct.

What this literature tells us is that both the reality and the potential use of *hybrid* mechanisms and models of governance require much more atten-tion in the security context than they have received. In this article we explore ideas about hybrid or nodal governance. We do not put forward a concrete proposal, but rather make the more modest point that new designs for governance must recognise, and even embrace, plurality in the institu-tions that do, or could, play roles in 'steering' (Osbourne & Gaebler 1992) and rendering accountable the provision of security goods.

In the following section we outline established approaches to the gover-nance of state security provision with a focus on the domain of public policing. We do not intend to be exhaustive in this review, but rather to point to dominant tendencies. We then outline practical developments in public policing in different parts of the world that have served to challenge this thinking by introducing hybridity into the mix. Following this we will discuss security provision by non-state providers, drawing on examples from private policing and commercial military service delivery, to raise some gov-ernance problems related to such provision in the context of established governing modalities. We will then enter into a more general discussion of the field of security delivery and the potential for new modes of nodal gov-ernance in the future.

Governing state security provision: The case of the public police

Public police powers are extensive and potentially oppressive. They include the ability to stop, question, detain, arrest and charge a person; the ability to search and seize property; fingerprinting, photographing, DNA testing, body searches; listening to people's telephone conversations, placing listening devices in their homes, vehicles or place of work; and using force, even violence, to control a situation. Public police are able to deprive people of their freedom, their dignity and, under very extreme circumstances, their life. They have been granted these powers to help govern and protect society in general and people's individual rights; security at the accepted price of liberty. The way in which the institutions bestowing these powers ensure that citizens are protected from their misuse defines in a fundamental way the nature of a sovereign state.

A variety of institutions now participate in the governance of policing. In addition to traditional forms of vertical accountability which involve governments, parliaments and the courts, 'horizontal' accountability institutions and processes (Floroni 1999; Schedler et al. 1999), such as freedom of information, judicial review, and independent agencies that oversee the conduct of public servants (including the public police), have been established. Individual police forces and police are also held accountable through internal processes that include rules, regulations, codes of conduct and internal investigation units. In response to continuing scandals about police corruption and abuse of power, internal 'ethical standards' units have been established and/or expanded and are more adequately resourced. In some jurisdictions they are disciplining members or bringing them before the courts in greater numbers than ever before. As well, most Australian police forces have been subject to some form of external, independent oversight since 1985 (Lewis & Prenzler 1999).

The recent rapid increase in the powers granted to public police, primarily in response to terrorist attacks in America and Indonesia, has seen the start of a gradual winding back of governance in relation to public police and other public servants engaged in intelligence and security matters. The context of this winding back is relatively straightforward. The terrorist attack on the World Trade Center in New York City in September 2001 altered the way in which citizens and democratic governments perceive crime and security. Prior to this event, community safety and security were commonly linked to traditional notions of crime. Post-September 11 there has been a shift which has broadened perceptions of insecurity to include fear of terrorist attacks. Governments have enacted laws which create terrorism as a particular category of illegal behaviour, one which they say necessitates the granting of exceptional powers to public police and other security agencies. Because these powers potentially threaten sacred demo-cratic legal principles and freedoms, parliament's role in the protection of such principles and freedoms becomes critical. Parliament can act as a 'rubber stamp' for government policy, or as a 'deliberate assembly' (Uhr 1998). The former suggests a timid, lazy or uninterested parliament (or a combination of all three), whereas the latter reflects a parliament which takes seriously its role in monitoring and ensuring Australia's commitment to its own democratic norms.

The integrity, and ultimately the future, of parliament as a governance institution, is now challenged more than ever. At the same time, there is much more at play, and much more at stake when it comes to the protection of dem-ocratic norms in the field of security delivery. There is much that is happening behind the scenes in terms of institutions and practices of security delivery. These developments, and their implications, are given short shrift partly because they fall outside established understandings of security provision and established understandings of how such provision should be governed.

In the following section we discuss issues of governance in relation to new forms of state-sponsored security delivery, which involve both state and non-state providers, as well as developments in security delivery that are authorised and sponsored by non-state institutions. The third section of this chapter will explore conceptualisations of hybrid governance that may have the potential to inform normative responses to issues associated with nodal security provision.

Nodal security provision:
State and non-state developments

Several chapters in this collection seek to describe and explain the emer-gence of nodal or networked policing and security delivery in light of con-temporary security challenges (Dupont, Chapter 2; Keelty, Chapter 5; Wardlaw and Boughton, Chapter 6; Wood, Chapter 11). Some examine the challenges involved in making networks function well, both in the short and the long term (Rhodes, Chapter 1; Fleming, Chapter 4). Other contrib-utors explore new ways of conceptualising networks in furtherance of diverse security delivery outcomes (Bradley et al. Chapter 8; Braithwaite 9).

This section explores some of the challenges and governance implica-tions of pluralisation in security provision. In the context of the analyses provided by our co-contributors, we would suggest that there are at least two stories to tell about the de-centring or pluralisation of security provision (Shearing & Wood 2000). The first story – and the dominant one to date – is a neo-liberal (O'Malley & Palmer 1996; O'Malley 1997) or 'new regulatory' (Braithwaite 2000) narrative about state devolution. It is a story about the particular mentalities and practices involved in a shift away from state provision of security goods and towards the governance of provision undertaken by non-state actors and/or devolved state actors to whom responsibility has been delegated.

The second story moves us beyond state-led devolution to a story of the 'steering' and 'rowing' (Osbourne & Gaebler 1992) being undertaken by a variety of actors within and across public, private and other non-governmental sectors (Parker & Braithwaite 2003). The de-centring or pluralisation of the provision of security goods has thus been the outcome not only of explicit state actions and agendas, but also of private actors taking on roles – in both the provision of security goods and its governance (Hermer et al. 2005).

Mapping policing and security provision

The contemporary world of multiple providers is characterised by numerous developments at local, national and transnational/global levels, some of which are captured in the previous chapters. Programs of 'responsibilisation' (O'Malley & Palmer 1996), for example, include all manner of 'community policing' initiatives devoted to creative problem-solving and crime prevention. The classic example in this regard is the mandatory reporting of suspicious conduct, ranging from child abuse and neglect to unusually high financial transactions. Such state-led initiatives fall rather easily under the heading of 'rule at a distance' (Latour 1987; Rose & Miller 1992) programs – about which we have more to say later – whereby states explicitly co-ordinate and authorise the security-producing activities of actors ranging from civil society groups to private corporations.

One can add to this picture the 'quiet revolution' (Shearing & Stenning 1981, 1983) in private policing, whereby private 'rowing' has been sponsored and 'steered' by both public and 'private governments' (Macauley 1986; Shearing 2006). Private governments are *enabled* or at least tacitly supported by state law such as that pertaining to private property, whereby owners are given the authority to operate as auspices of governance within their private spaces (Shearing & Stenning 1981, 1983). In the case of transnational private policing, private authority is global in reach, spanning the sovereign jurisdictions of territorially based governments (Hall & Biersteker 2002).

We continue to have 'poor analytical maps' (Joh 2005: 576) of private security provision, which limits our ability to identify and assess issues of democratic governance (Sarre & Prenzler 1999; Sklansky 2006). What we can say in the context of local security provision – and increasingly also in respect of national and global security – is that 'it is increasingly difficult to identify policing tasks and responsibilities which are the exclusive preserve of public rather than private police' (Stenning 2000: 326). We do know that private security provision involves a plethora of activities carried out by individuals and a multitude of small businesses, corporations and multinational companies and that their involvement in policing is becoming pervasive (Shearing & Stenning 1981; 1987; Kempa et al. 1999; Rigakos 2002; Wakefield 2003; Crawford et al. 2005; Hermer et al. 2005; Prenzler 2005; Joh 2005).

Analyses to date have attempted to distinguish private from public providers of security according to different dimensions. One such dimension is legal authority and power. For instance, private police do not have the same statutory coercive powers as those bestowed on public police. Nevertheless, as Stenning (2000: 333) notes, while they are different in fundamental ways, 'the legal powers available to private police frequently provide them with the authority for substantial intrusion on the privacy and liberty of individuals (such as random surveillance and searches) which we typically deny to the public police in democratic societies'. In private sector workplaces, for example, employees can be subject to intrusions by private sector agents – through, for example, access to employees' computers – which would not normally occur through the actions of public police (Joh 2005: 604).

Private police have considerable legitimate powers derived from private contracts and exercised in the policing of private property (Stenning 2000: 322) and mass 'communal spaces' (Kempa, Stenning et al. 2004; Hermer, Kempa et al. 2005) to which members of the public have access. For example, private police are able to deny people right of entry, they can search a person's bags as they enter or leave a department store, and they can eject them from a shopping complex (Wakefield 2003; Hermer, Kempa et al. 2005; Joh 2005). The privatisation of some buses, trains and airlines has seen the introduction of laws and regulations which give private police the power to question and detain, to search personal property, and to deny people access to transport. They can also exercise coercive power in relation to laws which govern employer–employee relations (Stenning 2000: 322).

By focusing analytically on differences in formal legal authority, one undoubtedly fails to capture the empirical realities of those 'informal' practices that both public and private police undertake within the discretionary spaces available to them and in accordance with the non-legal powers available in their 'toolkits', such as those emanating from their symbolic authority (Mopas & Stenning 2001). At the same time, some scholars (Shearing & Stenning 1983, 1985, 1987; Johnston 1999, 2000; Johnston & Shearing 2003) have stressed the importance of distinguishing public and private policing in terms of the mentalities and associated goals (Joh 2005) underlying their respective security practices. Essentially, private security providers are concerned with loss-reduction through risk-reduction technologies, while public police retain a backward-looking orientation centred on upholding laws and righting past wrongs by bringing offenders to justice (Johnston & Shearing 2003).

This distinction between mentalities, as a way of drawing a conceptual line between private and public providers, is proving increasingly inadequate. It is not simply the case that security technologies and practices can be understood by looking at who sponsors provision (corporate versus state institutions, for instance) and what their goals are (Joh 2005: 592). There is, rather, hybridity in mentalities and practices. It is increasingly apparent, for example, that public police organisations have adopted ways of thinking about security delivery that originated in the private sector. The adoption of risk-based thinking is a case in point, and can be illustrated in 'community policing' programs (Shearing 1997) and, in particular, initiatives such as 'zero tolerance' policing (Johnston 1997; Herbert 2001; Johnston & Shearing 2003). At the same time, private providers, in some cases, adopt a 'punishment mentality' (Johnston & Shearing 2003) whereby particular security objectives are met through criminalisation and the use of criminal justice processes: in efforts to control 'cybercrime' (Wall in press), for example. Mentalities and practices from private and public security providers and sponsors thus mix and meld (Johnston 2000; Braithwaite 2003), which poses a challenge for those concerned with keeping our analytical maps of the security field up to date.

Where this strategic and ideological melding is perhaps most stark is in regard to the exercise of violence. Whilst the classic Weberian conception of the state has centred on its monopoly over legitimate violence, this core essence of public governance is increasingly challenged by what Avant (2005) characterises as a 'market for force'.

The 'marketization of violence' is not simply about non-state entities exercising violence on behalf of states (Singer 2001: 208–209). The interests that lie behind the exercise of force do not derive from state-centred concerns with national identities or political affiliations, or even the physical integrity of nation states. Since the private military industry is an 'independent, globalized supplier operating beyond any one state's domain' (Singer 2001: 208), clients ranging from individuals to corporations to states and international organisations engage private military firms (PMFs) for a multitude of purposes (Singer 2001: 189). Clients are not necessarily of legal origin or character either. While private actors have long participated in warfare (Singer 2001: 190–91), it is the 'modern corporate business form' (Singer 2001: 191) that features centrally in contemporary military service delivery.[2]

The capacities and resources available to state military organisations have not proven sufficient in the context of the 'new wars' (on the 'new wars', see Kaldor 1999; Duffield 2001). It is now the case that skills and technologies developed in the corporate sector, by civilians, are increasingly required in military efforts, such as extensive systems that support fighting, weaponry and other activities associated with the use of coercion (Singer 2001: 195). Here we find another example of hybridity in security provision, as capacities and resources flow between public and private actors.

As we have suggested, private actors do not simply participate in supporting state military organisations while the latter exercise violence in the name of state or 'homeland' security. Johnston points out rather that 'governments are now turning to contractors for operational services that either require or make more likely their use of force' (2006:44). In the case of Iraq, for example, the interrogation of prisoners is itself not the legitimate monopoly of state military operatives. Out of the 37 interrogators working at Abu Ghraib Prison, 27 were employees of CACI International, a private contractor based in Virginia (Johnston 2006). Thus the use of violence reflects a security delivery mentality that is shared across public and private actors both nationally and transnationally; risk-based thinking and associated technologies (in areas such as intelligence gathering and surveillance) flow between the sectors as well (Johnston 2006).

Acknowledging hybridity in the mentalities and practices of security delivery does not require one to assume that there are no differences between public and private actors in policing or in military service provision. Rather, one is simply reminded to allow as much nuance as possible when developing explanatory maps of the security delivery field. While Joh (2005) attempts to advance this mapping exercise in the context of policing, Singer's work provides a useful typology in regard to private involvement in military service provision. He suggests that the private military industry consists of three types of firms: (1) military provider firms, (2) military consulting firms, and (3) military support firms.

Military provider firms operate at a tactical level and participate in operations that may require some element of coercion (Singer 2001: 201). In contrast to military provider firms, military consulting firms do not engage in combat: they offer a range of training and advisory services at strategic, operational and organisational levels. Such firms, Singer explains 'can reshape the strategic and tactical environments' (2001: 201). Military support firms provide 'rear echelon and supplementary services' rather than participating in strategic or tactical planning and/or operations. Services include logistical and technical support and transportation (Singer: 2001: 202).

In view of the above kinds of developments, one can assert that policing and security provision are undertaken through various nodes, which originate in the public sector (typically, police and military), the private sector, and other parts of civil society, including community groups. In many, but not necessarily all, cases, nodes come together in the form of security delivery networks. These are constituted in different ways, ranging from co-operative strategic partnerships such as 'community policing' to contractual arrangements between sponsors and providers. Given what we know about the nodal field of security provision, how do we approach the governance question? In what ways is it possible to shape the arrangements and practices of multiple nodes in ways that conform with various standards of conduct, particularly those that concern the protection of democratic principles? In the following section we outline some established critiques of existing governance mechanisms before we discuss the future (or more appropriately, possible futures) for the governance of nodal and networked policing and security provision.

Governing nodes of policing and security

As noted above, public police are now subject to several layers of accounta-bility. The governance of public policing has also evolved in other ways. Just as we see in the case of provision arrangements, the governance of that pro-vision has hybridised through the incorporation of mentalities and practices associated with private sector governance into public sector thinking.

Through a neo-liberal lens one can find newly 'responsibilised' actors, as well as existing state providers, being governed through existing structures and mechanisms which have been transformed according to a 'new manage-rial' logic (McLaughlin & Murji 1995, 1997). Metaphors from the world of business now inspire attempts to govern local providers of policing and security 'at a distance' (Latour 1987; Rose & Miller 1992), through tech-nologies such as 'business plans' and 'performance indicators' (Wood 2000) and audits (Power 1997). In line with conceptions of the 'bottom line' and 'core business', police organisations are required to engage in practices of 'commensuration' (Espeland & Stevens 1998) that aim to quantify security delivery practices and processes in order to demonstrate the achievement of particular outcomes. The 'Compstat' model (Bratton & Knobler 1998) is emblematic of this infusion of a results-based, business mentality into the public sector. Operational commanders are in effect required to operate small crime-reduction businesses that are accountable to the broader objec-tives of the policing corporation through a rigorous process of accounting for the achievement (or lack thereof) of crime-reduction targets.

One can also find an increasing reliance on contractual arrangements for the delivery of state-sponsored services; this too can be seen as part of the neo-liberal or new regulatory story. State institutions, like police depart-ments, 'farm out' the provision of services to private entities that are gov-erned through the terms of their contract. The increasing prominence of 'contractual governance' (Crawford 2003) represents not simply a men-tality shift in the public sector, but rather, 'as metaphor and instrument, ... a pre-eminent form of social regulation in today's individualistic consumer age' (Crawford 2003: 480). As part of this 'consumer age', diverse sponsors of services are governing the provision of particular goods through contrac-tual arrangements. Included in this are Business Improvement Districts (Murphy 1997) that establish their own tax base for security, and residen-tial communities who engage 'private cops on the block' (Noaks 2000).

Private governance authorities thus come in many forms, and are often participating in forms of 'regulated self-regulation' (Crawford 2003). Shopping mall owners, for example, enlist the services of private policing companies through contractual relationships and govern that provision through the terms and conditions set out in the contracts. At the same time, these private auspices are governed by state authorities through instruments such as criminal law, as well as by private authorities such as insurance companies, who require owners of mass private spaces to provide a certain level of security in return for insurance coverage.

Just as neo-liberal managerial reforms were designed to address inadequacies in established public sector governance, purely market-based governance mechanisms have been seen as grossly inadequate in respect to service delivery standards and other process-level standards that have been the preoccupation of public sector governance. From this perspective, it is perhaps the 'mix that matters' (Fleming & Rhodes 2005), rather than one governance form being naturally more effective and democratic than the other.

It is nevertheless common practice to compare the governance of private policing with the governance of public policing and to find the former considerably problematic. The evidence to support this comparison and the conclusions it generates is compelling. Like public police, private police, for example, have been subject to allegations of corruption and misconduct. For instance, private security guards have been involved in shooting incidents causing death and injuries to others and themselves, fraudulent behaviour, improper behaviour with public police, and the illegal accessing of information. Some private agents involved in misconduct scandals have been former police officers (Prenzler & Sarre 1998; Prenzler & Sarre 1999; Prenzler & King 2002). Other concerns pertain to the lack of education standards and the resulting poor pay, limited career paths and high turnover (Zedner 2006).

We now find these kinds of critiques aimed at private military service providers. In particular, the contractual governance of such services is seen as replete with gaps and leaks. For example, it is argued that the monitoring of outsourced services is compromised in the first instance by a lack of timely and comprehensive information regarding such services as they are delivered on a daily basis. Oversight, particularly of an 'extraterritorial' nature, is difficult in the 'fog of war' (Singer 2001: 203). Contractual arrangements can also involve third parties as recipients of services, which can complicate the oversight process. It is sometimes the case that the recipients of services are different from the parties that contracted the services, as in instances where PMFs are contracted by states to supply personnel on their behalf to international organisations (Singer 2001: 205).

The possibility that private military firms will fail to meet their contractual obligations altogether is a concern. If firms identify heightened levels of risk in terms of their financial operations or in terms of physical risks to their assets and/or personnel, and they fail to fulfil their contractual obligations, there are currently no severe consequences for them. Whilst it would not be in the interests of firms to jeopardise their reputations through such non-compliance, Singer points out that 'there are a number of situations in which short-term considerations could prevail over long-term market punishment' (Singer 2001: 205–206).

When inappropriate or abusive conduct on the part of private actors has been exposed, there has been clear evidence of such behaviour being rendered accountable (or not) according to different standards and mechanisms from those used in the governance of state military personnel. As widely seen in newscasts across the world, seven reservists accused of malpractice at Abu Ghraib Prison faced criminal trials, while civilian interrogators escaped such scrutiny (Singer 2001: 214; Johnston 2006: 44). There are many other related governance problems in military service provision, and they are captured extensively by scholars such as Avant (2005), Singer (2001, 2003) and Johnston (2006).

In the midst of these kinds of concerns, there have been attempts at governance reform. In the case of private policing, both governance authorities and service providers have not fundamentally challenged the market-based character of their arrangements. Rather, reforms have taken place within a market-based paradigm and have been devoted to improving the standards, professionalism and legitimacy of private actors and the services they provide.

In an effort to improve the reputation of private policing in Australia, the security industry has implemented forms of self-regulation. The government too has imposed accountability processes which will help set minimum standards of behaviour. The Olympic Games in Sydney in 2000, which by necessity required the establishment of several policing networks, prompted the NSW government to introduce legislation which required all those involved in private policing and security to be licensed. They were also required to pass stringent entrance requirements and to adhere to particular performance standards (Prenzler & Sarre 1998, 1999).

In Victoria, Australia, new laws which came into effect in July 2005 (through the Private Security Act 2004) are designed to raise industry standards, increase public confidence in the private security industry and assist in improving public safety. Several occupations within the private policing industry are affected by the new laws, including security guards, crowd controllers, investigators (formerly inquiry agents) and bodyguards. Those working in these occupations will be required to obtain licences. Private security business wishing to contract out the services of these people will also require a licence. If individuals or businesses wish to operate as security advisers or installers of security equipment, or want to hire out the services of other persons operating in these capacities, they will have to obtain registration (see <http://www.police.vic.gov.au/content.asp?Document_ID=109> [all websites listed were correct at the time of writing]).

The fact that market-based security provision remains unchallenged at an ideological level is something that continues to worry some commentators. Zedner warns, for example, that neo-liberal states are less devoted to constituting ethical markets for security delivery than they are to being 'pimps' to the security industry (Zedner 2006:279). She is also cautious about the motives of individual customers of security, who can be compelled to engage in 'grudge purchases' due to pressures from insurance providers or due to public relations concerns. In this way, customers are less concerned with policing as a public good and more concerned with minimising their own security costs (Zedner 2006:271).

Zedner's comments point to the gravity of the 'security goods problem' when considered within a 'state versus market' conceptual frame. It may be the case that within a neo-liberal environment, states have become 'pimps' to market institutions and that 'public goods' – as we have traditionally conceived them – are disintegrating through new security delivery arrangements that both reflect and reinforce new conceptions of 'club goods' (Crawford 2006) or 'common goods' (Shearing & Wood 2003). We would argue instead that the future of governance is a normative matter that can only be settled by rethinking the state-versus-market dichotomy, as scholars of regulation have been suggesting for some time now (Grabosky & Braithwaite 1993). In other words, the normative question should be something like, 'What mix of governance mechanisms might best contribute to the protection of fundamental democratic principles like equity, fairness, access to justice, and human rights whilst at the same time allowing innovative arrangements to "bubble up" (Braithwaite, Chapter 9) in ways that acknowl-edge local needs and preferences?" In the final section of this chapter we examine some ideas in this regard. Our goal, as previously indicated, is not to propose an over-arching solution to this problem, but to suggest that there may be spaces for innovation that call for further exploration.

Where to from here? Thinking about nodal governance

An important point that scholars of regulation increasingly make is that it is not simply state agencies that can, or should, act as central auspices of governance (Black 2000; Scott 2000, 2002, 2004; Parker & Braithwaite 2003). As Drahos puts it, 'Theories recognizing that regulation is more than a two-actor play and making a virtue of regulatory innovation are more likely to be able to provide strategies for dealing with problems relating to the supply and maintenance of public goods' (2004: 323–24). One means of moving beyond a two-actor play is to take a 'de-centred' approach: that is, to assume that a return to a state-centred model of hierarchical, top-down, command and control governance is no longer conceivable. Rather, models of hybrid, de-centred or nodal governance, carried out by actors across sectors, all with their own distinct qualities and strengths and weaknesses, should be calibrated and co-ordinated in ways that maximise the effective-ness of a governance regime as a whole. Whilst each of the parts is limited, the assumption is that individual weaknesses will be cross-checked by other parts of the governance network (Scott 2000; Goodin 2003).

In the field of policing and security, state actors have begun to recognise this. In Australia, for example, the Victorian government has pointed out that a 'monolithic command and control' approach is unlikely to work in the networked management environment that is a feature of anti-terrorism policy. The Secretary of the Victorian Department of Premier and Cabinet, Terry Moran, suggests:

> a more networked management arrangement which takes advan-tage of existing agencies and so forth at both levels of govern-ment, where relationships between them are well established and trialled through various exercises ... our experience is that that works reasonably well (Joint Standing Committee on Foreign Affairs, Defence and Trade 2003: 67).

This kind of approach is inclined towards a 'meta-governance' model (see Grabosky 1995; Parker 2002) whereby providers of policing and security are – despite the nodal and networked character in which they are organised – ultimately responsible to a singular set of norms and standards as set down by government. One can understand the role of parliament in this light. It is the responsibility of democratically elected parliaments to ensure that executive power is kept in check and decisions to grant exceptional powers to public police and government security agencies, for example, are open and inclusive. Parliaments have an established and proven process which allows them to do this: the committee process. In circumstances where a parliament is considering something as fundamental as whether citizens' civil rights and the rule of law are to be compromised, the committee process should be used. It provides the opportunity for many voices to be heard: those who support the proposed laws and those who do not. It also promotes discussion and communication across disciplines, professions and sectors (Lewis 2000: 37) and can lay the foundation for a networked approach to the implementation of an over-arching policing policy.

The meta-governance concept is consistent with Loader and Walker's argument for an 'anchored pluralism' (2006), whereby the state 'should remain the anchor of collective security provision' (2006: 194). This does not suggest, however, that forms of non-state governance would not be recognised, valued, even encouraged by the state as meta-governor (Loader & Walker 2006: 194). The meta-governance framework should rather allow for provision and governance arrangements that arise out of the innovative practices of state and non-state actors. In this regard, Loader and Walker stress that the state must remain an active guardian of the public interest:

> [T]he aim of the state is both positive and negative. Positively, it is to ensure the widest possible community consistent with the minimum affective ties necessary to deliver the regulatory and cultural infrastructure of a single security space with all the risk-reducing and fear-abating benefits that such a common security environment can bring ... Negatively, it is to ensure that other ordering and cultural sites ... do [their ordering] in a way which does not frustrate the attainment of a more inclusive regulation of security and security of regulation, either through regulatory norms which contradict the wider regulatory field or through forms of parochial solidarity which may be inconsistent with

membership of the wider security community, or indeed, with the equal security of their own members. The challenge remains one of finding the necessary commitment and institutional imagina-tion to strike the optimal balance (Loader & Walker 2006: 195).

Shearing and Wood reassert that the future of governance does not rest with a contest between the state and the market (see Grabosky & Braithwaite 1993). Markets are constituted, just as states are, through the governance regimes they are subject to (Shearing 1993). In other words, the debate can no longer be one about unfettered free market capitalism versus overly interven-tionist states that quash the spirit of entrepreneurialism. Rather, 'There is no unconstituted market to which to turn nor is there market ordering that will relieve us of the task of regulation' (Shearing 1993: 72).

At local levels, new ways of constituting more ethical markets for policing and security have been explored. For example, the Independent Commission on Policing for Northern Ireland (Independent Commission on Policing for Northern Ireland 1999), recommended a shift from a Police Board concept to a Policing Board concept to capture the reality of nodal policing and to ensure that members of that board would have a say not only in the allocation of public police resources, but also in the distribution of security resources more generally.

For Shearing, who was a member of the Independent Commission, this conceptual move to policing must be accompanied by a shift in the way budgets are conceived and allocated. In order for the people of Northern Ireland – represented by the Policing Board – to take advantage of what policing and security nodes can offer, they must have access to budgets (even nominal in the first instance) that can provide them with choice. In other words, they must have the opportunity to participate – albeit to a limited extent – in markets for policing and security. This would occur within an established meta-governance framework.

The idea of 'security budgets' has been explored elsewhere. In the UK context, Crawford and colleagues report that 'increasingly, local authorities are devolving certain budgets to neighbourhood committee structures, often including a community safety or security element, thus giving local people a greater say over how additional security is to be provided' (2005: 81). The city of Leeds, for example, is broken down into area committees, each of which has access to a 'wellbeing' budget. While these budgets must be spent in ways that contribute to council objectives, a certain degree of flexibility in their allocation is devolved to the committee structures. Such committees decide, for example, whether to spend money on neighbour-hood wardens or on community support officers (Crawford et al. 2005: 82). The authors point out that one advantage of the 'security budget' approach is that they 'invest a novel degree of local ownership over the purchased policing resource. They potentially allow for a re-engagement on the part of communities with locally based policing processes' (Crawford et al. 2005: 82).

The overall distribution of policing and security resources in society reflects deep inequities in wealth that are being exacerbated by the engine of capitalism in today's consumer culture. In light of this, it is arguably not enough to devolve some relatively modest budgets to local committee struc-tures within a meta-governance framework. One possibility is to explore ways to enhance the buying power of poor and marginalised groups that are otherwise left to deal with the consequences of decisions made by more vocal, articulate and wealthy members of society. In this vein, Bayley and Shearing imply that it is not markets themselves that are essentially prob-lematic. Rather, it is the ways in which they are constituted that generate bad outcomes for the poor. One way out of this, they suggest, is to provide block grants to particular communities to allow them to participate more effectively as customers in the policing and security market (Bayley & Shearing 1996). While this idea remains largely at a conceptual level, it is based on the assumption that states – at least in the first instance – would be required to provide such block grants. The assumption therefore is that the security *distribution* problem is a problem for which the state, as pro-tector of the public interest, is ultimately responsible.

The meta-governance idea – captured in the notion of an 'anchored pluralism' – provides a relatively neat and elegant means of tackling the governance problem, at least at local levels. At the transnational level, the picture is a bit more blurry. In the case of military service provision, a range of very powerful (as well as some less powerful) actors in state, cor-porate and non-governmental sectors participate as consumers in increas-ingly sophisticated markets. Powerful groupings, such as transnational corporations, have enormous buying power. We could further extrapolate from Zedner and suggest that some states do act as 'pimps' to transna-tional security markets due, for example, to their own interest in reaping the benefits of overseas economic investment.

That aside, there remains the challenge of governing the *conduct* of private actors at both local and transnational levels, conduct which may be in breach of democratic norms such as those associated with the protection of human rights. In the military context, Singer argues that it is the diffusion of responsibility among corporate actors for the provision of services that significantly compromises the governance of their conduct. It remains unclear which entity/ies is/are responsible for monitoring corporate conduct and carrying out appropriate sanctions or other regulatory measures (Singer 2001: 215). Responsibility for corporate conduct is further diffused at the level of those actors that pay for, and subsequently 'steer' security provision. As indicated above, it is not simply states that contract military services from private providers. A plethora of private actors, ranging from companies like Shell and British Petroleum to international non-government organisations, purchase security either directly or through the financing of state-sponsored security (Avant 2005).

If we consider the meta-governance idea in the transnational area, one can begin by appealing to the evolution of transnational normative standards, such as those pertaining to human rights, that are influencing various areas of regulation and shaping the practices of new types of transnational governance authorities. Such norms are not tightly linked with the territorial interests of nation states, but rather reflect, as well as constitute, a burgeoning 'global civil society' (Kaldor 2003). With that in mind, while our present concern may be to build a transnational ethic guiding the field of policing and security, and informing its governance (Sheptycki & Goldsmith in press), there are developments in other areas of regulation from which we may be able to draw inspiration.

The introduction of laws which govern the behaviour of individuals and businesses engaged in private policing has prompted attempts at greater self-regulation by the private security industry (Prenzler & Sarre 1998, 1999; Sarre & Prenzler 2005; <http://www.police.vic.gov.au/content.asp?Document_ID=109>). On the subject of self-regulation, general advances in regulatory theory are useful. Scholars have pointed out for some time now that the motivations of organisations to comply with ethical and other standards of conduct are many and varied, and cannot simply be traced to rational-choice type decisions. In the field of environmental regulation, Gunningham and colleagues' work reveals very clearly that the desire of companies to be reputable as ethical actors can trump even profit-making motives (Gunningham, Kagan et al. 2003; Gunningham, Kagan et al. 2004). Furthermore, it has been shown that non-government organisations can exercise considerable power in inducing compliance with normative standards through shaming and other measures targeted at corporate reputation (Grabosky 1994; Gunningham, Kagan et al. 2003; Gunningham, Kagan et al. 2004).

Furthermore, regulatory theory tells us that there is a role for non-state actors in manipulating complex motives towards collective ends. Scott reminds us of a 'neglected facet of contemporary governance': the governance of the public sector by private actors. He argues that whilst analysts of the new regulatory state have focused on regulatory change within government, there has also been a trend towards the regulation of state actors by non-state actors, particularly firms and non-government organisations (Scott 2002). One of the reasons such private governance has escaped the gaze of scholars is because in some contexts the activities in question may not be formally understood as regulation, though they are nonetheless regulatory in their effects in terms of standard-setting, monitoring, sanctioning or other actions designed to achieve compliance of state actors. A simple example can be found in international non-government organisations such as Amnesty International, Transparency International and Greenpeace International, all of which aim to promote global standards of conduct that are not tied to particular national concerns or interests (Scott 2002: 60).

If we draw inspiration from regulatory arenas outside the security field, we thus may come to the same conclusion as Johnston, who, in the context of transnational security governance, suggests that 'there are no immutable contradictions between the objectives of commercial, civil and collective partners' (2006: 34), and further that 'strategies for the democratic governance of transnational commercial security are bound to involve both state and non-state auspices' (2006: 51). This is not to suggest that a meta-governance framework is not desirable, but rather that it is more desirable, and – perhaps more importantly – more realistic, to conceptualise such a framework in terms of a strong, yet skeletal one that both supports and encourages nodal governance.

If one thinks nodally about the future of governance, it would therefore seem sensible not to develop a one-size-fits-all solution to current weaknesses in governance regimes. Rather, one would be required to conduct extensive 'maps' of security provision and its governance in particular local, national and transnational contexts. These maps could then inform an assessment of how particular governance mechanisms can be strengthened, both individually and collectively, in terms of how they can be co-ordinated and calibrated.

One particular means of guiding this calibration exercise is to assess weaknesses and failures in governance regimes from the perspective of what they provide in 'upwards' or vertical governance, 'horizontal' governance' and 'downwards' governance, levels we briefly mentioned in the first section of this chapter. This framework draws from Scott's extension (2000) of Elcock's work (1997) on 'upwards', 'outwards' and 'downward' accountability. 'Upwards' governance can include the accountability and control of providers and distributors of security to 'higher' authorities, such as parliament in a national context or supra-state organisations in a global context. 'Horizontal' governance can involve governance by 'parallel' authorities, such as other service providers and distributors within a market-based setting, and 'downwards' governance could entail governance by lower-level organisations, committees or other groups, such as consumers or everyday citizens (Scott 2000: 42). As part of such an assessment exercise one would examine the different governance modes in operation (as revealed through the mapping process) in order to think creatively about how to enhance them, such as by improving how they operate or by introducing new modes into the mix to strengthen hybridity in the system as a whole.

In summary, our argument is that new conceptual directions with respect to the future of policing and security governance must be pursued more vigorously than they have been to date. We have not aimed to provide concrete proposals of any sort, but rather to suggest that there is much that we can take inspiration from in thinking normatively about today's nodal world of provision, distribution and governance of security goods. We can draw inspiration from policing scholars themselves, such as Loader and Walker, who advance the notion of 'anchored pluralism'. More broadly, there is much we can learn from regulatory theory, which reminds us that motivations of service providers to comply with normative standards of conduct are complex, and that hybrid governance systems that involve the participation of diverse governance authorities are perhaps the most robust systems that we can have. To come back to Joh (2005) then, we must first get our analytical maps right and then move forward with conceptual frames that provide us with the greatest potential to be innovative in our governance model-building efforts.

Conclusion

In this chapter we have stressed that 'there is much more to the regulatory process than the activities of governments' (Grabosky 1997: 197). Just as policing and security provision are performed by a multitude of actors within and across the public–private divide, so too is the governance of policing and security, both now and in the future. The contemporary litera-ture on policing and security has focused primarily on describing and explaining the ways in which the provision of order and security has been gradually reconfigured within our nodal or networked era. The chapters in this book seek to further contribute to this explanatory work. The question of what has been happening, or perhaps more importantly, what *should* be happening to governance in this nodal or networked context, has received much less attention (as exceptions, see Loader 1999; Johnston, 2000; Shearing 2001; Kempa & Johnston 2005).

More empirical research is needed to determine how nodes and net-works of policing and security operate so that appropriate governance solu-tions can be designed and implemented. What we know from our current explanatory maps is that there is hybridity in the governance arrangements that already exist, involving mixes of command and control mechanisms, market-based incentives and other mechanisms for inducing compliance on the part of targeted actors. Recent transformations in governance have emerged in some cases as rather linear trajectories of a broader logic or rationality, such as neo-liberalism, while in other cases inventions have emerged as rather *ad hoc* contingent experiments undertaken by practical actors as they seek to both manoeuvre through and constitute the nodal field of policing and security provision. As part of such innovations, authority to govern has been delegated or otherwise dispersed through various processes, ranging from legislative change to new contractual rela-tions (Scott 2000) to 'commodification' (Loader 1999).

Our broader point, consistent with the work of scholars such as Goodin (2003), is that each governance strategy or regime is, in its own way, limited and insufficient. The challenge of how to most effectively combine, or hybridise, governance strategies so as to draw on the strengths of all, would appear to be a positive step forward. In taking this step, one must fundamen-tally challenge the tendency to distinguish private actors from public actors in terms of an assumed lack of governance of the former and an assumed robust governance of the latter (Scott 2000: 41). As we return to Stenning's (2000) point, this dichotomised understanding continues to retain a strong conceptual foothold within the policing and criminological literatures, serving to stymie progress in the development of innovative governance models.

Notes

1 Braithwaite understands governance in terms of three key processes: provision, distribution and regulation of goods such as security (Braithwaite 2005). Rather than conceiving of regulation as a fundamentally different process from governance, we thus adopt Braithwaite's understanding of the former as a 'large subset of governance that is about steering the flow of events, as opposed to providing and distributing' (Braithwaite 2005: 1). In this way, we at times use the terms 'governance' and 'regulation' interchangeably in this chapter, particularly when we are drawing from the literature on regulation.
2 See Singer (2003) and Avant (2005) for a historical discussion of the evolution of the private military firm and the military market as a whole.

References

Avant, D. (2005) *The Market for Force: The Consequences of Privatizing Security.* Cambridge: Cambridge University Press.
Bayley, D. and Shearing, C. (1996) The future of policing, *Law and Society Review*, 30(3): 585–606.
Black, J. (2000) Decentring regulation: Understanding the role of regulation and self-regulation in a 'post-regulatory' world, *Current Legal Problems*, 54: 103–146.
Braithwaite, J. (2000) The new regulatory state and the transformation of criminology, *British Journal of Criminology*, 40: 222–38.
—— (2003) Restorative justice and corporate regulation, in E.G.M. Weitekamp and H-J. Kerner (eds), *Restorative Justice in Context: International Practice and Directions.* Devon: Willan Publishing.
—— (2003) What's wrong with the sociology of punishment?, *Theoretical Criminology*, 7(1): 5–28.
—— (2005) *Neoliberalim or Regulatory Capitalism?* Canberra: Regulatory Institutions Network, Research School of Social Sciences, Australian National University.
Bratton, W., with Knobler, P. (1998) *Turnaround: How America's Top Cop Reversed the Crime Epidemic.* New York: Random House.
Crawford, A. (2003) 'Contractual governance' of deviant behaviour, *Journal of Law and Society*, 30(4): 479–505.
—— (2006) Policing and security as 'club goods': The new enclosures? in J. Wood and B. Dupont (eds), *Democracy, Society and the Governance of Security.* Cambridge: Cambridge University Press.

Crawford, A., Lister, S. et al. (2005) *Plural Policing: The Mixed Economy of Visible Patrols in England and Wales*. Bristol: The Policy Press.

Daniels, R.J., Macklem, P. et al (eds) (2001) *The Security of Freedom: Essays on Canada's Anti-Terrorism Bill*. Toronto: University of Toronto Press.

Drahos, P. (2004) The regulation of public goods, *Journal of International Economic Law*, 7(2): 321–39.

Duffield, M. (2001) *Global Governance and the New Wars*. London: Zed Books.

Elcock, H. (1997) What price citizenship? Public management and the citizen's charter, in J. Chandler, *The Citizen's Charter*. Aldershot: Dartmouth.

Espeland, W.N. and Stevens, M.L. (1998) Commensuration as a social process, *Annual Review of Sociology*, 24: 313–43.

Fleming, J. and Rhodes, R.A.W. (2005) Bureaucracy, contracts and networks: The unholy trinity and the police, *Australian and New Zealand Journal of Criminology*, 38(2): 192–205.

Florini, A. (2000) Does the invisible hand need a transparent glove?, in Proceedings of the 11th Annual World Bank Conference on Development Economics. Washington DC: World Bank, at <http://info.worldbank.org/etools/docs/library/18299/florini.pdf>.

Goodin, R.E. (2003) Democratic accountability: The distinctiveness of the third sector, *European Journal of Sociology*, 44(3): 359–96.

Grabosky, P. (1994) Green markets: Environmental regulation by the private sector, *Law and Policy*, 16(4): 419–48.

—— (1995) Using non-governmental resources to foster regulatory compliance, *Governance*, 8: 527–50.

—— (1997) Inside the pyramid: Towards a conceptual framework of the analysis of regulatory systems, *International Journal of the Sociology of Law*, 26(3): 195–201.

Grabosky, P. and Braithwaite, J. (eds) (1993) *Business Regulation and Australia's Future*, Australian Studies in Law, Crime and Justice. Canberra: Australian Institute of Criminology.

Gunningham, N., Kagan, R.A. et al. (2003) *Shades of Green: Business, Regulation and Environment*. Stanford: Stanford University Press.

Gunningham, N., Kagan, R.A. et al. (2004) Social license and environmental protection: Why businesses go beyond compliance, *Law and Social Inquiry*, 29(2): 307–41.

Hall, R.B. and Biersteker, T.J. (eds) (2002) *The Emergence of Private Authority in Global Governance*. Cambridge: Cambridge University Press.

Herbert, S. (2001) Policing the contemporary city: Fixing broken windows or shoring up neo-liberalism?, *Theoretical Criminology*, 5(4): 445–66.

Hermer, J., Kempa, M. et al. (2005) Policing in Canada in the 21st century: Directions for law reform, in D. Cooley (ed.), *Re-imagining Policing in Canada*. Toronto: University of Toronto Press.

Hocking, J. (2004) Protecting democracy by preserving democracy, *University of New South Wales Law Journal*, 27(2): 319–38.

—— (2005) Liberty, security and the state, in P. Saunders and J. Walter (eds), *Ideas and Influence: Social Science and Public Policy in Australia*. Sydney: UNSW Press.

Independent Commission on Policing for Northern Ireland (1999) *A new beginning: Policing in Northern Ireland.* Norwich: Independent Commission on Policing for Northern Ireland.

Joh, E.E. (2005) Conceptualizing the private police, *Utah Law Review*, 2: 573–617.

Johnston, L. (1997) Policing communities of risk, in P. Francis, P. Davies and V. Jupp (eds), *Policing Futures: The Police, Law Enforcement and the Twenty-first Century.* Houndmills, Basingstoke: Macmillan.

—— (1999) Private policing in context, *European Journal on Criminal Policy and Research*, 7: 175–96.

—— (2000) *Policing Britain: Risk, Security and Governance.* Harlow: Longman.

—— (2006) Transnational security governance, in J. Wood and B. Dupon (eds), *Democracy, Society and the Governance of Security.* Cambridge: Cambridge University Press.

Johnston, L. and Shearing, C. (2003) *Governing Security: Explorations in Policing and Justice.* London: Routledge.

Joint Standing Committee on Foreign Affairs, Defence and Trade (2003) Roundtable, 15 August, Melbourne, at <http: //www.aph.gov.au/hansard/joint/committee/j6808.pdf>.

Jones, T. (2003) Accountability in the era of pluralised policing, paper presented at In search of security: An international conference on policing and security, Montréal, Law Commission of Canada.

Kaldor, M. (1999) *New and Old Wars: Organized Violence in a Global Era.* Stanford CA: Stanford University Press.

—— (2003) *Global Civil Society: An Answer to War.* Cambridge: Polity Press.

Kempa, M. (2004) *Contesting and Shaping Liberal Governance: The Case of Policing Reform in Northern Ireland.* Canberra: Research School of Social Sciences, Australian National University.

—— (in press) Tracing the diffusion of policing governance models from the British Isles and back again: Some directions for democratic reform in troubled times, *Police Practice and Research: An International Journal.*

Kempa, M., Carrier, R. et al. (1999) Reflections on the evolving concept of 'private policing', *European Journal on Criminal Policy and Research*, 7(2): 197–223.

Kempa, M., Stenning, P. et al. (2004) Policing communal spaces: A reconfiguration of the 'mass private property' hypothesis, *British Journal of Criminology*, 44: 562–81.

Latour, B. (1987) *Science in Action.* Cambridge MA: Harvard University Press.

Lewis, C. and Prenzler, T. (1999) Civilian oversight of police in Australia, Trends and Issues in Crime and Criminal Justice, 141, at <http://www.aic.gov.au/publications/tandi/ti141.pdf>.

Loader, I. (1999) Consumer culture and the commodification of policing and security, *Sociology*, 33(2): 373–92.

—— (2000) Plural policing and democratic governance, *Social and Legal Studies*, 9(3): 323–45.

Loader, I. and Walker, N. (2001) Policing as a public good: Reconstituting the connections between policing and state, *Theoretical Criminology*, 5(1): 9–35.

—— (2006) Necessary virtues: The legitimate place of the state in the production of security, in J. Wood and B. Dupont (eds), *Democracy, Society and the*

Governance of Security. Cambridge: Cambridge University Press.

—— (in press) Locating the public interest in transnational policing, in J.W.E. Sheptycki and A. Goldsmith (eds), *Crafting Global Policing*. London: Hart.

Macauley, S. (1986) Private government, in L. Lipson and S. Wheeler (eds), *Law and the Social Sciences*. New York: Russell Sage Foundation.

MacSherry, B. (2005) Terrorism offences in the *Criminal Code*: Broadening the boundaries of Australian criminal laws, *University of New South Wales Law Journal*, 27(2): 353–72.

Makkai, T. and Braithwaite, J. (1994) Reintegrative shaming and regulatory compliance, *Criminology*, 32(3): 361–385h.

McLaughlin, E. and Murji, K. (1995) The end of public policing? Police reform and 'the new managerialism', in L. Noaks, M. Maguire and M. Levi (eds), *Contemporary Issues in Criminology*. Cardiff: University of Wales Press.

—— (1997) The future lasts a long time: Public policework and the managerialist paradox, in P. Francis, P. Davies and V. Jupp (eds), *Policing Futures: The Police, Law Enforcement and the Twenty-First Century*. London: Macmillan.

Mopas, M. and Stenning, P. (2001) Tools of the trade: The symbolic power of private security — An exploratory study, *Policing and Society*, 11(2): 67–97.

Murphy, J. (1997) The private sector and security: A bit on BIDs, *Security Journal*, 9: 11–13.

Noaks, L. (2000) Private cops on the block: A review of the role of private security in residential communities, *Policing and Society*, 10: 143–61.

O'Malley, P. (1997) Policing, politics and postmodernity, *Social and Legal Studies*, 6(3): 363–81.

O'Malley, P. and Palmer, D. (1996) Post-Keynesian policing, *Economy and Society*, 25(2): 137–55.

Osbourne, D. and Gaebler, T. (1992) *Reinventing Government: How the Entrepreneurial Spirit is Transforming the Public Sector*. New York: Plume.

Parker, C. (2002) *The Open Corporation: Effective Self-regulation and Democracy*. Cambridge: Cambridge University Press.

Parker, C. and Braithwaite, J. (2003) Regulation, in P. Cane and M. Tushnet (eds), *Oxford Handbook of Legal Studies*. Oxford: Oxford University Press.

Pue, W.W. (2000) Policing, the rule of law, and accountability in Canada: Lessons from the APEC Summit, in W. Wesley Pue (ed.), *Pepper in our Eyes: The APEC Affair*. Vancouver: UBC Press.

Power, M. (1997) *The Audit Society: Rituals of Verification*. New York: Oxford University Press.

Prenzler, T. (2005) Mapping the Australian security industry, *Security Journal*, 18(4): 51–64.

Prenzler, T. and King, M. (2002) The role of private investigators and commercial agents in law enforcement, *Trends & Issues* (Australian Institute of Criminology), 234: 1–6.

Prenzler, T. and Sarre, R. (1998) Regulating private security in Australia, *Trends & Issues* (Australian Institute of Criminology), 98: 1–6.

—— (1999) A survey of security legislation and regulatory strategies in Australia, *Security Journal*, 12(3): 7–17.

Queensland Government (2005) Government response to the Parliamentary Crime and Misconduct Committee Report No. 64 – Three Year Review of the Crime and Misconduct Commission. Brisbane.

Rigakos, G. (2002) *The New Parapolice: Risk Markets and Commodified Social Control.* Toronto: University of Toronto Press.

Rose, N. and Miller, P. (1992) Political power beyond the state: Problematics of government, *British Journal of Sociology,* 43: 173–205.

Sarre, R. and Prenzler, T. (1999) The regulation of private policing: Reviewing mechanisms of accountability, *Crime Prevention and Community Safety: An International Journal,* 1(3): 17–28.

—— (2005) *The Law of Private Security in Australia.* Sdyney: Thomson LBC.

Schedler, A., Diamond, L. and Plattner, M. (eds) (1999) *The Self-restraining State: Power and accountability in new democracies.* Boulder CO: Lynne Rienner Publishers.

Scott, C. (2000) Accountability in the regulatory state, *Journal of Law and Society,* 27(1): 38–60.

—— (2002) Private regulation of the public sector: A neglected facet of contemporary governance, *Journal of Law and Society,* 29(1): 56–76.

—— (2004) Regulation in the age of governance: The rise of the post-regulatory state, in J. Jordana and D. Levi-Faur (eds), *The Politics of Regulation: Institutions and Regulatory Reforms for the Age of Governance.* London: Elgar.

—— (2006) Spontaneous accountability, in M.W. Dowdle (ed.), *Accountability: Designs, dilemmas and experiences.* Cambridge: Cambridge University Press.

Shearing, C. (1993) A constitutive conception of regulation, in P. Grabosky and J. Braithwaite (eds), *Business Regulation and Australia's Future.* Canberra: Australian Institute of Criminology.

—— (1997) The unrecognized origins of the new policing: Linkages between private and public policing, in M. Felson and R. V. Clarke (eds), *Business and Crime Prevention.* Monsey: Criminal Justice Press.

—— (2001) A nodal conception of governance: Thoughts on a Policing Commission, *Policing and Society,* 11: 259–72.

—— (2006) Reflections on the refusal to acknowledge private governments, in J. Wood and B. Dupont (eds), *Democracy, Society and the Governance of Security.* Cambridge: Cambridge University Press.

Shearing, C. and Stenning, P. (1981) Modern private security: Its growth and implications, in M. Tonry and N. Morris (eds), *Crime and Justice: An Annual Review of Research.* Chicago: University of Chicago Press.

—— (1983) Private security: Its implications for social control, *Social Problems,* 30(5): 125–38.

—— (1985) From the panopticon to Disney World: The development of discipline, in A.N. Doob and E.L. Greenspan (eds), *Perspectives in Criminal Law.* Toronto: Canada Law Book.

—— (eds) (1987) Private policing, in *Sage Criminal Justice System Annuals.* Newbury Park CA: Sage.

Shearing, C. and Wood, J. (2000) Reflections on the governance of security: A normative inquiry, *Police Practice,* 1(4): 457–76.

—— (2003) Governing security for common goods, *International Journal of the*

Sociology of Law, 31(3): 205–25.

Sheptycki, J.W.E. and Goldsmith, A. (eds) (in press) Crafting Global Policing. Oxford: Hart.

Singer, P.W. (2001) Corporate warriors: The rise of the privatized military industry and its ramifications for international security, International Security 26(3): 186–220.

—— (2003) Corporate Warriors: The Rise of the Privatized Military Industry. Ithaca NY: Cornell University Press.

Sklansky, D.A. (2006) Private police and democracy, American Criminal Law Review, 43(1).

Stenning, P. (2000) Powers and accountability of private police, European Journal on Criminal Policy and Research, 8: 325–352.

Uhr, J. (1998) Deliberative Democracy in Australia: The Changing Place of Parliament. Cambridge: Cambridge University Press.

Vincent-Jones, P. (2000) Contractual governance: Institutional and organizational analysis, Oxford Journal of Legal Studies, 20(3): 317–351.

Wakefield, A. (2003) Selling Security: The Private Policing of Public Space. Devon: Willan Publishing.

Wall, D. (in press) Policing cybercrime: Situating the public police in networks of security within cyberspace, Police Practice and Research: An International Journal.

Wood, J. (2000) Reinventing Governance: A Study of Transformations in the Ontario Provincial Police. Toronto: Centre of Criminology, University of Toronto.

Zedner, L. (2006) Liquid security: Managing the market for crimes control, Criminology and Criminal Justice, 6(2):267–88.

11 | DARK NETWORKS, BRIGHT NETWORKS AND THE PLACE OF THE POLICE

Jennifer Wood

In the midst of the social and economic devastation left by Hurricane Katrina, American authorities have been exploring innovative approaches to the delivery of policing and security.[1] Take as an example St Bernard Parish, Louisiana, which will soon (at the time of writing) be home to Katrina evacuees through its newly established trailer camp. The Sheriff's Department – which is itself in rather dire financial straits – predicts that this camp will create the conditions for rising crime and disorder, including activities such as fighting and the harbouring of criminals. Major Pete Tufaro, of the Sheriff's Department, has developed a proposal for the parish, involving subcontracting DynCorp International LLC, a company from Texas that has a large security contract in Iraq and provided personal security services to Afghan President Hamid Karzai. This proposal, which is subject to approval by the Federal Emergency Management Agency (FEMA), would involve an expenditure of US$70 million over three years, which would cover the costs of up to 100 deputised DynCorp staff, who would have the authority to make arrests, carry weapons and wear the uniforms of the Sheriff's Department. Major Tufaro goes so far as to say, 'You wouldn't be able to tell the difference between us and them' (Merle 2006).

One of the interesting things about this proposal is that the 'hired guns' would earn more than experienced officers in the Sheriff's Department. It would seem that competition in the security market is not sufficiently rigorous to drive prices down. Indeed, the St Bernard Parish Sheriff's Department recommended DynCorp in its proposal without arranging for competitive bidding, as it was assumed that this firm would provide the cheapest service: compared to, for example, Blackwater USA (Merle 2006).

This development of a new networked arrangement for the provision of policing and security – involving a mix of public and private providers – is significant in many other respects as well. To begin with, it represents the classic economic challenge of constituting markets in ways that avoid monopolies, promote fair competition, and provide customers with various high-quality services to choose from. Linked with these economic problems is the array of governance issues that Lewis and Wood mention (Chapter 10) and which are elaborated more fully by scholars such as Singer (2003), Avant (2005) and Johnston (2006). For example, Singer notes that in the context of this particular proposal, it is unclear how well DynCorp officers will be supervised (Merle 2006).

Another most interesting aspect of this proposal is that it may serve as a marker of what could be regarded as a broader existential crisis in public policing. As Singer suggests, the kind of role that DynCorp would take on in this arrangement certainly raises the general question of whether there is anything 'core' any more about the public police function (Merle 2006). For the public police it would seem that it is essential, now more than ever, to reflect on their own identity and the ways in which they see themselves being placed within networks of policing and security provision (Fleming, Marks & Wood 2006).

The chapter in this volume by Lewis and Wood (Chapter 10) attempts to think slightly differently about ways in which nodes and networks of policing and security can be governed, recognising the considerable 'hybridity' that already exists in the mentalities, organisational arrangements and strategies of security providers. This chapter explores a different but related issue. It is concerned with the future identity of the public police as an institution. If the police, as a social institution, are uniquely knowledgeable and skilled and remain a symbol of law and order (Loader 1997), what is their place in policing and security networks? If there is something 'core' about who the police are and what they do, how do they retain this uniqueness in the face of an increasingly ubiquitous set of providers boasting a growing set of security-enhancing skills, capacities and resources? Put another way, will participation in networks ultimately threaten the identity, and possibly the very existence, of the public police and state security provision more generally?

As the chapters in this volume make very clear, police organisations the world over are being encouraged to establish partnerships and networks. This ambitious strategic direction is seen as inevitable given a range of factors, including the cost of policing and public demand for services, and the fact that contemporary forms of insecurity, such as organised crime, illicit drugs and terrorism, are themselves nodal and networked in their operations and organisational features. Even if one disregarded the imperatives of neo-liberal restructuring, empirical evidence tells us that 'bright' networks are required to manage 'dark' ones (Raab & Milward 2003). This is the position taken in the 9/11 Commission Report (2004), and it is similarly taken by other reformers embroiled in efforts to improve the governance of terrorism, organised crime, illicit drugs and other forms of activity that thrive with the pulse of globalisation.

This chapter reviews ways in which public police organisations are developing networks of policing and security provision. It then explores ideas about what police *ought* to do, or at least what they ought to make sure they keep doing, as they build networks that are dedicated not only to short-term strategic improvements but to the betterment and democratic advancement of the field of policing and security generally. As part of this discussion I will put forward the notion that the self-identity of the public police organisation, as a uniquely skilled and knowledgeable as well as legitimate and symbolically significant organisation, can no longer be taken for granted in our nodal and networked era. This is an implicit strand that runs through this collection, and one which I would like to bring to the fore. As such, this chapter serves as something of a conclusion to this volume, focusing on what its contributors have to say, as well as on what others have to say about how police must position themselves in networks for the future in order to retain, or perhaps newly establish, a distinctive place for themselves vis-à-vis other policing and security providers.

The following section will briefly review the need for policing and security networks at local, national and international levels. It will then outline key ways in which police organisations are forming networks to address forms of insecurity expressed through 'wicked problems' (Rittel & Webber 1973) and 'dark networks' (Raab & Milward 2003).

Wicked problems and dark networks

The now extensive literature on crime prevention and community policing has long recognised that security is a 'wicked problem', as Rittel and Webber would put it:

> The information needed to *understand* the problem depends upon one's idea for *solving it*. That is to say in order to *describe* a wicked problem in sufficient detail, one has to develop an exhaustive inventory of all conceivable *solutions* ahead of time. The reason is that every question asking for additional information depends upon the understanding of the problem – and its resolution – at that time. Problem understanding and problem resolution are concomitant to each other (Rittel & Webber 1973: 161, italics in original).

Consistent with this understanding of wicked problems, Goldstein, in his ground-breaking work on 'problem-oriented policing' (Goldstein 1991 [1979]), advanced a vision of police as 'problem solvers' rather than 'law enforcers'. 'The police job,' he argued, 'requires that they deal with a wide range of behavioural and social problems that arise in a community – the end product of policing consists of dealing with these *problems*' (Goldstein 1991 [1979]: 242, italics in original). To deal with these problems effectively requires an understanding of their multiple dimensions and a recognition that the traditional means available to the police, bound in their legal authority and law enforcement mandate, are simply some among many means they should consider. This shift from a law enforcement orientation to a problem-solving one would enable them to break out of the 'means over ends syndrome' that, in Goldstein's view, characterises police institutions (Goldstein 1991 [1979]).

As Fleming summarises (Chapter 4), police-led partnerships and networks are central to reform agendas in the English-speaking world, and in the case of the United Kingdom, are required through legislation. Despite the kinds of implementation challenges she identified, the need for local networks of policing and security is now accepted as a new kind of common sense which is embedded in the strategic plans of police organisations. Such plans articulate a vision of police as mobilising the knowledge, capacity and resources of a wide array of police and non-police actors. As stated in *The Way Ahead*, the strategic plan for Victoria Police (2003–08), 'Often, the solutions lie within the capacity and capability of other agencies, community groups and individuals to participate in and contribute to crime prevention and community safety strategies. Sometimes, by influencing others' behaviour, the need for police intervention can be avoided altogether' (2003: 16).

The question of how precisely police organisations form partnerships and networks is not an easy one to answer and put into practice, despite the simplicity of the vision articulated in documents such as *The Way Ahead*. This practical problem is of course amply demonstrated in the research conducted by Fleming (see also Fleming & Rhodes 2005) as well as in other studies that have confirmed the organisational, cultural, economic and other obstacles to realising the problem-solving vision of Goldstein and others. A recent critical commentary on 'implementation failures' is found in Bullock and Tilley's edited collection titled *Crime Reduction and Problem-oriented Policing* (2003) (for a review, see Bradley 2005).

Whilst recognising the need to harness other forms of knowledge and capacity in their strategies and tactics for addressing wicked problems, police are also required to harness non-police resources in furtherance of their traditional mission of law enforcement. This is the focus of Ayling, Grabosky and Shearing's chapter (Chapter 3) in this collection. The police simply do not have the resources to effectively monitor and enforce a wide variety of laws, so they require other individuals and organisations to help them do so. Within a paradigm of what Mazerolle and Ransley describe as 'third-party policing' (Mazerolle & Ransley 2005), police enlist others through a range of mechanisms that Ayling and her colleagues describe in terms of three key forms of exchange: coercion, sale and gift.

The chapter sheds much light on the variety of ways in which police constitute what we may describe in simple terms as 'bright networks' (Raab & Milward 2003). Mechanisms for enlisting others range from being highly coercive in nature – through, for example, the use of criminal sanctions for non-compliance – to being largely voluntary, as in many instances of community policing. These authors explain their category of 'sale' in terms of the constitution of 'market networks', which consist of a range of activities including the selling of public policing services as well as the outsourcing of services previously provided by the police to private providers through contracts. The example with which this chapter began is an illustration of the latter, and demonstrates the degree to which contracted services delivered by private providers can resemble those delivered by public providers, as least as far as appearances go. With this in mind, as Crawford reminds us, and as Lewis and Wood discuss (Chapter 10), it is not simply state institutions like the police that constitute market networks. A plethora of private organisations, community groups and citizens are contributing significantly to the 'commodification' of policing and security (Loader 1999). As Crawford states, 'The near monopoly that the public police enjoyed for over a century is at an end and policing, like security, has become a commodity to be bought and sold' (Crawford 2003: 496).

There is thus a variety of ways in which public policing organisations have gone about, and continue to go about, developing networks – made up of multiple forms of knowledge, capacity and resources – to support their traditional role of law enforcement as well as their more contemporary role of crime prevention. The chapters by Fleming and by Ayling, Grabosky and Shearing illustrate such attempts at the more local and national levels of policing and discuss the implementation challenges (Fleming) as well as the various normative implications (Ayling et al.) of such attempts. Other chapters in this volume, particularly those by Keelty, and Wardlaw and Boughton, speak to the current preoccupation that police organisations have with forming networks at national and international levels. These chapters demonstrate the considerable efforts made by the Australian Federal Police (AFP) to advance this agenda, and reveal that one of the biggest challenges associated with global network formation is the need for police organisations like the AFP to remain constantly flexible and adaptable to the activities of what Raab and Milward describe as 'dark networks' (2003).

Raab and Milwaard state that the general literature on networks tends to take a positive view with respect to the necessity – as well as the potential – of collaborative approaches to public sector governance. Networks are seen as superior to hierarchies in tackling the wicked problems that fall outside the mandate of any one public sector organisation. They point out, however, that wicked problems are understood by advocates of networked governance as 'socially nonreactive'. What if the problem that governments seek to tackle, they suggest, is 'not an unorganized set of poor or cognitively impaired clients but another network, perhaps engaged in illegal activity' (Raab & Milward 2003: 414)? In essence, they argue, there is much we need to learn about dark networks if we are to develop an adequate understanding of bright networks and their effectiveness.

Policy-makers and practitioners increasingly recognise that dark networks, as seen in areas such as organised crime and terrorism, are sophisticated and agile, to a point where they have easily outmanoeuvred existing systems of criminal monitoring and enforcement. In Dupont's words (Chapter 2), 'the myth of the fight against crime and the war-like metaphors on which it relied were seriously undermined by the discovery that organised crime was much less organised than initially thought and that crime syndicates were loosely coupled alliances of individuals who retained a large degree of autonomy'.

When broken down into their component parts, networks can be seen in terms of 'nodes' that come together in a variety ways (bonds of kinship, exchange of resources, for example) (Williams 2001: 66) for a variety or purposes, such as the generation of profits or the production of terror based on religious principles. Indeed, the dynamism of contemporary transnational crime makes it difficult to develop any single, elegant theory of dark networks. Beare stresses the importance of avoiding any uniform notions of how transnational crime operates except to perhaps suggest that the desire for profit is what unites organised crime networks. It is even problematic to assume that illicit markets operate independently of legal markets. It is more likely that there is an intersection between the two at different points in time and space. In alerting us to this, Beare is implying that practitioners and scholars must remember to conceptualise policing as part of a broader process of social and economic regulation that shapes the behaviour of otherwise 'legitimate' organisations as well as of illicit enterprises (2003). The ways in which legitimate economies are governed have direct implications for illegitimate actors in terms of opportunities created for them and loopholes they may be able to take advantage of (Ruggiero 2003).

Furthermore, in his analysis of several cases of transnational organised crime, Ruggiero suggests that such crime may 'mingle with entrepreneurial and, at times, governmental deviance'. This can occur, for instance, 'when legally produced goods are illegally marketed, or when the illegal marketing of goods produced in one country is supported by the complicity of corrupt politicians in a country in which those goods are officially banned'. Thus, according to Ruggiero, collusion between illegitimate and legitimate actors is essential to the success of transnational organised crime (2003: 177).

Paoli adds that organised crime groupings that come closer to their mythological construction, such as the La Cosa Nostra or the Japanese Yakuza, cannot be understood simply in terms of their involvement in illegal activities. Most organisations that Paoli depicts as 'mafia-type associations' 'pre-existed the formation and expansion of modern illegal markets' and 'throughout their existence ... have carried out a plurality of functions, most of which are not related to the provision of illegal goods and services' (2002: 63, 72).

Paoli further points out that 'organised crime' is much less 'organised' than what has traditionally been assumed in the literature and in police practice (2002). Due to the illegal and hence covert nature of the activities carried out by dark networks, large and static organisational structures are not the form in which members of the networks are brought together. Rather, different individuals and groups come together to form networks in particular time and space moments. Hence there is a distinction to be made between the activities of the networks and the individuals who carry out such activities, as the movement of individuals in and out of particular functions within illegal markets does not jeopardise the illegal market itself (Paoli 2002; Watkins 2004). Paoli explains:

> The concept of a network is indeed a useful construct to describe the distribution system of illegal commodities. The strength and cohesion of most illegal networks, however, should not be overestimated. Although long-term relations may develop among network members, the majority of them are arm's-length buyer-seller relationships, which are neither exclusive in any sense nor centrally organized. Each illegal entrepreneur is free to look for other partners to execute the next transaction and usually belongs to more than one network at the same time since he has contact with several suppliers and has numerous customers to whom he can sell his merchandise. Moreover, in any point of the network, the actors generally know only their imme-

diate supplier(s) and buyer(s) and have no idea of its overall extent and structure. Finally, it must never be forgotten that illegal networks are volatile constructions. They constantly change their form and extension, as new partners are included, others are occasionally or permanently discarded, and others are replaced because they have been targeted by law enforcement action (2002: 67–68).

The redundancy, and hence resilience, of dark networks achieved through ebbs and flows of people in and out of particular functions is something that Gross Stein highlights in her analysis of terrorist networks. She too uses the language of 'nodes' and 'networks' in an attempt to shift thinking away from the assumption that security threats can be eliminated through traditional command and control governance exercised in the wielding of military might. She explains:

> A network is a collection of connected points or nodes, gener-ally designed to be resilient through redundancy. It can be one terminal, connected to the Internet, or one expert communi-cating with another expert in a common network devoted to a shared problem. The design of the network determines its resilience, its flexibility, its capacity to expand, and its vulnera-bility (2001: 74).

For Gross Stein, this nodal understanding must guide strategic and tactical planning: 'No single approach against a single site – even the headquarters, to the extent they exist – will be effective. The implications are clear: removing a single node, or even several, will not destroy the network' (2001: 74).

Australian and other police organisations around the world have begun adopting the language of nodes and networks in the strategic plans they are developing for organised crime, terrorism and related dark network activity. The newly developed Organized Crime Strategy (2005–09) of Victoria Police states that the organisation 'needs to change some of its internal struc-tures, culture and thinking in order to succeed in matching and combating the fluid, flexible, dynamic and networked characteristics of organised crime net-works' (2005: 8). Central to this change is the development of its research and analytical capacity – one based on a nodal and networked perspective – that provides the organisation with a timely and comprehensive knowledge base that can guide strategic and tactical planning.

The need for intelligence-led policing within networks of public agencies, communities, the private sector and international organisations is the focus of Wardlaw and Boughton's chapter (Chapter 6). This involves a shift in emphasis away from a narrow understanding of 'information' that is used to deal with specific criminal actors to 'intelligence', which they describe as 'value-added analysis for decision-making'. In their chapter, they describe a variety of challenges associated with quality collection, dissemination and analysis of intelligence within and across police and non-police organisations that have varying capabilities as well as interests.

Based on the above, we see that in the face of contemporary security challenges that come in the form of wicked problems and dark nodes and networks, the public police are required to participate in the development of networks – and indeed to actively constitute them. The previous chapters provide much insight into the imperative for networks as well as the ways in which this imperative is met. A central theme cutting across these chapters is the need for police organisations to strategically position themselves in ways that enable them to most effectively take advantage of the capacities, resources, and knowledge/intelligence residing in other nodes and networks.

The challenge of network formation, though, is not simply one of effective strategic positioning. The various analyses of challenges associated with network formation, as provided by contributors to this volume, reveal that every strategic choice is a normative one, even though some choices are less controversial than others. As Lewis and Wood mention at the beginning of their chapter, requests by governments to enhance the powers of their police agencies are currently very controversial, because according to some critics, they hit at the heart of core democratic principles such as freedom. Of course there are a variety of other issues and principles at stake that may receive less attention in the public domain. Ayling, Grabosky and Shearing provide a comprehensive discussion of the normative issues associated with practices of coercion, sale and gift in the harnessing of resources for networked policing. Wardlaw and Boughton discuss issues pertaining to the quality, integrity and security of information within a networked context. Lewis and Wood focus on the challenge of governing networks of policing and security provision both at nodal levels and in the totality of their operations. I do not wish to revisit such discussions here, but rather to move on to a discussion of what might be regarded as some generic 'design principles'[2] for guiding the public police in their network-building efforts, principles that could underlie ways in which they engage with, mobilise and connect to other forms of capacity, resources and knowledge/intelligence.

Making networks bright: Generic design principles for the police

As Dupont's chapter reminds us, there is much we still don't know about how networks are formed by the various nodes within them. As Dupont observes, it is not just the public police or other state security organisations that play an active role in establishing the kinds of networks they desire. Rather, a plethora of other state institutions, private actors and community groups are active in this regard, shaping strategic and other alliances in ways that contribute to their particular interests, be they parochial or communal in some fashion (see also Crawford 2006). Furthermore, it is not just policy networks, or other formal ways of networking, that matter. There is also much that occurs informally, at the 'coal face', that builds new networking habits. Networks, Dupont writes, 'are established and maintained largely within the context of routine activities associated with the production of security'. We are also reminded by Rhodes (Chapter 1) that networks have not simply replaced bureaucracies and markets as forms of organisation. All three governance forms co-exist, albeit in often uneasy ways, and it is naive to assume that any one particular form is necessarily, on its own, better than any other.

If we take stock, however, of what we do know about the need for networks as well as the need for police organisations to actively build them, what might be some generic principles that guide this network-building process? As indicated previously, identification of such principles is gleaned largely from the insights of other contributors to this volume. Such authors revealed principles with varying degree of explicitness; for the most part, they did not describe them in terms of principles at all. What I wish to attempt is to repackage some of these insights into generic design principles. This discussion is based on the assumption — expressed in the analyses of the previous chapters — that police do not simply want to become a node that is indistinguishable from others. In that case, how must they position themselves in networks to maintain a privileged identity and role within them? Expressed differently, how does a police organisation, as a node that is connected to other nodes, stand out for who they are and what they do? I offer the four following principles for consideration.

Maintain the symbolism of police

The continued emergence of private providers of policing and security that look like, and often act like, their counterparts in the public sector is significant not only in terms of the role confusion – and an associated confusion in legal authority – that may be created in the minds of the public. Nor is it simply significant from a governance or regulation perspective, which is the focus of Lewis and Wood's discussion. It is also significant as an (albeit colloquial) example of a possible erosion of police symbolism. Nodal and networked policing has the potential to gloss over what is distinctive about particular nodes – in terms of both their identities and their roles – unless great care is taken in constituting nodal relationships. Lewis and Wood point out, drawing largely from Johnston's observations (Johnston 2000, 2006), that mentalities of policing and security provision – particularly those centred on punishment and risk – also mix and meld between providers. Not only has risk-based thinking penetrated the public sector; punitive practices of security delivery can be found creeping up in areas such as commercial military service provision (Johnston 2006).

Let us focus for a moment on the symbolism and identity of the police. We do know that this social institution continues to maintain considerable symbolic capital (Dupont 2003, 2006). According to Loader, the continued cultural significance of the police is not given sufficient attention in contemporary analyses of policing:

> [P]opular attachment to policing is principally *affective* in character, something which people evince a deep emotional commitment to and which is closely integrated with their sense of self. Policing, it seems, can provide an interpretive lens through which people make sense of, and give order to, their world; the source of a set of plausible stories about that world which help people sustain 'ontological security' (Giddens 1991). As such, the attachment to policing is unlikely to be shifted merely by demonstrating that it is in some sense or other irrational or wrong-headed (1997: 3).

It is against this backdrop that one might refer to the police as having not only coercive power, but also symbolic power:

> The symbolic power of the police has become the power of legitimate pronouncement: a power to diagnose, classify, authorize,

and represent both individuals and the world, and to have this power of 'legitimate naming' not just taken seriously, but taken-for-granted ... the police's entitlement and capacity to speak about the world is seldom challenged. They start from a winning posi-tion (Loader 1997: 3).

Based on Dupont's analysis of 'power struggles' in the field of policing and security (2006), it is not sufficient for police to assume that their symbolic power and cultural significance will carry them through changing times. Indeed, other providers of policing and security are amassing various forms of capital (economic, political, social and symbolic) and are doing so rather successfully. Police managers know this, as do unionists (Fleming, Marks & Wood 2006), and as such are themselves accumulating and deploying various forms of capital as they 'jockey for position' in the field. Dupont observes that an important objective guiding the power struggles of police managers is to achieve a central and 'professional' place in the field of policing and security provision (2006).

Before I discuss Dupont's observation regarding police profession-alism, I will turn to an example of a 'power play' that is currently being carried out by Sir Ian Blair, Commissioner of the London Metropolitan Police. It is devoted to the accumulation of economic capital through attempts to monopolise the market, particularly the market for 'reassur-ance policing'. It is not, however, simply a strategy for re-producing police hegemony. It is a way of asserting an identity for the police as a culturally significant, publicly legitimate and highly skilled and professional service that, through its monopoly of the field, will optimise security outcomes for all. This is not a strategy that I necessarily advocate. But it provides one example of how to realise the next design principle, which is to constitute markets in ways that align public interests with other common interests (Shearing & Wood 2003), or what Crawford describes as 'club goods' (2006).

Constitute markets to promote public interests

Sklansky argues that much greater attention needs to be paid to the potential threats to democracy posed by the growth in private security. One such threat comes in the form of 'dampening political support for public law enforcement committed, at least nominally, to protecting everyone against illegal violence'. He goes on: 'The result may be a system of policing even less egalitarian than the one we have today' (2006:91). This threat constitutes a key part of the 'public goods' problem that has been of great concern to many scholars, including Loader and Walker (2001, 2006) and Crawford (2006).

One way of approaching this challenge is to conceptualise it as a problem of governing all nodes and networks of security providers in new and 'hybrid' ways in accordance with public interest norms (Lewis Wood, Chapter 10). Another way of approaching it is for police to become highly successful participants in the security market so that they can, in effect, monopolise that market. Sir Ian Blair, Commissioner of the London Metropolitan Police, has been attempting to do just that, having recognised the importance of jockeying for position in the security market if the police are to remain instrumentally effective as well as symbolically dominant.

Blair has been relatively open and transparent in revealing his own existential angst about the identity and role of the police in the context of 'little dispassionate, thought-through, public examination of just what it is we are here to do in the 21st century' (2005). He regularly prepares and delivers papers for conferences, such as for the British Society of Criminology Annual Meeting (2002) and the Law Commission of Canada's *In Search of Security* conference (2003), and recently delivered the Dimbleby Lecture (November 2005). In these presentations he has argued that it is not enough for the police to position themselves as simply one service provider among many within a policing and security market, even if this position is a privileged one as a certifier or regulator of some sort. His position now is that the police must compete aggressively in this market (Blair 2003), to the point where he stated that the Metropolitan Police was now 'trying to monopolise the market' (*The Economist* 2005).

The reasons for this are both instrumental and symbolic. Instrumentally, such a monopoly would maximise police effectiveness in relation to local, wicked issues of security as well as to the new forms of insecurity produced through dark networks. Blair explains that the mission of the public police has widened, given current preoccupations with antisocial behaviour which is 'threatening our ability to lead free lives' as well as with new forms of terrorism, as experienced in the London bombings of July 2005. The knowledge and capacity required to understand and act upon the range of local, national and international threats to security must, he argues, be housed within a 'single police service'. He explains:

What we should seek to avoid, at all costs, is a separation of local, neighbourhood policing from either serious criminal investigation or counter terrorist investigation. Every lesson of every police inquiry is that, not only the issues that give rise to anti-social behaviour, but also those that give rise to criminal activity and to terrorism, begin at the most local level (Blair 2005: 12–13).

He goes on to say:

Thus national security depends on neighbourhood security.

It will not be a Special Branch officer at Scotland Yard who first confronts a terrorist, but a local cop or a local community support officer.

It is not the police and the intelligence agencies who will defeat crime and terror and anti-social behaviour; it is communities.

We do not want one kind of police force being nice to people and another one arriving in darkened vans wearing the balaclavas.

Whoever is responsible for the one has to be responsible for the other (Blair 2005: 12–13).

A big component of Blair's plan has been the establishment of Police Community Support Officers (PCSOs) (mentioned in the above passage) who operate effectively as a second-tier police service, as part of the 'extended police family', owned and operated by the Metropolitan Police but wielding less power than a regular police officer. The PCSOs are in the market for work with organisations such as shopping malls, local authorities and housing associations (*The Economist* 2005: 41). This forms part of Blair's vision for a single police service that is 'engaged with and accountable to the community and being shaped by the needs of citizens, capable of dealing with every requirement from truancy to terror, from graffiti to gunmen'. He argues passionately, however, for more active engagement by members of the public in debates about their vision for policing. As he puts it, 'You need to decide what kind of police service we want' (Blair 2005: 14).

Blair's remarks serve to reaffirm the link between policing and the public good. In forging this link, an understanding of the police as a highly skilled, professional and democratic organisation is reinforced. The desire to reimagine policing as an 'exclusive domain of practice' (Australasian Police Professional Standards Council 2006) is also on the minds of police managers and leaders, and constitutes the next design principle.

Reassert policing as an 'exclusive domain of practice'

To return to an earlier point, scholars have observed a mixing and melding of mentalities among police and security providers. Sklansky raises a concern related to this observation when he talks about the 'transfer of norms' between public and private police (2006:100). This includes the transfer of private sector thinking into the management of public policing (that is, the 'new managerialism'). He points out that one way of distinguishing between public and private policing organisations – and clearly an important way, in his view – is to see private organisa-tions being concerned with 'efficiency and goal achievement' and public organisations being concerned with '[taking] into account broader values such as integrity, the accommodation of interests, and morality' (Selznick 1969, cited in Joh 2004, and see Sklansky 2006). 'Community policing,' Sklansky explains:

> has meant reducing the organizational insularity by opening new channels of communication and co-operation with a variety of outside groups, both governmental and nongovernmental. Officers in these departments have been forced, regularly and sys-tematically, to confront and to accommodate conflicting views of their mission and conflicting notions of how best to balance liberty and security. They have been pushed away, in other words, from a single-minded focus on a narrow set of performance goals ... There is no corresponding trend in the private security industry (2006:100-01).

In this particular passage, Sklansky is also reasserting a link between policing and public interest objectives. Their public mission is what dis-tinguishes police from other providers. At the same time, police leaders are seeking to clarify what it is that is distinctive about the knowledge and capacities required for police work, and this is partly an existential exercise. For example, the Australasian Police Professional Standards Council (APPSC) (2006, and see Burgess, Chapter 7) has taken the posi-tion that while a professionalisation agenda is further advanced through initiatives in areas such as education and training and ethics, it is essen-tial to begin with a deep understanding of what professional policing is and how it can be defined. It is instructive to hear a lengthy passage:

In order for an occupation to claim professional status, the domain of professional practice must be identified and delineated from the work of others in similar, related or complementary occupations. This will demonstrate to the community that police, as experts, have claim to an *exclusive domain of practice*.

... This involves defining the nature of the profession that will be the basis for future strategies and the establishment and maintenance of a professional police occupation. Within public policing, the skills base and knowledge base of practice have rapidly expanded. Police services have responded to the need to keep abreast of technology and criminal techniques by the creation of more specialised and highly educated police in areas of technical support, forensic science, fraud investigation and high tech crime. This has been accompanied by increasing employment of non-sworn specialists and professionals. Outside public policing, there has been a growth of specialised investigative and regulatory agencies within federal and state jurisdictions, with many government employees exercising powers that intersect with traditional police roles. In the security sector, the traditional work of police is supplemented by government and private suppliers providing patrol guardianship and protection services ... The parameters of the policing profession impact on what courses form part of a university degree in policing, what ethical standards are established and how they are regulated, the criteria for competency and accreditation and who will be eligible for registration as a policing professional. A definition also educates and informs the public and allied professions about what it is that police do, and what they stand for, rather than leaving the profession as a situation where a definition is imposed from outside the field (APPSC 2006: 2–3, italics added).

Thinking about what the police do and what they stand for is therefore partly a project on identity and partly a project on capacity/capability. The identity work, as the above suggests, is something that is urgently needed given the kinds of developments seen in the example of St Bernard's Parish, Louisiana. In practical terms, it may be very difficult for everyday citizens to distinguish between an officer from the Sheriff's Department and an officer from DynCorp, particularly if they are sporting the same uniforms. Yet what the APPSC is saying is that there is, or at least ought to be, something very distinctive about what the Sheriff's Department does and what it stands for in that parish, including within the parameters of its newly established trailer camp.

The above passage also highlights the degree to which police have been required to expand their knowledge and capacities in order to meet the strategic challenges of the 21st century. They have done so in various ways, including, as the passage suggests, through the creation of new specialist units and specialist police skills in areas such as new technologies and investigative methods. They have also developed the capacity to identify the kinds of knowledge and skills that civilian personnel can bring to policing. Given this growing acceptance of non-police skills in policing, as well as the expansion of knowledge and capacities beyond the organisational confines of the police, the status of the police remains elevated. At the very least there is a yearning for this high status to be so. For instance, participants at the Police Commissioners' Conference of March 2005 proclaimed the need to 'progress policing from an occupation to a profession' (in APPSC 2006: 2).

From a police union perspective, Chapter 7 in this volume, by Burgess, expresses the importance of seeing the police first and foremost as 'professionals with a unique set of skills and ethics'. Wardlaw and Boughton (Chapter 6) emphasise the importance of continuous capacity development. In discussing the 'professionalisation of intelligence', they argue that, 'Surviving and contributing to the new era of policing requires significant investment in the continued development of competencies for intelligence officers, new training and education options and a major push for the continuous development of new analytical techniques.'

As Bradley, Nixon and Marks suggest, it is not simply the quality and distinctiveness of the skills and ethics that contribute to the professionalism of policing. The ways in which police undertake and engage with research to inform strategic and tactical innovation can, and must, distinguish the police from others. The vision they have for police research is one that, like other transformations discussed above, requires organisational and cultural change. It requires new ways of bringing together academics and practitioners in knowledge-generating networks. Complementing Wardlaw and Boughton's views then, they suggest that it is not simply enough to produce high standards in 'intelligence'. In advocating a 'participatory action research' (PAR) approach, Bradley and colleagues envision deeply collaborative research whereby practitioners 'are directly involved in the research process from the point of problem identification to research design to data collection and analysis and thereafter to dissemination and uptake of research findings and recommendations'. One of the assumptions behind the PAR model is that as 'owners' of the research process, police knowledge and experience will be valued and integrated into new practical applications.

The above ideas about enhancing police knowledge and capacity are thus central, and by no means exclusive, components of a broader agenda devoted to enhancing and improving the status of the police as professionals. At the same time, other policy-makers, practitioners and academics have emphasised the privileged role of the police in enabling and developing other knowledge and capacities that contribute to public policing and security objectives. This leads us to the last key design principle, which relates to police as facilitators and shapers of multi-capacity policing.

Enable and develop other knowledge and capacities

Within a nodal environment, police play an important 'brokering' role to other nodes and to the other specialised domains of practice that may distinguish them. There is a variety of ways in which brokering can take place and a variety of directions in which it can occur. A simple typology can be constructed in terms of downward, horizontal and upward brokering. Downward brokering to forms of 'local capacity governance' is something that Shearing has advocated for many years, particularly in respect to community peace-building practices (Shearing 2001). For Shearing, part of the brokering role involves giving non-police actors the space, in figurative terms, to develop new and innovative solutions to local security problems, provided such solutions are lawful (Shearing & Wood 2003). This could involve brokering to a vast array of crime prevention groups who, for example, explore social development or environmental design approaches or, in the case of Shearing's work, local 'peace committees' (Johnston & Shearing 2003: 151–60) that undertake conflict resolution and related 'micro-governance' processes (Burris 2004) that contribute to the social and economic development of a particular (in this case poor) community. Police do not lead such groups, but simply link to them. At the same time, the police can be mobilised by such groups if it is seen that police specialist knowledge and skills must be brought in to address a particular security or broader governance problem. As brokers, the notion of policing as a specialised domain of practice is reinforced. That being said, police officers must have the capabilities required to broker effectively, which means that they must have a grasp of alternative ways of thinking about and promoting security and be aware of which actors lay claim to these alternative views and advance them effectively. In essence, police must be experts on the nature of wicked problems.

This vision complements that put forward by Braithwaite (Chapter 9) on peacemaking networks and restorative justice. Not only must police allow the space for local knowledge and capacity to flourish in ways that build peace; they must also 'secure islands of civility as nodes from which peace-building networks are built outwards'. As part of this, they must protect peace-builders and others, such as human rights activists, whose campaigns for peace threaten those who have a stake in ongoing conflict and war. The theory of 'responsive regulation' (Ayres & Braithwaite 1992) that informs Braithwaite's analysis maintains a privileged place for the police as legitimate specialists in the exercise of coercion. The nature and degree of coercion that is required in pacifying any one conflict depends on the effectiveness of more deliberative security solutions (such as restorative justice) lower down on the regulatory pyramid. The base of the pyramid must consist of skilled local peacemakers, because, 'Local creativity, and familiarity with local custom, are crucial to turning ripples into waves of peace that wash across a nation.'

For Braithwaite then, the police's unique knowledge of 'sympathetic combatants' who could be 'drawn into reconciliation processes' informs their role. It is possible, Braithwaite writes, that the 'key combatants who first step in to the circle can then become translators of the mentalities of the peacemakers to the mentalities of the war-makers, and vice versa'. According to Braithwaite's analysis, the essential role of the police is thus to protect and nurture islands of civility.

There are also those who continue to place a high priority on more direct forms of capacity-building and knowledge transfer – as undertaken by, for example, organisations such as the AFP for the benefit of police agencies in other parts of the Asia-Pacific region, particularly those operating in weak and failing states. This is the focus of Keelty's chapter in this volume (Chapter 5), and is part of how the AFP reassert their exclusive domain of practice. While there are explicit instrumental reasons for transferring particular skills and knowledge to recipient organisations, such as to enhance uniformity and integration of operations across countries, Keelty also recognises that forms of indigenous knowledge and capacity, and the cultural traditions that inform them, must be respected and privileged in international capacity-building networks.

As previously indicated, the above design principles are largely gleaned from the insights of various contributors to this volume. As principles they are very broad and serve more as normative guides than concrete prescriptions. In Dupont's terms (Chapter 2), the police are best understood as operating within a 'securisphere' – one that is fluid and ever changing – rather than as exercising a state monopoly in security provision. That this securisphere is ever changing does not mean that the police have no control over its ebbs and flows. And indeed, as research has shown, police leaders know this, for the most part. They know that the police must always reflect on their place within this securisphere vis-à-vis other security providers and must be cognisant of how it operates normatively as well as strategically. There is much that police leaders and unionists are doing to think proactively about their positioning within the securisphere, but as most observers concede, there is still more to be done. Central to moving forward will be a clear position on the place of the public police in society.

Conclusion

There is much we don't know about how dark networks operate and there is much we don't know about how bright networks are formed. What we do know, however, is that the language of nodes and networks provides a crucial guide in the development of new tactics and strategies on the part of public police organisations. Bright networks involve the identification, mobilisation and integration of various forms of knowledge, capacity and resources from within and outside public policing. All the chapters in this volume recognise the need for knowledge networks, capacity networks and resource networks, notwithstanding the difficulties of forming and sustaining such networks in practice.

The chapters herein illuminate a variety of ways in which such networks are currently constituted, and reveal some of their normative implications. This chapter has attempted to take stock of what these authors, and others, imply, in normative terms, as to how the police should position themselves in networks of policing and security provision. The consensus seems to be that as the police seek to adapt to the contemporary challenges stemming from wicked problems and dark networks, and even if they are required to do so in rather *ad hoc* and contingent ways, they must be guided by a vision of themselves and their distinctive role in society. As part of this, they will be required to explore smarter ways of policing that confirm rather than undermine their commitment to democratic principles. In so doing, the police must play an active role in the constitution of networks, mindful that their current symbolic importance and operational distinctiveness cannot be taken for granted. A clear and bright vision of what police do and what they stand for will guide them through the increasingly amorphous securisphere.

Notes

1   I'm very grateful to Monique Marks, whose insights have contributed significantly to the shape of this chapter.
2   I wish to acknowledge Clifford Shearing's insights into the importance of establishing design principles.

References

Australasian Police Professional Standards Council (2006) *Defining the Australasian Policing Profession.*

Avant, D. (2005) *The Market for Force: The Consequences of Privatizing Security.* Cambridge: Cambridge University Press.

Ayres, I. and Braithwaite, J. (1992) *Responsive Regulation: Transcending the Deregulation Debate.* New York: Oxford University Press.

Beare, M.E. (2003) Introduction, in M.E. Beare (ed.), *Critical Reflections on Transnational Organized Crime, Money Laundering, and Corruption.* Toronto: University of Toronto Press.

Blair, I. (2003) Surprise news: Policing works – a new model of patrol, paper delivered at In Search of Security: An International Conference on Policing and Security, Montreal, Canada: Law Commission of Canada.

—— (2005) The Richard Dimbleby Lecture, *Guardian Unlimited*, 16 November, at <http://www.guardian.co.uk/crime/article/0,2763,1643995,00.html>.

Bradley, D. (2005) Crime reduction and problem-oriented policing, *Police Research and Practice: An International Journal*, 6(4): 391–94.

Bullock, S. and Tilley, N. (eds) (2003) *Crime Reduction and Problem-oriented Policing.* Devon: Willan Publishing.

Burris, S. (2004) Governance, microgovernance and health, *Temple Law Review*, 77: 335–59.

Crawford, A. (2003) 'Contractual governance' of deviant behaviour, *Journal of Law and Society*, 30(4): 479–505.

—— (2006) Policing and security as 'club goods': The new enclosures?, in J. Wood and B. Dupont (eds), *Democracy, Society and the Governance of Security.* Cambridge: Cambridge University Press.

Dupont, B. (2003) Public entrepreneurs in the field of security: An oral history of Australian Police Commissioners, paper delivered at In Search of Security: An International Conference on Policing and Security, Montreal, Canada: Law Commission of Canada.

—— (2006) Power struggles in the field of security: Implications for democratic transformation, in J. Wood and B. Dupont (eds), *Democracy, Society and the Governance of Security*. Cambridge: Cambridge University Press.

Fleming, J., Marks, M. et al. (2006) Standing on the inside looking out: The significance of police unions in networks of security governance, *Australian and New Zealand Journal of Criminology*, 39(1).

Fleming, J. and Rhodes, R.A.W. (2005) Bureaucracy, contracts and networks: The unholy trinity and the police, *Australian and New Zealand Journal of Criminology*, 38(2): 192–205.

Giddens, A. (1991) *Modernity and Self-Identity*. Cambridge: Polity.

Goldstein, H. (1991 [1979]) Improving policing: A problem-oriented approach, *Crime and Delinquency*, 25(April): 236–58 reprinted in C.B. Klockars and S.D. Mastrofski (eds), *Thinking About Police: Contemporary Readings*. New York: McGraw-Hill.

Gross Stein, J. (2001) Network wars, in R.J. Daniels, P. Macklem and K. Roach (eds), *The Security of Freedom*. Toronto: University of Toronto Press.

Johnston, L. (2000) *Policing Britain: Risk, Security and Governance*. Harlow: Longman.

—— (2006) Transnational security governance, in J. Wood and B. Dupont (eds), *Democracy, Society and the Governance of Security*. Cambridge: Cambridge University Press.

Johnston, L. and Shearing, C. (2003) *Governing Security: Explorations in Policing and Justice*. London: Routledge.

Loader, I. (1997) Policing and the social: Questions of symbolic power, *British Journal of Sociology*, 48(1): 1–18.

—— (1999) Consumer culture and the commodification of policing and security, *Sociology*, 33(2): 373–92.

Loader, I. and Walker, N. (2001) Policing as a public good: Reconstituting the connections between policing and state, *Theoretical Criminology*, 5(1): 9–35.

—— (2006) Necessary virtues: The legitimate place of the state in the production of security, in J. Wood and B. Dupont (eds), *Democracy, Society and the Governance of Security*. Cambridge: Cambridge University Press.

Mazerolle, L. and Ransley, J. (2005) *Third Party Policing*. Cambridge: Cambridge University Press.

Merle, R. (2006) Storm-wracked parish considers hired guns, *Washington Post*, 14 March.

9/11 Commission (2004) *Final Report of the National Commission on Terrorist Attacks upon the United States*. New York: W.W. Norton & Co.

Paoli, L. (2002) The paradoxes of organised crime, *Crime, Law and Social Change*, 37(1).

Raab, J. and Milward, H.B. (2003) Dark networks as problems, *Journal of Public Administration Research and Theory*, 13(4): 413–39.

Rittel, H.W. and Webber, M.M. (1973) Dilemmas in a general theory of planning, *Policy Sciences*, 4: 155–69.

Ruggiero, V. (2003) Global markets and crime, in M.E. Beare (ed.), *Critical Reflections on Transnational Organized Crime, Money Laundering, and*

Corruption. Toronto: University of Toronto Press.

Shearing, C. (2001) Transforming security: A South African experiment, in H. Strang and J. Braithwaite (eds), *Restorative Justice and Civil Society*. Cambridge: Cambridge University Press.

Shearing, C. and Wood, J. (2003) Governing security for common goods, *International Journal of the Sociology of Law*, 31(3): 205–25.

Singer. P.W. (2003) *Corporate Warriors: The Rise of the Privatized Military Industry*. Ithaca NY: Cornell University Press.

Sklansky, D.A. (2006) Private police and democracy, *American Criminal Law Review*, 43(1):89-105.

The Economist (2005) A thicker blue line, *The Economist*, 376: 41.

Victoria Police (2003) *The Way Ahead: Strategic Plan 2003–2008*. Melbourne: Victoria Police.

—— (2005) *Organised Crime Strategy 2005–2009*. Melbourne: Victoria Police.

Watkins, R. (2004) Victoria Police Organized Crime Strategy Project: Organised Crime Template.

Williams, P. (2001) Transnational Criminal Networks, in J. Arquilla and D. Ronfeldt (eds), *Networks and Netwars: The Future of Terror, Crime, and Militancy*. Santa Monica CA: Rand.

INDEX

www.ingramcontent.com/pod-product-compliance
Lightning Source LLC
Chambersburg PA
CBHW031412270326
41929CB00010BA/1421